RAILPOLITIK

Bringing railways back to the community

Paul Salveson

Lawrence & Wishart 2013

First published 2013

Copyright © Paul Salveson 2013

The author has asserted his rights under the Copyright, Design and Patents Act, 1998 to be identified as the author of this work.

A catalogue record for this book is available from the British Library

ISBN 9781907103810

Text setting E-type, Liverpool

CONTENTS

FOREWORD

Maria Eagle MP, Shadow Secretary of State for Transport

Our railways don't work for fare-payers or tax-payers. Passengers face inflation-busting fare rises year after year, while public subsidy helps boost private profit. For too long there has been a misguided consensus that there are no credible alternatives to the current industry model. It's time this was challenged and this book does so passionately, effectively and with considerable expertise.

The creation of Network Rail as a not-for-dividend infrastructure manager began the task of reform. Yet not enough was done to improve accountability or champion devolution. The costs of fragmentation and excess profit that are the legacy of a botched privatisation have not been tackled and continue driving up costs.

The truth about the rail industry's finances has now been revealed by the regulator. In addition to the £3.9 billion of annual investment that is delivered through Network Rail, the tax-payer also pays train operators £51 million a year more than they return to government in franchise payments. Yet these private companies walk away with over £300 million in profit. That isn't a system that is delivering value for money at a time of serious pressures on the public finances.

A serious programme of reform must have three elements. First, it is surely right to at least look at alternative options for delivering our InterCity rail network when existing franchises come to an end, including whether the not-for-dividend model that has worked so effectively on the East Coast in recent years could credibly be extended.

Second, we need to create a rail network that is far more accountable and responsive to the communities it serves. That means a bold programme of devolution of the non-InterCity services to transport authorities, enabling proper integration of local transport.

Third, we must also look at how best to bring the rail network back together. That must include looking at the case for bringing Network

Rail, HS2, Directly Operated Rail and the Rail Delivery Group together within a single not-for-dividend organisation – tackling inefficiency and providing stronger leadership. This organisation could then take on the vital task of planning and procuring rolling stock in a way that better supports British manufacturing, jobs and apprenticeships.

There is a consensus in the country that privatisation has been a costly failure. This book sets out an alternative vision for the future. It should be read by any politician serious about reforming our railways to deliver a better deal for fare-payers and tax-payers.

Preface and acknowledgements

This book brings together a range of thoughts, ideas and experiences about Britain's railways, based on sixty years of close proximity to them. (I was born in the maternity wing of Bolton General Hospital, which directly overlooked the now-closed Bolton to Manchester railway, and was brought up within earshot of Bolton locomotive sheds. The rest was inevitable.)

The aim is to put the contemporary railway in the context of a proud history that stretches back to the early nineteenth century. It is a political book, not a railway history, and still less is it a technical description of how railways operate. It puts railways into a wider context of modern socialist thinking, and seeks to avoid old certainties. It draws lessons not only from the experience of the nationalised railway, but also the last twenty years of privatisation.

Too often for the left in British politics the solution to contemporary problems is to go back to some mythical 'golden age' when everything was fine. Yet the apostles of the 'return to BR' policy should look at the realities of Britain's railways following nationalisation, when they were subject to political whims and short-term financing, and run by a managerial elite that had little sympathy with the ideals of social ownership. The call for a return to BR is the policy equivalent of a plan for modern rolling stock based on building a new fleet of coal-burning steam locomotives. Both ideas are based more on nostalgia than reality.

This book argues for a future railway which is in touch with the communities it serves and offers value for money to the taxpayer, the passenger and industry – as well as being really accountable to the people as a whole. It also recognises the changed political landscape in the UK, with devolution of rail responsibilities to Scotland, Wales and – in all likelihood – the English regions.

The main focus of the book is 'bringing railways back to communities' – the area in which I've been working for the last twenty years. There have been many exciting initiatives in local and regional rail during this period, some of which offer pointers to the future of the network as a whole. This is an area where immediate change could be easily implemented, given that so much groundwork has already been done; and it is also a field that has sometimes been neglected in national thinking. However the book does not neglect the national InterCity and inter-regional railways. Rather, it looks at them from a different perspective.

Rail is still of massive importance to the country, despite the best efforts of Beeching and his political masters fifty years ago. More people are travelling by train than ever before and the health of our towns and cities – and countryside – depends on having a reliable, affordable and efficient railway. Rail could do so much better if the primary motive force was not private profit but public benefit.

We need to combine social responsibility with enterprise and creativity. The last twenty years have seen railway management develop high-level commercial skills which complement their traditional expertise in railway operations and civil engineering. Those commercial skills should be put to the service of a railway which is enterprising and efficient and meets the wider social, economic and environmental needs of the country as a whole – and not a minority of shareholders. Railways work best as a network, but they also need to be part of *wider* networks promoting sustainable development and an inclusive society.

Rebuilding Rail, the 2012 report by Transport for Quality of Life, highlighted the substantial additional costs of the privatised railway, suggesting a cumulative figure of around £11.5 billion additional costs since privatisation (Ian Taylor and Lynn Sloman, *Rebuilding Rail*, 2012). That's a lot of money, which could have been spent on making a better railway. We need a workable strategy which doesn't cost any more than railways currently do. Last year we spent a total of £4 billion on rail: it would be politically wrong-headed to say that the problem has been lack of cash. What needs to change is how the money is spent.

There has to be another way. This book represents a view from the left, but one that isn't based on a rigidly centralist and statist approach, and which recognises the importance of freeing up local and regional initiative where it makes sense – whilst retaining a centralised focus when that is necessary. It is rooted in that important but often ignored socialist tradition of co-operation, community, mutuality and decentralisation. I hope that some of the proposals and arguments that follow will make sense to people who do not necessarily share all of my political prejudices.

ACKNOWLEDGMENTS

Special thanks to the following friends and colleagues who commented on earlier drafts. I should stress that they are not responsible for the conclusions or opinions expressed in the book, for which I take sole responsibility:

Ian Ambrose, Roger Bell, Jonathan Bray, Brian Burdsall, Malcolm Bulpitt, Alex Burrows, John Chapman, Allan Dare, Hester Dunlop, Rod Fletcher, Roger Ford, Bertil Hylén, Stephen Joseph, Richard Knowles, Jenny Lynn, Andrew McNaughton, Mark Barker, Heidi Mottram, John Nelson, Tim Owen, Dave Prescott, Liam Robinson, Lynn Sloman, Chris Stokes, Ian Taylor, Dave Walsh, John Walton, Karen Wilkie.

And special thanks also to Paul Stevenson for the index and bibliography.

Paul Salveson, Huddersfield, May 2013

INTRODUCTION

Britain's railways have always been profoundly political. Ever since the inauspicious opening day of the Liverpool and Manchester Railway on 15 September 1830, when the popular Liverpool MP William Huskisson was mown down by Stephenson's *Rocket*, railways have had an uneasy relationship with politicians.[1]

This book offers an overview of the history and current performance of railways in Britain and sets out a radical alternative both to the current system and to the old corporate British Rail. One challenge for rail governance in the early twenty-first century is to find a model that recognises devolution within the UK, whilst at the same time recreating a comprehensive UK-wide rail network that has benefits of scale. The second major challenge is to create a viable structure that combines democratic accountability with value for money, and meets the needs of passengers, communities and industry. We already have the technical and managerial expertise for this: what we lack is the political vision. Finally, we need to make sure that the technical and commercial expertise we have on the railways is allowed to blossom, with a 'people's railway' that is innovative, growing and puts the needs of customers first.

In 1997 the Blair government inherited a railway that had been privatised by John Major with a commitment to creating a 'publicly-owned and publicly accountable railway'. It never happened, and since then, far from privatisation reducing the costs of a bloated state-run bureaucracy, the cost of running our trains has risen dramatically. In the meantime Labour has veered between advocating what is in effect a return to a nationalised railway and accepting the current system as it is, with minor changes around the edges. Yet there is a 'third way', that can combine service quality, commercial acumen and accountability – through that neglected labour movement tradition of mutuality and co-operation.

Many of the nineteenth-century calls for state ownership included innovative ideas, including alternative ownership models as advocated by some railway trades unionists. These ranged from the syndicalist 'workers' control' approach to a form of consumer and workers' participation that included chambers of commerce alongside the unions and government. The Independent Labour Party, formed in 1893, developed some of these demands further, with leading figures like Philip Snowden articulating a detailed strategy both for taking railways into public ownership and for their democratic administration.

Railways were seen by Snowden and other early pioneers as providing the perfect exemplars for socialist enterprise. They impinged on the lives of most people, and were vital to the economic and social life of Britain, but they also offered some of the worst examples of profiteering and poor service to the public. Railways, and transport generally, was a means to many ends but above all it was the basic infrastructure that allowed life to carry on, be it economic activity or a trip to the seaside.

After the First World War Britain's railways went through a process of consolidation into four monopolies, and this was followed by a period of state ownership (1948-1994) and then, after 1994, a form of state control with private delivery. Arguably, we now have the worst of both worlds – although there are pockets of progress. In recent years the performance of Britain's railways has shown some steady improvement in reliability; more trains are running on time and a degree of confidence has returned to the system across the country. Investment totalling over £9 billion was announced by the Coalition government in July 2012, which will see many routes electrified and some lines re-opened. But all this is at a cost. We are pumping £4 billion of public money a year into the railways, over three times the amount that went into railways in the last year of BR ownership. We need to draw on the experiences – good as well as bad – of the last twenty years but to move on towards something better.

There is much to learn here from the experience of continental Europe, in both their highly successful intercity networks, which remain state-owned, and the developing regional networks, which are often specified by democratically controlled regional authorities with the right level of expertise to be 'an informed client'. Few other European countries have adopted the same approach as Britain, although a degree of private operation, particularly in the regional passenger sector, has been introduced. Having said this, we shouldn't be too romantic about 'Europe'. There are bad examples as well as good; there has been worsening performance in some countries, as well as rows between contract bidders, and loss of inter-availability of tickets.

In most books on rail policy one particular interest is often absent – that of the passenger. Yet the UK has a very strong network of passenger organisations, some voluntary and some sponsored by transport authorities. There is a statutory body representing rail and bus passengers, Passenger Focus, and Britain has developed a flourishing network of volunteer-led rail user groups, along with community-rail partnerships.

What should rail offer to UK in the twenty-first century? Can we combine modernisation with a community focus? Is there a way to create a more realistic and deliverable high-speed rail network that offers better synergies with the 'conventional' network? This book looks at ways of expanding the network that bring the maximum social, economic and environmental benefits to the country as a whole. It also takes on board the fact that trains don't operate in isolation from other forms of transport. Getting maximum possible integration with buses, trams, cycling and walking is vital – and we've been useless at doing it. And we should also acknowledge the continuing importance of park and ride; it is far better for people to make short car journeys and transfer to rail than to drive all the way. It also looks at opportunities now being explored in Wales, Scotland and the North of England for running new, social-enterprise train companies, which could provide an outstanding service and offer direct lessons for other parts of the UK.

NOTES

1.　One railway manager commented to me: 'You could say that this is where politicians ignoring railwaymen's advice for political gain stems from – he got down onto the tracks to go and talk to the Duke of Wellington against instructions from the railway company! The rest is history.'

1. THE FIRST RAILWAY AGE
THE PRIVATE RAILWAY 1830-1948

Railroad travelling is a delightful improvement of human life ... Everything is near, everything is immediate – time, distance and delay are abolished.[1]

Britain gave the world railways. They grew out of the roughly-constructed tramways using horse or man-power that developed to serve coal mines. The first record of what we would recognise as a railway was in 1604, in Nottinghamshire. However, it was in the North-East that railways began to take shape, in order to serve the expanding coalfields of Durham and Northumberland. Steam power was applied to 'locomotives' as early as 1804, and crude but workable steam traction soon began to spread to some of the larger North-East collieries, using the designs of men like George Stephenson and Timothy Hackworth. But it was Stephenson who recognised the real potential of steam railways and he persuaded others – with capital – to support his vision.

Stephenson is rightly called 'the father of railways', and he epitomised the Victorian romantic image of the self-made 'working man'.[2] But even at the time this was contested as a simplified view, and Samuel Smiles's glowing biography, published in 1857, was heavily attacked for its unstinting praise of Stephenson (and this led to a revision of subsequent editions). There were also limits on how far 'the self-made working man' could reach, and the working-class Tynesider had a hard struggle in overcoming class prejudice. His broad regional accent was often an object of ridicule, and it contributed to some of his early setbacks in promoting parliamentary bills for lines such as the Liverpool and Manchester. Yet Stephenson was a very astute operator, and was able to marshal substantial financial interests behind his projects, particularly in the North. As well as becoming a very rich man, he transformed the geographical, and to an extent political, landscape of Britain. The 'railway interest' became one of the most powerful forces in Parliament during the late Victorian and Edwardian eras.

THE FIRST RAILWAYS

The break-through came in 1825 with the opening of the Stockton and Darlington Railway.[3] It has often been forgotten, however, that this was a coal railway, not a passenger route, though hundreds of locals took a ride on the first train. Its purpose was very simple – to bring coal from the West Durham coalfield around Shildon and Bishop Auckland to the Tees ports of Stockton and rapidly-growing Middlesbrough. Much of the finance came from those progressive capitalists, the Quakers. The Pease family of Darlington were the Stockton and Darlington Railway's main backers, and many other Quakers – with their combination of commercial skills and social responsibility – played a central role in early railway development, recognising as they did that railways were a catalyst for economic growth.[4] The success of the Stockton and Darlington Railway proved that railways were viable for moving large tonnages of coal, more quickly than canals or rivers. Other, mainly freight, railways quickly followed.

The Liverpool and Manchester Railway, which opened on 15 September 1830, was in quite a different league from anything that had gone before and Stephenson was the genius who engineered it. The railway linked two of Britain's most important – and rapidly growing – cities and was built for both passenger and freight traffic. The infrastructure was not that of a basic 'works line' carrying coal, but pre-figured the grand statements of Victorian capitalism. The 'Moorish Arch' at the Liverpool end of the railway, at the city's Crown Street terminus, was meant as a harbinger of a new era. And so it was. The railways acted as the motor of the industrial revolution, transforming the country's economic base, social relationships and even our concept of time. The opening of the Liverpool and Manchester Railway in 1830 was undoubtedly a watershed, but at that time railways were already spreading across much of the North of England; and they were supported – and opposed – with all the energy and vigour that today's plans for high-speed rail attract. Railways involved substantial land-take, and disturbed long-established settlement patterns across Britain. Some landowners promoted the new form of transport, particularly if it involved quicker and more profitable means of conveying the coal that was mined on their lands to ports and towns. Others, usually representing the still powerful agricultural interests, were less enthusiastic, and sometimes violently resisted the incursion of railways onto 'their' estate.

Many more 'main-line' railways followed on from the Liverpool and Manchester. They included Leeds and Selby (1834), Newcastle and Carlisle (1838), London and Birmingham (1838) and Manchester and Leeds (1841). Brunel's Great Western Railway, built to a larger 'broad-gauge', opened between London and Bristol in 1840 and set new standards of speed and comfort.

Railways developed as prime examples of innovation and enterprise in early Victorian England. They were not promoted by the state but by private capital, using the skill and ingenuity of people like Stephenson and the labour of thousands of 'navvies' recruited from among local agricultural workers, or from further afield in Ireland and Scotland. Although the influence of the state was considerable from the beginning of the railway age, the ideology of Victorian liberalism shrank from having too much state involvement; and whilst Germany and France moved towards full state ownership (at least of infrastructure) as the century wore on, in the case of Britain the extent of state 'interference' was confined to marginal regulation and safety improvements. And even these were strenuously opposed by 'the railway interest'.

The railways conformed to the classic model of capitalism that Marx delineated so well in *Capital*. The larger companies swallowed the smaller fry and continued to develop as semi-monopolistic giants. The London and North Western Railway, with its empire based at Euston (and its huge engineering centre at Crewe), became one of the biggest joint-stock companies in the world. Others, such as the Great Western, Midland and North Eastern, were not far behind. Each, by the end of the nineteenth century, enjoyed near or complete monopolies in much of the areas within which they operated. The railway towns – Crewe, Swindon, Darlington and many others – were ruled by the railway; employees and their families were expected to abide by the moral norms laid down by 'the company'. Only in towns like Derby, where other industries and interests challenged the railways' hegemony, was any degree of independence tolerated. And it was the Derby brewer, Bass, who encouraged the first signs of trades unionism on the railways.

The early railway companies tended to cover one line, or at most a small handful. Unlike Belgium, which was entering into a process of rapid 'railway-isation' planned by the state, the British network grew piece-meal. Jack Simmons commented:

> Since the State ... had nothing to do with the planning and laying-out of the railways, they grew up haphazardly, not necessarily where there was most need for them, but where capital and leadership were most readily forthcoming, and – often quite as important – where opposition to them was weak or negligible.[5]

As the 'First Railway Age' progressed, feeder routes were constructed and mergers became commonplace. The Liverpool and Manchester Railway merged with the Grand Junction Railway in 1845, and in the following year became part of the London and North Western Railway; the new company was formed out of the merger of the Manchester and Birmingham, Grand Junction and London and Birmingham railways. The Stockton and Darlington grew from being a basic pit-to-port railway to become a major regional operation that eventually merged with the larger North Eastern Railway in 1863. The Great Western Railway grew with its absorption of the London and Bristol Railway, South Devon and Bristol and Exeter.

By the early 1850s, a basic national network of railways had been created, with London linked to most major centres in Scotland and the North of England; and the process of amalgamation continued throughout the early years of the railways, with some degree of state regulation being enforced. Gladstone's 1844 Railways Act subjected the railways to 'such conditions as are hereinafter contained for the benefit of the public', including cheap 'workmen's' fares. The legislation also started the long process of regulating railway safety, initially through the Board of Trade; and in addition it established the possibility of railways being brought back into state ownership, although these provisions were to remain dormant for several decades (see Chapter 3).

Railway workers were recruited to the growing railway centres of Crewe, Derby, Swindon and Doncaster from 'over the railway fence' – that is, from neighbouring farms – as well as from further afield.

Naval and army personnel were also favoured, particularly the former, who were attuned to doing skilled work whilst being part of a larger organisation. This workforce was hammered into a disciplined body by military-style discipline, often enforced with great ruthlessness. Early attempts at industrial action, such as a strike by drivers on the Liverpool and Manchester, resulted in ring-leaders being imprisoned, often with a stretch on the notorious tread-mill.[6] The threat of eviction from company-owned housing was another threat as much feared as imprisonment. This militaristic discipline had the full backing of the state. A select committee in 1839 stated that:

> it is essential to the safety of the Public and to the maintenance of regular intercourse by railroads that the Companies should have a more perfect control over their servants … where the lives of many persons depend on the good conduct and ready obedience of subordinate officers, and where the smallest irregularity may be attended with fatal consequences, a system of exact discipline should be encouraged …[7]

Women, in general, were kept out of railway employment. However, certain traditional female roles were required, including catering, laundry work and attendants in ladies' waiting rooms; and as early as 1836 women were employed in some railway workshops as seamstresses and French polishers. When the Swindon Works of the Great Western Railway took the 'bold' decision to employ young women in 1874, as French polishers in the Carriage Department, they were provided with a separate entrance from the men, and given different start and finishing times.[8] As the century wore on, some women were employed in railway offices as 'lady clerks'.[9]

There is a widespread and nostalgic image of railways in nineteenth century Britain as models of enterprise and service, but this is far from the reality. The early, largely unplanned, network produced duplication and triplication of routes in some cases, but gave little benefit to passengers. Many of the complaints of today's passengers – about late trains, poor customer service and high fares – could be heard, every bit as strongly, in the so-called halcyon years of Britain's railways, between 1880 and 1914. In fact the railways became popular targets for editorial writers and politicians – a role they never quite managed to relinquish.

PROFITS BEFORE SAFETY

Railway safety also quickly became a major area of public concern. Huskisson's death had confirmed popular prejudice about the dangers of railways (leaving aside the deaths of the hundreds of navvies who were killed during railway construction), and there was no shortage of further deaths to whet the Victorians' morbid fascination with the new steam monster. A particularly serious accident occurred on Brunel's Great Western Main Line at Sonning, on Christmas Eve 1841, when a train ran into a landslip. Eight passengers, mostly travelling in basic third-class wagons, were killed, and nearly twenty were injured. The accident fuelled public calls for improved safety, and it was these that paved the way for Gladstone's act of 1844. A pattern became set for most railway safety improvements in the nineteenth century: with each major accident some additional safety feature became legally enforced.[10] This was the case with the problem of inadequate braking systems, which led to a number of serious accidents over a period of decades. At first, although the Amalgamated Society of Railway Servants launched a campaign for improved railway safety in 1878, and won some support in the House of Commons, the railway lobby ensured that the campaign got nowhere. Then came the Armagh 'accident' of 1889, in which an inadequately-braked train ran away, resulting in the deaths of eighty passengers (mostly young children). This entirely man-made tragedy then led to legislation that enforced continuous brakes and signalling improvements.

The pressure for better safety came partly from public opinion, often expressed through the media of the day, and also from the frequently selfless and principled conduct of the largely ex-army railway inspecting officers of the Board of Trade. The recommendations of the latter were routinely opposed by the railway companies, however, who saw every instance of state intervention as an assault on their rights.

Many of the worst of the nineteenth-century railway accidents were caused by over-work. Exhausted railway workers, who often worked shifts of fourteen hours or more, were often made scapegoats for inadequate safety arrangements. When in 1858 the Chief Inspecting Officer of Railways at the Board of Trade reported that many accidents arose from men being excessively overworked, his comments were refuted by the companies. In 1875 767 men were killed on the railways, representing one in 334 of the workforce.[11] A Board of Trade report in 1890 showed that out of around 16,000 signalmen employed in fifteen of the larger companies, over a thousand regularly worked more than fifteen hours a day. The proportion of drivers and firemen working over fifteen hours a day was even higher.

Trades unionism came late to the railways. Whilst textiles and coal were increasingly unionised by the 1840s, railway trade unionism took a long time to take root.[12] This reflects another aspect of railway development in the nineteenth century – its militaristic nature. To build and then manage a rapidly-growing railway network required the sort of management skills which only the military could supply. Many of the first managers of the bigger railways came from military backgrounds, and applied a very clear management model, based on tight discipline and close adherence to the rule book. Trades unionism was seen as the equivalent of mutiny, and early attempts at organisation were stamped on. The unionism which eventually emerged in the 1870s was moderate and – initially – rooted in class compromise. The Amalgamated Society of Railway Servants was the first union to establish strong roots – and its title says it all. But the docile approach of the early ASRS gradually began to change, and other unions were formed, first for locomotive drivers and then for workers in the less skilled sectors. Maintaining inter-grade rivalry was used by railway management as a means of 'divide and rule', and the unions faithfully complied by establishing separate unions for different grades. The legacy of those divisions, which led to a fragmented and divided workforce, have remained with us to this day.

It was the issue of over-work and its impact on safety that helped the early rail unions gain support, and even a degree of respectability. But in this the unions encountered stiff resistance from most of the railway companies. The general manager of the London and North Western railway told members of a parliamentary select committee as late as 1893 that 'you might just as well have a trade union in Her Majesty's Army' as have unions on the railways.[13]

CONSOLIDATION AND MONOPOLISATION

By the late 1860s Britain's railway network was largely complete. The last major projects were the London extension of the Midland Railway, completed in 1868, the Settle-Carlisle Railway, finished in 1876, and the extension of the Manchester, Sheffield and Lincolnshire Railway to London (Marylebone) – and its transformation into 'The Great Central Railway' in 1899.

The haphazard nature of railway building had given the country a network that lacked efficiency but at the same time had little of the 'competition' so fervently espoused by Victorian liberal ideologues. At one extreme was the small rural branch line, often built with local capital in the hope that the railway's coming would transform the fortunes of the investors' area of rural England and make them rich. In all probability the railways did make a major contribution to the rural economy, enabling agricultural products to get to urban markets and stimulating extractive industries, notably coal but also quarry products. But it is doubtful whether any of the small investors got much return on their investments.[14] At the opposite extreme, the early pioneers had a good idea of which were likely to be the main and most profitable routes, such as Manchester–Birmingham, Liverpool–Manchester, London–Bristol and Birmingham–London, creating what looked pretty much like our modern British inter-city network.

Railways were essential to the continuing momentum of Victorian industrialisation. As well as linking growing industrial centres, the bigger railway companies built or expanded many of the major ports that exported coal and manufactured goods across the world: on Teesside, Humberside, Cardiff, Barrow, Southampton and Bristol.

Yet as early as the end of the nineteenth century some local railways were suffering from tramway competition in urban areas. Whilst rail passengers had to make do with worn-out third-class accommodation, many of the tram companies were noted for their high standards, efficiency and enterprise. And many of them were owned by the local council.[15] Complaints were rife about overcrowding on the trains. In 1898 nationalisation campaigner Clement Edwards wrote that:

> the deficiency of accommodation is a feature from which none of the companies running into London, at least, are free ... on several lines, as Lord Chief Justice Russell has put it, 'men and women and children are forced into trains in a way they would not herd sheep or bullocks'.[16]

Punctuality was another area of concern. According to a *Times* report in 1891, railway time-keeping left 'much, very much, to be desired'. It reported that in September, the punctuality of 'up' trains on most lines had been under 10 per cent.[17] The much-feted Great Western Railway in June 1895 recorded 72 per cent of its Paddington arrivals as more than five minutes late.[18]

LACK OF COMPETITION

Competition became a thing of the past: rates on apparently competing routes, such as London to Birmingham, were agreed between the rival companies. Thus, for example, as early as 1851 eight of the main companies operating supposedly competing Anglo-Scottish services had come to an agreement to pool receipts. A Parliamentary enquiry into 'rate fixing' in 1872 concluded that 'there is now no active competition between different railways in the matter of rates and fares'.[19] This was amply confirmed in the recollections of Sir George Findlay of the London and North Western railway, who observed that:

> in days gone by, it cannot be denied that the railway companies incurred great losses and sacrificed a considerable portion of their revenue by extreme competition amongst themselves, but in this matter, as in many others, they have gained wisdom by experience and profited by the uses of adversity.[20]

At a parliamentary select committee hearing in 1882, the general manager of the Great Western, when asked whether passenger rates, as well as goods charges, were 'fixed', replied 'Yes, the fares between all competitive places are agreed'.[21]

Clement Edwards argued that:

> The competitive principle has practically ceased to operate upon our railways. Superficial appearances might seem to indicate otherwise. There are still several hundred railway companies with their distinct organisations, their separate directorates, their duplicated services, and all the usual concomitants of competition. In fact the present system may be fittingly described as Monopoly in the guise of Competition.[22]

The record of the railway companies in investing in better services was also mixed, with some railways worse than others. Whilst Stephenson, with remarkable foresight, had prophesied that electric traction would eventually power the railways, few of the companies took much interest in this emerging technology. Productivity was poor. For the three decades up to 1914 it was static.[23] Whilst productivity on the US railroads was increasing, with investment in modern freight operation and high-speed passenger trains, Britain lagged behind.

A we have seen, there was some competition from urban tram systems, which were among the greatest achievements of 'municipal socialism' before the First World War. Many local authorities invested in state-of-the-art electric tramways, and these acted as the arteries of urban expansion. Indeed, it has to be said that some of the early tram networks contributed to the decline of several urban 'heavy rail' networks that suffered from poor penetration of city centres, and dirty and unattractive steam traction. For a while, publicly owned entrepreneurial municipal tramways were seeing off private, under-invested urban rail networks. Yet by the 1930s, as tram networks started to come up for major renewal, all too many were scrapped in favour of buses. Most continental countries, however, even war-ravaged Germany, kept their systems and modernised them.

THE FIRST WORLD WAR AND AFTER

The railways were effectively taken over by the state during the huge strains of the first world war, with the railway companies providing a service 'on contract' to the government. And after the war there was widespread expectation that part of the peace dividend would be a publicly-owned railway system.[24] But what actually happened was the passing of the 'Ministry of Ways and Communications Act' in 1920, which gave government the powers to bring the principal forms of transport into state ownership without actually doing it. The influence of 'the railway interest', which still had 45 railway-director MPs in the House of Commons, had triumphed. The rail unions were offered some palliatives, including representation on the boards of the private companies, but this was politely declined.

The government introduced further legislation in the following year. The Railways Act of 1921 grouped over one hundred of the railway companies into just four regional monopolies – the Southern, London Midland and Scottish, Great Western and London and North Eastern Railway ('The Big Four'). Suggestions for a distinct 'Scottish Railway' were dropped, with the LMS and LNER sharing routes north of the border. Railway regulation by government continued as before, with the assumption that the railways had a monopoly which needed to be controlled – completely ignoring the rise of competitive road transport. Rail management had virtually no freedom to react to these or any other market changes, and because of this they had very limited ability to attract capital for much needed modernisation. A present-day railway manager with both UK and American experience made the observation that a similar thing had happened in the USA:

> ... where the old Interstate Commerce Commission strangled the railroads with ridiculous regulation and cumbersome bureaucracy right up to 1981, and almost killed the industry stone dead. The huge revival in railroad traffic following the ICC's abolition shows what could have happened here if wiser counsels had prevailed.[25]

As well as imposing poorly conceived regulation, the 1921 Act also reinforced the lack of competition on the railways: the 'grouping' accelerated a process that had already been underway for several decades. Any pretence of 'competition' – other than PR exercises involving a handful of accelerated 'streamlined' express services on the LMS and LNER – was abandoned.

The 'Big Four' inherited a railway that had lacked investment for decades; and the problem had been compounded by the additional strains that had been placed on the railway during war-time. To make matters worse, the economy was sliding into recession and there was serious competition from the roads. The room for manoeuvre by the four companies was increasingly restricted, and wage reductions and service reductions became the order of the day.

The situation was no different in other industries – including the coalfields, which were soon to be the setting for the biggest confrontation between labour and capital ever seen in this country, the General Strike of 1926. The strike had a profound effect on the railways, and virtually the whole system was closed down for the nine days of the strike. After the TUC's capitulation that ended the strike, many companies took advantage of the unions' defeat to victimise workers, and nowhere was this more obvious than on the railways. At the same time, the action had contributed to the long-term decline of rail, as some goods business transferred to road for good.[26]

The years after the General Strike saw the unions accepting their weakened position and opting for a period of 'industrial peace' during which wages and conditions were negotiated downwards. Philip Bagwell has described these years as being a time of 'backs to the wall'. A slow recovery began in the mid-1930s, however, and parts of the network now received the investment that they had lacked for decades. But the Southern Railway, under the visionary management of Sir Herbert Walker, was the only company to seriously invest in large-scale electrification, capitalising on the continuing economic growth of south-east England. The LNER did develop plans to electrify its East Coast Main Line, and some pilot schemes were started, mainly focused on the electrification of the busy Manchester–Sheffield via Woodhead route; but this was not completed until after the second world war. The Big Four's 'Square Deal' campaign of 1938 also tried to change things, but then the Second World War broke out.

The war halted any cautious steps towards developing new services, and the rail network was once more forced to shoulder a huge burden. Soon the railways were again brought under state control, but this time the railways themselves were key targets for German bombers. Railwaymen and women subsequently played an outstanding role in keeping trains moving under highly dangerous wartime conditions.

At the end of the war, the railways had taken a hammering but were perhaps not in quite as bad shape as politicians such as Hugh Dalton were suggesting (he quipped that the railways were 'a poor bag of assets'). However, the political landscape was very different from that of 1918. Labour won a huge majority in the 1945 election, and a central plank of its manifesto was transport nationalisation. Although the Conservatives mounted a strong rear-guard action against Labour's plans – particularly its intention to nationalise road haulage – the Attlee government had the whip hand.

The railways passed into public ownership on 1 January 1948. It had been a long time coming. Attempts to bring a degree of public accountability to the railways stretched back to 1840 and the setting up of the Railway Department of the Board of Trade, and Gladstone's legislation of 1844. The following chapter takes a closer look at this history.

NOTES

1. Sydney Smith writing in 1842. Quoted in Michael Robbins, *The Railway Age*, 1962, p44.

2. Biographies of George Stephenson are numerous, but see L.T.C. Rolt, *George and Robert Stephenson* (1960) for one of the most readable.
3. For a readable general introduction to railway history see Jack Simmons, *The Railways of Britain* (second ed. 1968); for a very brief introduction to railways in the North of England see Paul Salveson, *Northern Rail heritage* (2010). Christian Wolmar's *Fire and Steam: a new history of the railways* (2008) is a fine recent addition.
4. See booklet by Edward Milligan, *Quakers and Railways*, 2002.
5. Simmons, op cit, p72.
6. See P.W. Kingsford, *Victorian Railwaymen*, 1970; and Philip Bagwell, *The Railwaymen*, vol. 1, 1963.
7. Quoted in Salveson, op cit, p11.
8. Rosa Matheson, *Railway Voices: 'Inside' Swindon Works*, 2008.
9. Ibid.
10. See L.T.C. Rolt, *Red for Danger* (second ed. 1966) for the classic history of railway accidents.
11. Bagwell, op cit, p95.
12. See Kingsford, op cit. Frank McKenna's *The Railway Workers 1840-1970* (1980) is an excellent account by a former railwayman, with a strong focus on the culture of railway life.
13. Ibid, p95.
14. See M.C. Reed, *Railways in the Victorian Economy* (1969); and Jack Simmons, *The Railway in Town and Country*, 1830–1914 (1986), esp. Chapter 10, 'Rural England and Wales'; and D. St John Thomas, *The Country Railway* (1989).
15. See R.J. Buckley, *History of Tramways* (1975); and for a good local account, J.S. King, *Keighley Corporation Transport* (1964).
16. Clement Edwards, *Railway Nationalization* (1898), p85.
17. Ibid, p86.
18. In Paul Salveson, *British Rail – the Radical Alternative to privatization*, Manchester, 1989, p14.
19. Ibid, p12.
20. G. Findlay, *The Working and Management of an English Railway*, p265.
21. Salveson (1989), op cit, p15.
22. Edwards, op cit, p7.
23. See D. Aldcroft, 'The Efficiency and Enterprise of British Railways 1870-1914', in D. Aldcroft (ed), *Studies in British Transport History*, 1974.
24. See next chapter.
25. Personal communication to author, May 2013.
26. See Bagwell, op cit; also Malcolm Wallace, *Single or Return: the history of the Transport Salaried Staffs Association*, pp194-201, 1996.

2. CHALLENGING THE
RAILWAY BARONS

> For some years past a number of people have pointed out that the incompetent and amateur way in which the railroads of the United Kingdom were run was becoming a menace to the national welfare, and that the whole fabric of railway finance was becoming so top heavy that its collapse was merely a question of time ...[1]

In nineteenth century Britain the railways were as much in the public eye as they are today. And the public was increasingly dissatisfied with what it saw. Indeed, the history of state intervention in Britain's railways points to the inherent contradictions of Victorian laissez-faire 'political economy'. On the one hand the railways were encouraged to develop according to 'the laws' of the market, whilst on the other hand there was strong public concern over the creation of monopolies. Further, the new mode of transport brought significant safety risks to the travelling public which required some degree of state intervention. The increasingly powerful 'railway interest', which had a substantial number of MPs in parliament as well as a swathe of peers in the Lords, was implacably opposed to any attempts to reduce its power. [2]

EARLY STATE INTERVENTION

The state took an interest in railway development from the start. New railways, including most of the early colliery lines, required legislation to permit their development and the acquisition of land. The 'Railway Department' of the Board of Trade was established in 1840, with a safety remit that included inspecting new railways before they were pronounced fit to operate. A jumble of different legislative requirements were formalised in 1845 with the 'Railways Clauses Consolidation Act', providing a basic template for future railway bills.

Before that select committees had devoted considerable time to 'the railways question', and in 1844 Gladstone had acknowledged the need for greater state regulation of the railways, though the Railways Act of that year gave limited immediate powers to the government. The Act gave some scope to control railway rates, and a later piece of legislation in the same year provided for cheap 'workmen's' fares on certain trains, which went down in railway folklore as 'parliamentary trains'.

Gladstone's act made some provision for the compulsory purchase of railways built after 1844, with the owners to be compensated to the value of twenty-five years estimated profits from the time of purchase. But this could only take place twenty-one years after the passing of the act. As we shall see, the legislation was to form the basis of a campaign for full nationalisation during the 1890s. However this provision of the act was largely forgotten for several decades, until in 1865 a Royal Commission was formed to consider the issue. Well-known figures including Walter Bagehot and Edwin Chadwick argued for state ownership, but things went no further until in 1872 a select committee was set up to consider the issue, chaired by Captain Tyler, a former inspecting officer of railways at the Board of Trade.[3] The committee came out in favour of state ownership, with Tyler posing the question as to 'whether the state shall manage the railways or the railways manage the state.'[4] But no action was taken on the committee's recommendations.

Whilst Britain's politicians were taking an essentially non-interventionist approach to rail development, Belgium, and later Germany and the Netherlands, used rail development as a tool for industrial growth. Even in the United States the state intervened to assist private railway development. The American writer C.F. Adams commented in 1878: 'railroad competition has been tried all over the world and everywhere is being abandoned. In its place, the principle of responsibility and regulated monopoly is asserting itself'.[5] Adams was quoted by Clement Edwards in his critique of privately-owned railways; his view was that whilst monopoly may have asserted itself there was precious little responsibility being exercised, and insufficient regulation.

THE CASE FOR NATIONALISATION GETS MADE

Edwards, a Liberal MP, was one of the earliest critics of private owner-ship of the railways, and was a key figure in the Railway Nationalisation

League, formed in 1895. The league was supported by several of the railway unions and reflected the growing strength of the socialist movement in the 1890s.[6] Edwards's *Railway Nationalization* was published in 1897, and aimed to provide ammunition for implementation of the clauses of Gladstone's 1844 Railways Act that allowed for compulsory purchase of railways constructed after 1844. He set out a convincing critique of Britain's railways under private ownership, citing higher fares compared with continental railways, low pay and excessive hours of work for railway employees, high rates for carrying goods and wasteful competition with duplicating routes. Edwards made a detailed study of state-owned railways in other parts of the world and concluded:

> On the whole the experience of State-ownership of railways when tried side by side with private ownership – and that is the true basis of comparison – shows that charges for services are much less, the management is more economical, and there is a practical immunity from those grave ills and anomalies under which we suffer in the United Kingdom.[7]

Edwards did not set out a detailed vision for how railways under state control would be organised, but emphasised the wider benefits of a publicly-owned rail network, stressing 'the development of neglected districts' and the economic revival of rural areas following 'sweeping reductions in goods rates and passenger fares'.[8] He argued that nationalisation need not involve any outlay of cash, under the terms of compulsory purchase set out in Gladstone's 1844 Act. Whilst he estimated that the total cost would amount to £38.5 million, he envisaged that the state would not purchase the railways outright but would convert railway shares to bonds ('scrips' as Edwards terms them). He explains:

> ... it is exceedingly important to emphasise the fact that there will be no need to raise a single halfpenny of the purchase money by taxation. The process will be one of simple conversion. Assuming that Parliament decide that the Government shall acquire the railways for the people, then upon a given day a State scrip will be substituted for the present railway share-certificate. If shareholders desire to realise in cash, all they will have to do will be to sell the Government scrip as they sell Consols today.[9]

Similar arguments had been made a few years earlier with the publication of James Hole's *National Railways – an argument for state purchase*, published in 1893. Hole cited detailed examples of state ownership of railways within the British Empire, notably in India and Australia. And he also gave favourable mention to the work of another contemporary advocate of railway nationalisation, Liberal MP A.J. Williams. Williams had argued in *Appropriation of the Railways by the State* that five regional railways should be created, constituted as 'mutual trusts' – London ('Metropolitan'), Southern, Western, Midland and Eastern – with additional trusts for the railways in Scotland and Ireland. Hole was favourably disposed to these proposals, in which 'each system would become a trust … conducted with no reference to private gain but in the general interest alone'.[10]

Edwards' ideas were not adopted by Parliament, but the incremental approach was strongly espoused by both Labour and some Liberal politicians. Philip Snowden frequently lectured on 'railway nationalisation', and used Edwards's arguments as the basis for a socialist approach to state ownership.[11]

THE UNIONS AND PUBLIC OWNERSHIP

The railway unions adopted an increasingly pro-public ownership stance towards the end of the nineteenth century, influenced by the rise of socialism and the Independent Labour Party, which had a strong following on the railways.[12] The Amalgamated Society of Railway Servants passed a resolution in favour of nationalisation as early as 1894, and even the less militant Railway Clerks Association approved a resolution in favour of nationalisation at its conference in 1910. The union president, John Romeril, argued in 1913 that the industry should be managed by a 'National Railway Board'; and that one third of the membership of this board would be representatives of the users of the railways, including chambers of commerce; one third would be MPs, and the remaining third would be elected railway workers.[13] During the 1890s the locomen's union ASLEF carried regular articles in its *Locomotive Journal* by William Wilson of the Railway Nationalisation League, and ASLEF formally committed to state ownership at its 1909 conference.[14]

Syndicalist railway workers argued for a more radical approach, with the railways in their entirety being run by the workers themselves.

Syndicalism had gained a small but influential following on the railways during the period before the First World War – and *The Syndicalist Railwayman* also appeared at this time. The movement's high-point was between 1911 and 1913; in August 1911 there was a partial general strike on the railways, beginning in Liverpool, where the influence of syndicalists such as Tom Mann was considerable, though their actual number was small.[15] The action rapidly spread to many other parts of the network, and the grass-roots unity which emerged in the strike was a major factor in subsequent moves towards setting up a single union for all railway workers – a key issue for the syndicalists but also a development seen as sensible and pragmatic by many other railway workers. The National Union of Railwaymen (NUR) was formed in 1913, bringing together the ASRS, the more militant General Railway Workers Union and the smaller United Pointsmen's and Signalmen's Society. The locomotive workers in craft-conscious ASLEF and the white-collar workers in the Railway Clerks Association stayed out of the new body.

The more radical elements within the newly-formed NUR had strong support in the district councils, which were composed of rank-and-file activists. A national conference of the NUR's district councils in 1917 passed a syndicalist-inspired motion:

> That this Conference, seeing the railways are being controlled by the state for the benefit of the nation during the war, is of the opinion that they should not revert to private ownership afterwards. Further, we believe that national welfare demands they should be acquired by the State, to be jointly managed by the State and representatives of the National Union of Railwaymen.[16]

Slightly later, Guild Socialists put forward ideas for a 'national railway guild' to run the industry. In 1918 the National Guilds League published *Towards a National Railway Guild*, which argued for state ownership but not state control. It proposed that the state should take ownership of the railways, but that a 'Railway Guild', based on the railway unions, would run them, paying rent to the state:

> In this aspect, too, the State will represent the consumers and users of the railways. And, if the users decide that it is best for the community that railway transport shall be free for all, then instead of paying

a levy to the State the Railway Guild will receive its income from the State, out of the proceeds of those taxes levied on those Guilds which still sell their products and services.[17]

The Guild Socialists argued that the overall management of the railways should be done through a board, or 'central committee', half of which would be nominated by the government and the other half by the railway workers through their unions. The Guild Socialists recognised that simply having a handful of representatives on a national body was insufficient, and that 'control, to be real, must be local as well as national, and indeed, must be far more local than national'.[18] *Towards a National Railway Guild* did more than simply set out a utopian vision: it laid out a practical approach to achieving the vision.

New 'conciliation boards' had been formed in 1907, with limited powers over local issues, and further powers were granted after the 1911 strike; and although these were unequal bodies, in which railway management had most of the power, the Guild Socialists saw them as a possible means by which local control could be exercised. They argued for converting them into local 'negotiation boards' which would represent all grades of railway worker, 'gradually developing into managerial bodies'. Alongside this evolutionary approach to industrial democracy, merger of the rail unions into one industrial union for all railway workers was also seen as essential.

Guild Socialism had a limited life. As with the syndicalists, many of its proponents were drawn into the young Communist Party or the Labour Party. Yet its vision for industrial democracy, although framed in the somewhat medieval language of 'guilds', was far from backward-looking; and some of its aspirations for greater workers' control of industry had a continued relevance.[19]

THE INDEPENDENT LABOUR PARTY

The Independent Labour Party (ILP) was founded in Bradford in 1893, and railway nationalisation was one of its early, popular, causes. The ILP recruited strongly in the railway industry, and assisted in the emergence of a new generation of radicalised activists that challenged the timorous Liberal-inclined leadership of the ASRS. It was ILP activists in the Doncaster branch of the ASRS, including Tom Steels, who tabled the famous 1899 resolution at the Trades Union Congress which called for the formation of what was to become the Labour Party (initially the 'Labour Representation Committee').

The ILP saw the railways as the most obvious target for early nationalisation. Philip Snowden addressed a crowd estimated at over 2000 outside Huddersfield railway station on 2 July 1905, and argued that the people who worked the railway and the people who used the railway should own the railway. 'Socialism, therefore, as plainly as I can put it, means the merging of all land and machines into co-operative ownership.'[20]

ILP member Emil Davies wrote extensively on the subject. In *The Case for Railway Nationalisation*, published in 1912, he criticised excessive profits, poor and dangerous working conditions, lack of investment in improvements including safety measures and electrification, and the absence of any linkage with the needs of the nation's economy. He proposed a national management board, led by government-appointed commissioners but with a supervisory 'Railway Council' that would include representatives of local government, chambers of commerce and the trades unions. This would exert a degree of accountability on the proposed railway commissioners who would be responsible for the day-to-day running of the railway:

> As these Railway Commissioners would be as much autocrats in their own way as directors of the Railway Companies are at the present time, it would be necessary to temper their autocratic way by an admixture of popular control. It would be desirable, therefore, to constitute a Railway Council, which should act as a sort of Railway parliament, representative of all sections of the community. This should be an elected body, and could be formed on something like the following basis: each County Council could appoint two of its members, and each County Borough Council one representative, the Associated Chamber of Commerce, the Chambers of Trade, and the associated Chambers of Agriculture of the kingdom should appoint a certain number of members … whilst the Trade Union Congress might appoint twelve members as representative of labour.[21]

This was a move away from the neo-syndicalist approach of railway workers themselves having a direct stake in the management of the industry; presumably the rail unions would exert influence through the TUC-nominated members. The responsibilities of the Railway Council would relate to policy:

> Its duties would be to consider all questions of general improvements, rate and fare reductions or increases, wages etc. and its decisions should be binding upon the Railway Commissioners, provided, however, that such decisions were ratified by the Minister for Railways.[22]

Davies's work was influential amongst the more radical figures in the rail unions, and the Railway Clerks Association's John Romeril was clearly influenced by this approach towards governance of a state-owned railway. Davies, alongside the syndicalists and guild socialists, had recognised the potential problem of state-owned industry becoming bureaucratised and remote, though his solutions were quite different from the classic 'workers' control' stance. His idea of giving a role not only to local government but also to local and regional business associations was radical and – for the left – unusual.

This proposal for how to take the railways into state ownership echoed the suggestions of Edwards from the mid-1890s, which recommended making use of the still-extant provisions of Gladstone's 1844 legislation. As we have seen, these involved buying out the companies, with compensation being paid on the basis of a calculation of the expected profits for the ensuing twenty-five years. Davies developed this option in some detail, arguing that the economies of scale of a national railway organisation would avoid the financial burden caused by the enormous waste and duplication of the private system, and would give the state a net profit, year on year.

As we have seen, there were great hopes that the railways would be nationalised after the First World War. Liberal Prime Minister Lloyd George went so far as to tell a deputation from the TUC in March 1918 that he was 'in complete sympathy' with railway nationalisation; and many other senior Liberal politicians seemed to be in agreement – including Winston Churchill, who acknowledged at a meeting of Dundee Chamber of Commerce that railway nationalisation would happen sooner rather than later.[23] And the newly-constituted Labour Party also added its voice to calls for national ownership of railways. But in the end the railway interest won out, and it was not until after the second world war that nationalisation finally took place.

The model Labour in the end opted for was that of the 'Morrisonian' corporation, run by 'experts'. This is discussed in the next chapter.

When Morrison had outlined his approach in the early 1930s in *Socialisation and Transport*, he had used the proposed London Passenger Transport Board as a model (coupled with a highly idealised view of transport in Soviet Russia).[24] But not everyone had agreed with this approach. George Woodcock, writing in 1943, argued for the syndicalist model of workers' control, heavily influenced by the experience of the Spanish CNT railway unions during the Spanish Civil War.[25] And shortly after the war, Birmingham railwayman T.E. Nixon put forward a detailed model of industrial democracy, in a pamphlet called *First Stages of Workers Control of the Railways*. The industry would be run through a system of area and regional committees. Nixon made the point that the great potential for harnessing the ideas of railway workers was not being drawn upon:

> … inventive geniuses have not always come from the managerial class. Indeed all the great inventions which initiated the industrial revolution … came from the common people. Thousands of intellectually active railwaymen have been kept with their noses to the grindstone wearing out their energies and wasting their prospective contributions towards prosperity on the desert air of reactionary railway management.[26]

The views of Woodcock and Nixon largely fell on deaf ears – as we shall see.

NOTES

1. Emil Davies, *The Case for Railway Nationalisation*, 1912, p5.
2. See G. Alderman, *The Railway Interest*, Leicester 1973.
3. See Michael Simmons, *The Railway Age*, 1962, p116.
4. Ibid.
5. C.F. Adams, quoted in Salveson (1989), p12.
6. The Independent Labour Party was formed in 1893 though smaller socialist groups had been in existence since the 1880s. The ILP attracted many disenchanted Liberals who supported greater state intervention, including railway nationalisation. See Mark Bevir, *The Making of British Socialism*, 2012.
7. Edwards, op cit.

8. Ibid, p212.
9. Ibid, p201.
10. James Hole, *National Railways – an argument for state purchase*, 1893, p351.
11. See report of Snowden's speech in Huddersfield in *The Worker*, 1 July 1905.
12. See David Howell, *British Workers and the Independent Labour Party 1888-1906*, Manchester 1983.
13. See Malcolm Wallace, *Single or Return?* op cit; also Branko Pribićević, *The Shop Stewards Movement and Workers' Control 1910-1922*, 1959; and Colin Ward, *Freedom to Go – after the motor car age*, 1991.
14. Robert Griffiths, *Driven by ideals – a history of ASLEF*, 2005, p47.
15. For a short period a rank-and-file newsletter called *The Syndicalist Railwayman* was published during 1911. See Frank McKenna, 'Victorian Railway Workers', in *History Workshop* No. 1, Spring 1976, pp72-3.
16. Ward, op cit, p60. See also Bob Holton, *British Syndicalism 1900-1914*, 1976.
17. National Guilds, *Towards a National Railway Guild*, 1918, p9.
18. Ibid, p13. See also Mark Bevir, op cit, pp310-312, for a modern discussion on guild socialism.
19. See G.D.H. Cole and R. Page Arnot, *Trade Unionism on the Railways* (1917) for a useful discussion of workers' control on the railways. Cole was a leading advocate of 'guild socialism'.
20. *The Worker* (Huddersfield), 2 July 1905.
21. Emil Davies, *The Case for Railway Nationalisation*, 1912, pp249-250.
22. Ibid, p252.
23. Bagwell, op cit, pp405-6.
24. Herbert Morrison, *Socialisation and Transport – The organisation of socialised industries with particular reference to the London Passenger Transport Bill*, 1933. Morrison here argued for 'consultative committees' for employee representatives, but not direct involvement in management – using Soviet Russia as a model.
25. George Woodcock, *Railways and Society: for workers' control of the railways*, 1943.
26. T.E. Nixon, *First Stages of State Control of the Railways*, Manchester 1948, p6.

3. THE RAILWAYS UNDER STATE OWNERSHIP

This structure for nationalisation had arisen following a long debate over how nationalised industries should be organised and managed. The 1947 Transport Act was a far cry from workers' control. This issue had often been hotly debated within the labour movement, but was not seriously considered by Attlee's government.[1]

Britain's railways were nationalised in 1948 following the election of a Labour government in 1945. But the form of nationalisation which emerged did little to change things. The same managers carried on managing in much the same old way, and trades unions continued to be largely reactive, rather than pro-active, organisations. British Railways was never a well-loved organisation. At best, it was seen by the workers as an improvement on what they had experienced before.

Labour not only took the railways into public ownership, but also the canals and road haulage; and it created a 'British Transport Commission' to co-ordinate the various transport modes – though in reality each operation went its own way. The railways were run by a Rail Executive, but the in-fighting between the Executive and Transport Commission had a debilitating effect on the early British railways, which inevitably contributed to its decline.

The experiment in 'integrated' transport, such as it was, proved to be short-lived. The Conservatives won back power in 1951 and promptly de-nationalised road haulage. The railways continued much as they were, but they began to suffer from increasing road competition. Increased access to private car ownership was part of the contemporary ideology about what a modern Britain should look like (with ownership of 'your own house' also figuring strongly).[2]

But railway nationalisation had been more than just a pragmatic move by the Attlee government. It was the culmination of decades of campaigning by socialists and railway trade unionists, and great hopes had been placed on the new people's British Railways. Michael Young, writing in 1948, had argued that 'the nationalised industries should be models of industrial democracy which can later be followed elsewhere.'[3] That this did not happen is in large part due to the model of nationalisation that was adopted. Against a more co-operative approach, as we've seen, Herbert Morrison had already developed ideas for running transport in London in the shape of the London Passenger Transport Board. There was no room here for passenger interests, or even those of employees: the board was run by appointed 'experts'. This then became the model for the British Transport Commission and the Railway Executive.

Some of the railway unions had been hoping for more involvement. At the NUR's 1946 annual conference, general secretary John Benstead had argued that: 'It is an irrefutable fact that in the localities within the ranks of the working people there are latent all the necessary capabilities to make an effective contribution to the success of the transport undertakings'.[4] As a sop to the unions, Bill Allen of the locomotive drivers' union ASLEF was given a place on the Executive's board. But most of the key jobs went to senior figures from the old private companies.

THE BEECHING ERA AND ITS LEGACY

The experience of the railways under public ownership was mixed. The modernisation that was desperately needed after years of under-investment and war damage finally came, to a degree, with the 1955 *Modernisation Plan*, which augured the replacement of steam traction by diesel and electric, coupled with investment in infrastructure. But the plan had fatal weaknesses. One railway manager observed:

> The Plan was a disaster, largely cobbled together from pre-war projects with no clear idea as to what the railways were *for*. Political meddling, for example to favour certain loco builders, made matters worse. The mishandling of modernisation was a key factor in turning government opinion against the railway from 1960 onwards.[5]

The tide was running against rail transport in other ways, as car ownership began to grow. Some degree of rationalisation was therefore inevitable, and it was necessary to cut out some of the duplicated routes which were a legacy of the brief age of competition. But what actually came was the appointment of Dr Richard Beeching as chairman of the

British Railways Board (as the Railways Executive had been re-chris-
tened), with a mandate to take an axe to much of the network, in order
to achieve that increasingly impossible will o'the wisp, a profitable
railway. His subsequent report, *The Re-shaping of British Railways*, was
published in 1963, and was awesome in its implications – which were
eventually to deprive thousands of communities of their railway services.

Chris Austin and Richard Faulkner have stressed the unholy
alliance that emerged in the early 1960s to promote drastic cuts in
the network:

> There was no single conspiracy to destroy the railways, but individuals
> from various parts of the political spectrum were drawn to the supposed
> Holy Grail of a much smaller network and a 'profitable' core. They
> included right-wing free market ideologues opposed to the concept of
> public transport, well-meaning but misguided social democrats who
> saw rail subsidies as regressive, beneficial only to the middle classes, and
> a variety of lobbying interests who would benefit from the expansion of
> road building, car ownership and road haulage – including trade
> unionists opposed to the development of rail freight services.[6]

Following publication of the Beeching report, the programme of
closures followed quickly and ruthlessly, with few threatened lines
managing to survive the cull. The election of a Labour government in
1964 did little to halt the process under Tom Fraser's tenure as transport minister. Barbara Castle took over in 1965 and stopped some of
the closures, but many still went ahead.

The unions put up a lukewarm opposition, despite their members'
futures being on the line – nearly 9000 clerical and supervisory jobs
alone were under threat, and many more in the 'wages' grades. It is
hard to escape the conclusion that a stronger fight could have been
mounted. The National Union of Railwaymen's general secretary, Sid
Greene, was of the traditional right-wing school – most comfortable
when having 'a quiet word' with the men in power. William Evans, the
retiring general secretary of ASLEF, described the report as 'a very able
document and an entirely honest attempt to rationalise the railway
system', though his comments were repudiated by his executive. The
first statement from the TSSA came from future Labour minister Ray
Gunter, who told a TV interviewer that the Beeching report was 'one
of the bravest efforts I have known in industry to face the economic

facts of life'.[7] Labour's transport spokesman George Strauss welcomed the report, though he expressed concern about 'the proposals to curtail railway services on the drastic scale suggested'.[8] Fighting talk indeed. What we were seeing in these responses was the culmination of the post-war pro-roads consensus, which viewed railways as a thing of the past. At best, their future lay in a small number of main-line routes.

The report's targets were not just little-used rural branch lines. Important commuter routes such as Liverpool–Southport and Leeds to Ilkley and Wetherby were on the death list. Main lines such as Edinburgh to Carlisle via Hawick ('The Waverley Line') were also to disappear, leaving major Borders towns isolated.[9] Thankfully, some routes managed to survive, but many lines which could have played an important role in solving today's transport problems were mercilessly cut. Any BR manager who at that time had ideas for reducing costs of local lines (for example through 'pay-train' operation) was told in no uncertain terms to shut up if he wanted a career to look forward to.

Most rank and file rail union members were horrified at the implications of Beeching but felt helpless in the face of a government that was determined to implement the report. The rail unions discussed options for campaigning against the closures, including a national rail strike, but this was – probably wisely – rejected by the white-collar TSSA. Instead, the unions managed to extract improved resettlement and redundancy terms. The fight was lost before it had hardly begun. The unions could have reached out to a wider cross-section of the community, in business, threatened communities and local government, but they were not ideologically equipped to do that. Closures followed in rapid succession, making opposition difficult and fragmented. BR was under pressure to deliver results, and line after line went with hardly a whimper of protest. 'Last trains' became local carnivals, with trains carrying many times the number of passengers who normally used them. The last train from the railway town of Horwich ran in September 1965, hauled by a steam locomotive cleaned and embellished by young local enthusiasts the night before, its departure accompanied by dozens of exploding detonators. Cold reality set in very quickly, when Horwich and many other towns and villages were virtually cut off. The so-called 'replacement bus services' lasted a few years, sometimes months, before they were withdrawn. Hardly any made an attempt to connect into the rail network at surviving stations. We are still counting the cost.[10]

Jenny Lynn, a Calderdale Labour councillor, grew up in a railway family. Her father was station-master at Guisborough, at the end of a busy branch line from Middlesbrough, between 1960 and 1963:

> When we arrived there my dad made lots of suggestions to his higher ups to make various improvements, like making the timetable simple and easy to memorise – what we now call 'regular interval departures', with trains leaving at the same time past each hour. He got my mum, my sister and myself to push timetable leaflets through every door in the town (which at that time had a population of 15,000). He even got the local bus service to have a stop in the station yard. Needless to say he was ignored by his bosses. Instead they fiddled the figures to demonstrate that the line was making a loss, by the simple expedient of depreciating the diesel trains operating on the line over 10 years, instead of the 30-plus years which they actually went on to run. In the ensuing decades, Guisborough experienced lots of new housing development, with the population growing from 15,000 to 40,000, and many people commuting – now by car of course – into ICI Wilton and other industries on Teesside. And of course they ripped up the track and sold bits of the land off asap, for garden expansion or housing, just to make absolutely sure that it couldn't be reopened again![11]

Guisborough was depressingly typical of its time, with dedicated railway workers being told that their commitment counted for nothing in the brave new Beeching age.

Another former BR manager highlighted the cuts to routes in the prosperous south-east – which now suffer acute traffic congestion.

> Guildford to Cranleigh should never have closed. True, it would be unrealistic to argue the case for retention of the whole line between Guildford and Horsham but there was a good case for the retention of part of the branch between Cranleigh and Guildford, to relieve pressure on the congested A281. The particularly short-sighted and daft feature of this closure is that the decision to close the line was made at the same time as the decision, by the same Government, that the town of Cranleigh was to be developed significantly, with a consequent large increase in population. It was demonstrated at the time of closure in 1965, by a 'maverick' BR employee, that if the line had been retained as far as Cranleigh and electrified, a service could have been provided at

marginal cost using EMUs and crews that laid over at Guildford between services to and from London via the 'new line'. The report was suppressed by BR management and the employee told, in no uncertain terms, to mind his own business, reflecting the rather macho 'I can close more railways than you' culture that existed, to an extent, in BR at the time. The other outrageous feature of the closures was the indecent haste with which BR tended to destroy the infrastructure of lines that closed in order to ensure that it would be difficult and very costly, if not impossible, to re-instate them at some future date.[12]

The closure programme had run its course by the early 1970s, but a new round of cuts was proposed in the early 1980s in yet another report, this time produced by Sir David Serpell. This report was vigorously attacked both by the media and unions and also by BR itself. There have even been suggestions that the report itself was constructed to be ridiculed! One railway manager commented:

I was part of the BR team pointing out the idiocies in this report, and it was like shooting fish in a barrel! In fairness to Serpell, it has since been suggested that this was probably what he wanted, by making the pro-closure lobby (and in particular Thatcher's friend Alf Sherman) look ridiculous.[13]

The Serpell Report was shelved, but the early 1980s were probably the nadir of publicly-owned British Rail. The impact of Beeching's cuts was felt over a prolonged period; though closures were reduced to a trickle by the late 1970s, the threat as typified by Serpell remained. The prevailing management culture continued to be one of managing decline, with a sullen workforce which had lost trust in management. Yet there were pockets of resistance in railway management. A number of middle managers – John Davies in South Wales, 'Nobby' Clarke at Norwich, Ron Cotton in Liverpool, Peter Fox at Research, even then had expansionary mindsets.[14]

THE BEGINNINGS OF A FIGHTBACK

Beeching and Serpell were not the end of government attempts to trim the railway network. The Settle-Carlisle Line, which had been threatened with closure by Beeching but managed to survive, was again proposed for abandonment in the early 1980s. This led to the biggest campaign in railway history, as a result of which, finally, Conservative transport minister Michael Portillo bowed to pressure, telling BR to look instead at ways of developing the route. The fight for the Settle–Carlisle Line was in some ways the railway equivalent of the Miners' Strike – though with a better result! The campaigners' success in heading off closure made it difficult for BR or the Thatcher government to contemplate further cuts in the network. The broadly-based campaign that united Dales communities, trades unions and other supporters of the railway paid off. Since then, hardly any line closures have taken place.[15]

The role of the national transport and environmental campaign, Campaign for Better Transport (originally 'Transport 2000'), was central in shifting an increasingly receptive public opinion, which began to see the obsession with road building as increasingly unacceptable. Alongside the early Transport 2000, rail campaigners in the Railway Development Society, as well as highly localised groups, were having some impact on local authorities (see chapter five). By the mid-1980s the unions were no longer an isolated voice arguing for more investment in rail.[16]

THE SECOND RAILWAY AGE?

The BR of the late 1980s was increasingly at odds with the Thatcher government. A new breed of highly effective senior managers emerged who wanted to see an expanding, not contracting, railway.[17] Management re-structuring led to a clearer focus on markets, with the emergence of InterCity, Network SouthEast for the huge outer suburban network around London, and Provincial (later 'Regional Railways'). Each had talented managers who turned round the fortunes of a railway which had appeared to be in terminal decline. The 'closure' mentality of the 1970s was overtaken by a more positive spirit within railway management, with recruitment of a new generation of idealistic and public-spirited young managers through the highly acclaimed BR management trainee scheme. The traditionally all-male bastion of railway management began to crumble, as young women graduates joined the scheme and proved that they were quite capable of running a railway. Many stuck the course and later became directors in the privatised railway.

The British Railways Board was headed up by Bob Reid, who had the strength of character to take on the road-oriented civil servants in Whitehall, and by implication the Thatcher government itself. However, he also became close to arch-Thatcherite Nicholas Ridley, and succeeded in winning unexpected support for railways.

As BR was renewing itself, there was also a parallel shift in its local government, largely through the work of the passenger transport executives (PTEs) that had been created by Barbara Castle during her reign as transport minister in the late 1960s. The PTEs had substantial powers to fund passenger transport, and the results of their efforts started to become evident during the 1980s. During the following decade Tyne and Wear got its Metro system, Greater Manchester began to develop a light rail network, and bus-rail interchanges were built at major centres in all of the PTE areas. Local rail services which had been threatened with closure in the Beeching report, such as the Leeds–Ilkley–Bradford–Skipton network, were electrified. Looking back on that time, many railway managers comment on how relatively easy and cost-effective it was to open new stations and introduce new services. Despite the Thatcherite prejudice that state-run services were inefficient, by the late 1980s BR was probably the most efficient railway in Europe, working positively with the metropolitan PTEs to develop good quality local services as well as investing in an InterCity network which many continental railways rushed to copy.

The period between the mid-1980s and privatisation in the mid-1990s is curiously uncharted by railway historians.[18] Against considerable odds BR managed to develop new schemes – including the electrification of the Aire Valley lines in West Yorkshire – and to develop what had been seen as 'the hopeless case' of regional railways.

In the early 1990s BR introduced the 'Organising for Quality' reorganisation when the whole 'production line' of BR was put under sector management and the old 'regions' were abolished. At this time a large number of experienced older engineers and operators retired. As Andrew McNaughton, then a manager with BR, commented:

> They had coexisted with the sector business directors but weren't prepared to serve under them. I have to say that to those of us in our late 30s and early 40s this was wonderful, as suddenly we could advance without waiting for dead men's shoes to become available. Track quality and train performance improved with the new and more local management focus. However, investment in provincial railways stopped under the new 'maintenance holiday' regime.[19]

However, despite these achievements the political tide was running against BR, and by the early 1990s various right-wing think-tanks were suggesting their favoured approach of privatisation. In the end it was the John Major administration that bulldozed through the 1993 Railways Act, thereby ending the all-too-brief golden age of publicly-owned railways in the UK.[20]

NOTES

1. Kerry Hamilton and Stephen Potter, *Losing Track*, 1985, p32.
2. See David Kynaston, *Austerity Britain 1945-1951*, 2007; and *A World to Build 1945-48*, 2007.
3. Michael Young, *Small Man–Big World*, 1948.
4. John Benstead, speaking at the NUR AGM in Morecambe, July 1946.
5. Personal communication to author, May 2013.
6. Richard Faulkner and Chris Austin, *Holding the Line – how Britain's railways were saved*, 2013, p5.
7. Wallace, op cit, p349.
8. Philip Bagwell, *The Railwaymen* Vol 2, pp132-158.
9. See David Spaven, *Waverley Route: the life, death and re-birth the Borders Railway*, 2012.
10. See Mayer Hillman and Anne Whalley, *The Social Consequences of Line Closures*, 1980.
11. Personal letter to author, March 2013.
12. Personal letter to author from J. Chapman, March 2013.
13. Private email to author, 3 May 2013.
14. I am grateful to Allan Dare for reminding me of these men; Peter Fox went on to become a leading railway publisher and sadly died in 2011.
15. See Roger Henshaw, *The Line that Refused to Die*, for an insider's account of the closure campaign.
16. See Railway Development Society, *Fighting for Rail* (1983).
17. The ground had been laid by Sir Peter Parker in the mid to late 1970s. In the words of one manager: 'he did wonders for railway morale, was very effective fighting the railway conversion idiots such as Sherman, etc, and of course it was Parker who recognised and supported Reid. A great guy all round'. Personal email from Allan Dare to author, May 2013.
18. However, see Nigel Harris and Ernest Godward, *The Privatisation of British Rail* (1997), for an insightful outline of the period.
19. Andrew McNaughton, personal communication to author, April 2013.
20. See Salveson, op cit, particularly pp65-82, for a review of the right-wing arguments.

4. A BOTCHED PRIVATISATION

Our objective is to improve the quality of railway services by creating new opportunities for private sector involvement. This will mean more competition, greater efficiency and a wider choice of services more closely tailored to what customers want.[1]

The structure that emerged after the 1993 Railways Act was based on separation of operations and infrastructure, reflecting a neoliberal notion of 'freeing-up' the railway network to the benefits of competition, with a plethora of private operators buying 'slots' to operate trains. However, there was a fundamental contradiction at the heart of the new system. Passenger operations were bundled up into more than twenty franchises, and these were put out to tender by the Office of Passenger Rail Franchising (OPRAF), though with a notional commitment to 'open access' companies being able to provide niche services in addition to the core franchised network. The first bids were won by a mixture of established private companies and some management teams, though the latter (with some notable exceptions, e.g. Chiltern) were quickly bought out by larger companies.[2]

The establishment of the franchises failed to bring the expected results. Whilst some degree of innovation happened on the InterCity routes, the regional franchises were largely devoid of entrepreneurial flair, and were dependent on public intervention to 'buy' additional services. On the one hand the short term of the franchise arrangement provided little incentive to invest in growth and on the other the Department for Transport was reluctant to 'lose control', in case this created a need for financial support in future years. The Strategic Rail Authority, formed on the initiative of John Prescott in 2000 to take over OPRAF's functions and provide a more strategic framework for rail, did not make things any better. As one senior rail manager commented, 'the SRA hard-wired everything, constraining service improvements'.[3]

Far from freeing-up the network to new entrants, the obstacles placed in front of any potential open access operator, particularly for the provision of passenger services, were immense. Non-franchised passenger services have never really taken off, despite a few rare successes such as Hull Trains and Grand Central.[4] There was a freer rein for freight, with the former BR Railfreight business being sold off in chunks, and encouragement given to other private operators to enter the market. Like the companies operating passenger services, they did not own their infrastructure, but, unlike most passenger services operators, they could function as long-term businesses, and were not subject to the control of the Department for Transport.[5]

Part of the privatisation 'settlement' included the establishment of rail regulator (now the Office of Rail Regulation), with a remit to ensure fair treatment between the different players in the industry, and also to set a range of charges to provide the financial under-pinning of the railway, notably the track access charges that operators pay to Network Rail (formerly Railtrack).

The infrastructure company, Railtrack (privatised in 1997), was set up to own, manage and develop the railway infrastructure, and its main income stream was from track access charges levied on train operators. This created a fairy-tale land where Railtrack appeared to be a profitable enterprise, based on government-subsidised franchisees paying a heavily loaded 'track access' charge. However, in addition to track access charges which were fixed by state regulation, Railtrack also owned a vast property portfolio, which was potentially far more profitable than running a rail network. One senior rail manager observed that:

> Railtrack set itself up as a 'virtual company' with no maintenance and renewal staff, no proper asset base, and without the expertise to be an informed customer. This included a naïve and, with hindsight, totally unacceptable mindset that they had contracted out their infrastructure safety responsibilities to their contractors too.[6]

When the Conservatives introduced their privatisation legislation in 1993, they had not had the intention to sell-off Railtrack, at least in the short-term. However, around 1995 'the market' told the government that the sale of units like BR Infrastructure Service and the train operators would not be successful unless the company at the centre of the industry – Railtrack – was also privatised: 'Railtrack privatisation was conjured out of nothing in a hurry to satisfy this need – we had all understood that this was the one bit of BR that would stay in public ownership whilst all the other bits matured. So 1997 saw the business privatised'.[7]

Routine maintenance, let alone investment, in the rail network began to suffer accordingly. The result was the Hatfield accident of October 2000, when a train derailed at high speed owing to corroded track. In the words of former head of the Strategic Rail Authority Sir Alistair Morton, the system suffered 'a collective nervous breakdown' in its response to Hatfield. Ultimately the Blair government intervened, and a new body emerged, structured as a not-for-dividend company, to be called Network Rail. This fell short of the nationalisation that the rail unions demanded, but it took the railway infrastructure away from the short-termism of a profit-making business only accountable to its shareholders, as well as the equally short-term perspectives of the Treasury.

However, it is unclear as to whom the current Network Rail is accountable. It has a number of 'public members' (far too many to be effective), who exert little control over a company that has been criticised for awarding its directors huge bonuses on top of very generous salaries. Network Rail's recently-published Long-Term Incentive Plan gives each of its four executive directors a total of £600,000 a year. The company's Finance Director gets £168,000 a year bonus on top of his salary of £360,000.

Rail privatisation has also failed to secure another of its implicit aims – that of reducing the power of the unions. For, whilst union membership has declined, the industrial power of some sectors, notably drivers and signalling staff, has increased – along with their pay.

The orthodoxy of 'competition' being automatically a good thing is increasingly being questioned in the industry. One senior manager commented:

Is true competition in the operation of services really beneficial to the passenger or is it more likely a case of more *apparent* choice actually meaning less, particularly with our over-complex ticketing system? The early years of the railways took this to extreme, leading to an unbalanced network, but I would suggest that the proliferation of operator specific/train specific deals today is in danger of damaging something the railways can do well, which is 'turn up and go' mass transport. Also I would suggest that competition in procurement, whether it be rolling stock, service, franchises or anything else, has added to cost rather than reduced it – West Coast, Thameslink rolling stock are just two examples of many that spring to mind. That's not to say all competition is bad, but being slaves to the wrong ideology probably is![8]

A LOSS OF COLLECTIVE MEMORY AND RAILWAY EXPERTISE

The early period of privatisation was enormously destabilising for employees at all levels, in both infrastructure and operations. A direct consequence of privatisation has been an enormous loss of experience and knowledge that had been passed down from generations. The incoming leadership of the privatised railway made little secret of their contempt for 'the old railway', and the consequences of this attitude were literally disastrous. The same manager quoted above – who has spent a lifetime in railway engineering – commented:

> There was a total scramble for jobs, eye off the ball, with track quality and performance tumbling. Many senior engineers retired as they were told they were not entrepreneurial enough. Railtrack under John Edmonds continued to behave as a BR sectorised organisation and involved very highly centralised decision-making to retain control.[9]

Further loss of experienced and talented managers happened when the train operating companies and rolling-stock-leasing companies were sold at knock-down prices:

> It made a few multi-millionaires, especially in the ROSCOs, but most become slaves to the new bus company owners. The next five years or so saw a further steady trickle of managers leave. 1996 saw the sell-off of BR Infrastructure Services units to construction companies with no idea of asset. Track quality plummeted. Needless to say, this led to further losses in front-line engineering staff.[10]

It is hard to prove conclusively, but accidents such as Hatfield and Potter's Bar would have been unlikely to have occurred under BR's 'old-fashioned' management. McNaughton continues:

By 1997 John Edmonds had been ousted and Gerald Corbett took charge. Many remaining engineers retired and the centralised organisation was devolved to 'empowered zones' (regions). Control was lost. 1994 had marked a high point in track quality. It then deteriorated very badly in the following three years when the railway infrastructure managers were totally distracted by the BRIS reorganisation and sell offs. It then started to recover but it was 2002 before it recovered to 1994 levels – just as Network Rail took over.[11]

After the Hatfield crash a period of re-centralisation set in as the centre regained control from the zones. There was then further loss of invaluable railway expertise: 'The new regime under Iain Coucher made it quite plain that the remaining "BR generation" was no more welcome than the Railtrack era managers. Most left quickly and the remainder followed steadily'.[12]

The Co-operative Party's report on Network Rail identified some serious failures of governance, saying that 'its Board is not accountable to anyone in a meaningful way'.[13] As a former 'public member' (amongst some one hundred or more others) I can only agree. The public members have little or no real say in how the business is run, with appointed board members taking all the major decisions.

The privatisation and subsequent 'quasi-nationalisation' of Railtrack kept the basic structure of the industry intact, but the persistent reorganisation has hardly been good for an industry which works best with long-term stability. Franchising has meanwhile continued for passenger operations, with the market increasingly dominated by large groups such as First, Stagecoach and Go-Ahead. However, a growing number of European state-owned railways, such as Netherlands Railways, German Rail (through its Arriva subsidiary) and French operator SNCF have begun to win UK franchises, in some cases as joint ventures with UK-based private companies such as First and Serco.

WORST OF BOTH WORLDS? STATE CONTROL – PRIVATE DELIVERY

An often forgotten feature of the post-1993 system is the very high level of state control of the railways, through the government's management of franchises and control of the purse strings for much infrastructure and rolling stock investment. Some railway managers have suggested that there is more interference by civil servants in the running of the railway now than there was in BR days. They're almost certainly right, despite a much slimmed-down Department for Transport. And another aspect of the current system is the lack of incentive by private franchisees to invest. This is a structural fault of franchising, with the core 'franchise agreement' between train operator and government setting the terms of what will be delivered. The original contract may, in some cases, include new rolling stock, but this will be delivered through the complex mechanisms of the franchise contract and ultimately be the responsibility of government.

The scope for independent initiative by the franchisee is limited to the life of the franchise, and by whether or not a good enough business case can be made for improvements – for example to station facilities – within the remaining franchise time. The closer you get to the end of the franchise the more difficult it becomes to justify anything but the most essential investment, and the situation is not helped by franchise extensions which can't be planned for. Franchise extensions do little more than give breathing time to hard-pressed civil servants, while allowing the franchisee to carry on milking the franchise with no extra investment, unless specifically sanctioned by the Department for Transport. The government can 'buy' some additional benefits as part of the extension deal, such as extra car parking or CCTV at stations. But all this is totally ad hoc and short-term.[14]

One of the little-remarked aspects of short-term franchising on the railways is the effect on staff morale at all levels. Railway people have a strong and positive tradition of 'service', a word which counts for little in the profit-driven age of brands and 'the bottom line'. But the ephemeral nature of franchising prevents the development of any real company loyalty – though most railway employees, however long their 'length of service', remain loyal to their industry and the people it serves. One employee with over thirty years' service on the railway, from guard to senior manager, said:

> To give your loyalty to a here-today gone-tomorrow train operating company is unrealistic. We serve the people, the passengers and provide the service, those things that have real permanence and are beyond the 'brand' identity. It demeans our loyalty to suggest we can acquire it like a mere commodity – it is not just picked up with the

wage packet. Time, pain, pleasure, honesty, belief and history are the ingredients for loyalty, never shareholder value, 'being on message' or brand awareness. Anyone who says otherwise is just acting.[15]

You cannot quantify employee loyalty; it doesn't easily lend itself to a consultant's report, but when you get a decline in employee morale the results can be all too apparent to passengers.

THE CHANGING FRAMEWORK

Following abolition of the Strategic Rail Authority in 2005, franchising became the direct responsibility of the Department for Transport. However, there are notable exceptions. Scotland has responsibility for its domestic rail services, through the Scottish government's executive arm, Transport Scotland. On Merseyside, the region's passenger transport executive, Merseytravel, has responsibility for the Merseyrail electric network.[16] Transport for London manages the London Overground franchise. These concessions have proved highly successful; they have seen substantial passenger growth and long-term investment in the network, and are accountable to democratically elected bodies. It should also be pointed out that Northern Ireland Railways remains as a state-owned and vertically-integrated railway that has close synergies with bus services in the province, which are also publicly owned.

The current arrangements in England are under review, and the Department for Transport has been consulting widely on proposals to devolve responsibilities for franchising in England to a more local level, particularly in the metropolitan areas. The exclusion of Scotland and Wales from the review reflects the fact that in both cases 'decentralisation' has gone further there than in most parts of England (apart from Merseyside and Greater London).

The most radical option currently being looked at is for the passenger transport executives and Northern local authorities to take over complete responsibility for the 'Northern' franchise – and possibly TransPennine Express, which sits largely within the contours of the Northern Rail franchise, with the exception of its Scottish extension. A similar process is underway in the Midlands, with West Midlands PTE taking the lead in decentralisation plans for the region. But the Northern and West Midlands authorities are aware that taking on local rail networks has got to be accompanied by a fair funding settlement. As the Passenger Transport Executive Group has argued:

> Taking on greater responsibility for local rail is not without risks. As part of negotiating for more power, we want a full understanding of the costs, risks and liabilities associated with increased responsibility. At present the system for allocating costs lacks transparency, and is relatively unaccountable to local partners. Our ambitions can only be realised if we get a fair deal for funding on the railways.[17]

Transport Scotland (overseen by the Scottish government) is responsible for specifying, managing and funding the 'Scotrail' franchise, which is currently operated by First Group. It is also responsible for publishing its own High-Level Output Specification, which details the long-term development of the rail network, with accompanying funding arrangements. The Scottish government has been lobbying the Department for Transport to allow derogation from the provisions of the Railways Act 1993 that allow only private sector operators to bid for franchises, though this has, unsurprisingly, been rejected.

The DfT currently has responsibility for the Northern and TransPennineExpress franchises, though the passenger transport executives have considerable – and growing – influence. The North of England proposals bring together a total of 33 transport authorities across the North, including the integrated transport authorities which oversee the PTEs, with the objective of taking over responsibility for the two contracts in the next three years.

WINNERS AND LOSERS

The structure which was created by the Major government in 1993 and survived the Blair years (other than the re-structuring of Railtrack into Network Rail) has met few of the original objectives of rail privatisation. Costs have escalated, new entrants to the rail market have virtually dried up, and union power, at least in some sectors, has increased. The sheer complexity of getting things done has led to many local authorities shying away from rail projects.

The big winners from UK rail privatisation have been the banks. At privatisation, BR's rolling stock was sold off at bargain-basement prices to the highest bidder.[18] Not many companies wanted to take the risk of bidding in what was then an uncertain market, and so most successful bids were awarded to management buyout teams. But the new rolling stock leasing companies (ROSCOs) subsequently proved themselves to be very lucrative cash cows, and their new owners quickly sold up to various financial institutions, including HSBC. The ROSCOs have for some time now enjoyed a period of massive profits, in what is a protected market; nobody else has access to a large number of trains, and the ROSCOs can – and do – charge very high rates for leasing their trains to the franchised operators. The most basic type of train – the 'Pacer' railbuses which still see extensive use in the North, South Wales and South-West – cost around £60-70,000 a year to lease, before any allowance for maintenance. The train companies, and in turn the taxpayer, are thus paying for these fully-depreciated and woefully inadequate trains several times over. Newer trains (e.g. the class 172 diesel units leased by London Midland) cost around £240,000 per year for a two-coach unit. Little wonder that between 1996 and 2009 the ROSCOs made dividend payments to their parent companies totalling £2.52 billion.[19] A typical year, 2009, saw dividends totalling over £200 million.[20]

The ROSCOs would argue that they are playing by the rules established by the government, with high lease charges driven by short franchises. One railway manager commented:

> The structure of rolling stock leasing was set up specifically to *encourage* investment in new trains by virtue of avoiding tatty old stock being leased at depreciated prices. People had watched bus deregulation and wished to avoid a similar thing whereby old rubbish was kept in service in the northern cities rather than invest in new efficient modern vehicles. So it was done with the best of intentions. Of course the result was rubbish as TOCs on a seven-year franchise couldn't make a case to order new trains that might appear about three years before the franchise was re-tendered and ROSCOs could sit pretty on what they had. We still have this regime today which is at the heart of the problem. But that's the reason why.[21]

Another senior manager added:

> There is nothing to stop other parties building and/or buying trains, and several new players such as Beacon Rail have entered the market.

The big problem is the totally unnecessary risk engendered by the DfT's refusal to sanction long-term contracts or guarantees.[22]

The most comprehensive critique of rail privatisation so far was produced by a small transport consultancy based in mid-Wales, an area which was particularly hard-hit by Beeching. Its report, *Rebuilding Rail*, commissioned by the rail unions, tried to arrive at a realistic cost of rail privatisation, as well as its impact on passengers and freight, and the wider impact on railway jobs. According to the report, 'the most cautious view is that the public money going into the railways has increased from around £2.4 billion per year before privatisation (in the period 1990/1 to 1994/5) to approximately £5.4 billion per year in the last three years to 2009/10 (based on 2009/10 prices)'. The report cites higher interest payments in order to keep Network Rail's debts off the government balance-sheet; debt-write-offs; costs arising as a result of fragmentation; profit margins of complex tiers of contractors and sub-contractors; and dividend payments to private investors. 'Taken together, these represent a cumulative cost since privatisation of more than £11 billion of public funds ... This should be considered a minimum figure, as it only includes those costs which may be most readily quantified.' [23]

Whilst the profits of the train operating companies are not as high as the ROSCOs, they are still making respectable returns on minimal investment. As Christian Wolmar has observed:

Train operators made around £300m profit (2011/2) which represents the relatively low figure of 3 per cent of overall turnover ... but that is an unusual way of looking at profit as it is usually expressed in terms of return on investment. Since operators make very little investment, that figure is not published.[24]

The authors of *Rebuilding Rail* agree that the regional train operators are onto a good deal:

The present regional TOCs have paid their shareholders more than half a billion pounds over the terms of their franchises. Over the nine financial years 2003-2011 dividend payments by the five regional companies under consideration amounted to £555 million, an annual average of £62 million. The dividend payments are made to the parent companies that own the regional TOCs. These include Abellio, which is a subsidiary of state-owned operator of Dutch Railways (NS); Arriva, which is a subsidiary of state-owned operator of German railways Deutsche Bahn; and Keolis, which is a subsidiary of state-owned operator of French railways, SNCF. So these dividend payments are supporting the finances of rail services of other European countries whilst representing a loss of potential investment for British taxpayers and rail travellers. It might be argued that dividend payments are a fair recognition of the investment that the owners of train operating companies have made. However, relative to the private capital which has been committed by these companies, the return they are able to extract is high.[25]

As they point out:

... shareholders of Arriva Trains Wales have benefitted from an average 54 per cent return on shareholders' funds since 2003, First Keolis Transpennine and First Scotrail show average returns on shareholder funds running at about 150 per cent, whilst Merseyrail Electrics and Northern Rail show average returns in excess of 200 per cent. Investors might reasonably expect such rates of return from Virgin Galactic's experiment with space travel, but the risk faced by operators of train services is not in any way comparable, especially given that the history since privatisation has been that the government steps in when train operations run into problems.[26]

Add to the profits of ROSCOs, train operators and a plethora of contractors and sub-contractors and you get, in the view of the authors of *Rebuilding Rail*, a 'dividend leakage' of just under £500m on regional railways in the UK.[27] That is £500m that could be directly invested into local and regional railways.

There are additional costs reflecting the 'checks and balances' introduced into the railway industry following privatisation. The 'performance regime', through which operators and Network Rail pay for delays, has led to a Kafkaesque bureaucracy, employing, across the different companies, around six hundred staff, who spend all their time arguing with each other as to who is responsible for a particular delay. The cost has been very approximately assessed at around £600 million per year. It is debatable as to whether the performance regime actually drives up quality of service. It introduces a very strong disincentive to operators to hold connections from delayed trains, leaving inconvenienced passengers with the option of a long wait or a taxi journey. In addition, the various agencies established since privatisation – including the Office of Rail Regulation and the Railway Safety and Standards Board – add further overheads and fragmentation to the railway. That's not to say they don't have a role, but their work needs integrating with other functions.

So it's clear who the winners are. The losers are the British tax payers who are having to fund this expensive neoliberal adventure, currently costing £4 billion per year, and the passenger who has to pay some of the highest fares in Europe. A report produced by Passenger Focus in February 2009 measured ticket prices for people travelling to the principal cities in the eight biggest economies in Europe. It found that a commuter travelling between 10.6 miles (17km) and 25 miles (41km) each morning to London spent an average £1,859.96 on an annual season ticket, compared with £990 in the next most expensive country, France, and £443,69 in the cheapest country, Italy. A passenger travelling between 25 miles (41km) and 50 miles (80km) to London faced an average annual ticket cost of £3,188.68, compared with £1934.89 in the second most expensive country, Holland, and £683.20 in the cheapest, Italy. Unrestricted day returns to London for a trip of between 10.6 miles (17km) and 25 miles (41km) cost an average £11.57 but a similar journey was £6.88 in Germany and £3.63 in France. Meanwhile, a walk-up day return to London up to 50 miles (80km) away could cost more than £250, whereas no similar fare in France would exceed £100.[28] The Liberal Democrat transport spokesman at the time, Norman Baker (now transport minister in the Coalition government) was angry. He said:

> This report shows British passengers are the most ripped off in Europe. Every year ministers are forcing above-inflation price hikes on passengers who are being forced to stand on increasingly over-crowded trains. There should be an immediate fare freeze, paid for by taking money from the road-widening budget.[29]

Yet far from the Coalition imposing a fare freeze, it has done quite the opposite. A report in *The Independent* commented:

In 2011 it had intended to allow train companies to raise the average price of regulated fares – which include season tickets – by RPI inflation plus three per cent this year and next January. This would have meant rises of 6.2 per cent. David Cameron then announced in October that it would instead be limited to RPI plus one per cent – a 4.2 per cent rise.[30]

The Independent report compared UK fares with other large European countries, and found England in particular (compared to Wales and Scotland) to have by far the most expensive long-distance train fares.

THE GROWTH IN RAIL TRAVEL

A crucial change over the last twenty years has been the growth in passengers, which has increased dramatically. Britain's railways today carry 1.5 billion people each year. However, before this is counted as a success of privatisation, account has to be taken of external factors, including growing traffic congestion and the economic boom of the Blair/Brown years. Lifestyle changes, including the opportunity afforded by rail travel to use laptops and social media, are also certainly a factor, as are rising car insurance costs and the price of fuel. Another factor is house prices and the cost of moving home. It's cheaper to make a longer commuting journey than to move, and it also avoids disrupting partner's jobs and children's schooling.

So whilst it is undeniable that passenger numbers have increased since privatisation it is particularly remarkable that the growth has continued after the economic collapse of 2008. How much of this is down to a more pro-active approach by the privatised train companies, and how much can be ascribed to a mix of economic growth, worsening traffic congestion and other factors?

The reality is that the privatised railway emerged at the start of one of the longest periods of economic growth seen for decades. Rail patronage traditionally rises (and falls) with the fortunes of the economy. From 1994 there was a period of continuous increase in rail patronage, whether measured as number of passengers travelling, or passenger-miles. Some of the growth was undoubtedly a result of effective marketing by the train companies (TOC), though this can be exaggerated. The franchising system gives little scope to independent initiative by the train companies, outside a fairly limited boundary. In the case of the biggest franchise (in terms of trains operated), Northern Rail, growth took place despite the Department for Transport's assumptions in 2004 that it would be a 'no-growth franchise'. There was little investment in rolling stock, or in stations, yet passenger numbers continued to rise. In other franchises, growth was even greater as a result of government-funded investment in new trains, particularly in the south-east.

WHAT HAS WORKED WELL?

Outside the Coalition government, unqualified defenders of the UK model of rail privatisation are increasingly few. Following the West Coast Main Line debacle of October 2012, the government appointed the respected rail professional Richard Brown to 'review' the franchising programme. His report set out the case to retain the current system with relatively minor reforms, but it met considerable criticism from independent commentators outside government. Within the rail industry the report was met with much scepticism, but also the inevitable vet on the views of any manager who wanted to continue their careers.

The case for continuing the present approach was made by Nigel Harris, editor of RAIL magazine, one of the most widely-read industry titles, with a readership spanning managers, front-line workers and enthusiasts. In his 'comment' column in RAIL he argued:

> Private delivery of public rail services has given us more train services, a brighter, sharper, more customer-friendly and customer-focused environment, superb online retailing, fantastic ticket bargains if you shop around, newer trains, better performance management and an open readiness to compensate when it goes wrong ... Yes, there's still plenty to put right, but all these things have led to a doubling of passengers to 1.5 billion today. [31]

In the same issue (a tribute to Harris's editorial open-ness!) columnist Barry Doe argues that if BR had been allowed to continue as a single entity, albeit privatised, it would now be carrying about 2 billion passengers a year, because of the network benefits of keeping a single 'InterCity', and the avoidance of instability caused by the fragmentation and short-termism of franchising.

The most successful franchises in terms of passenger satisfaction and overall perception within the rail industry are geographically distinct but have one thing in common. They are small. The examples often given of a 'successful TOC' are Chiltern Railways, operating a relatively small and self-contained franchise from London northwards to Birmingham: c2c, primarily serving the Essex commuter market, once known as 'The Misery Line' but now with an outstanding reputation, though covering only a small network of routes east from London; Merseyrail, which operates the entirely self-contained electrified Merseyside network; ScotRail, seen as 'Scotland's railway', whose franchise is with the Scottish government and has developed a highly successful business; and, finally, the relatively new London Overground franchise, managed by Transport for London, which has demonstrated a degree of dynamism which puts other franchises to shame. In the case of Chiltern and Merseyrail, the franchise period is long, giving a strong element of stability which is welcomed by staff as well as passengers; while the Merseyrail franchise is let by the local passenger transport executive, Merseytravel.

A recent study commissioned by the Campaign for Better Transport suggests that the 'concession' approach brings better results than conventional franchising:

London Overground is run as a gross cost contract: Transport for London (TfL) takes the revenue and the risk associated with it, with the operator left with risks associated with the train operations. This mirrors other TfL experience and its learning from both London bus contracts and from the Docklands Light Railway (DLR). With the DLR the first contract for the operation and maintenance commenced in 1997 and transferred revenue and cost risk to the franchisee. When the franchise was re-let in March 2006 TfL decided to retain revenue risk, given the limited ability of the operator to manage the risk. This has been accompanied by the initiation of a more rigorous incentive or penalty regime based on punctuality, reliability and the availability of passenger facilities. TfL argue that the use of gross cost contracts in this way is a proven means of cost-effectively providing a public transport service. In particular it insulates the operator from the risks of fluctuation in the London labour market and economy, which means that the costs of the contract or concession are reduced. Merseyrail is not a pure gross cost contract, in that revenue risks rest with the operator. However, in practice it has some of the features of such a contract: detailed specification and a profit sharing arrangement giving 50 per cent of profits back to Merseytravel. Merseyrail is also a 25 year contract but with 5 year reviews, avoiding the cost of bidding for renewals.[32]

The highest-scoring companies in Passenger Focus's National Passenger Survey are open access operators Grand Central and Hull Trains. These are small operations, but provide valued inter-city services on markets which both BR and private franchised operators neglected. But open access passenger services in the UK have been slow to get off the ground, and one of the few initiatives in this field has failed.[33] The 1993 Railways Act enabled private operators to run passenger services outwith the franchised network, providing they met certain criteria, namely that they were not 'primarily abstractive' of the revenue of franchised operators on competing or overlapping routes. Hull Trains, now owned by First Group, has developed a successful niche serving Humberside and Lincolnshire to London. Grand Central, now owned by Arriva (in turn owned by German Rail), has developed routes to London from West Yorkshire and the North-East. The other main example, Wrexham and Shropshire, was developed as an independent venture but was then taken over by Arriva and failed to meet commercial targets, being hamstrung by restrictions on where it could and couldn't stop. Its last train ran to great regret, not only from its staff but also its passengers, who consistently gave it the highest passenger satisfaction score of any passenger train operator. Hull Trains and Grand Central also score very high levels of passenger satisfaction. Passengers point out the good customer service, comfortable trains and a sense of being 'local'. Staff appreciate the accessibility of management and the sense of being a valued part of a small team. The late managing director of Grand Central, Tom Clift, referred to his operation as a 'community railway operating an inter-city service', and he was right.

So it would be wrong to say that the experience of rail privatisation has been wholly negative. If you ask 'non-political' rail professionals for their view, they will point to freight, the very limited but successful open access operators, and some of the smaller franchises.[34] Each of these share some features in common. The most obvious characteristics, which apply to most of the examples, are size and a degree of long-term stability. The most successful franchises have generally been the smaller ones with long franchises, which have enabled them to plan ahead, invest and give their staff and passengers a degree of stability. The freight operators also tend to be relatively small and have long-term stability. The biggest freight operator is the German Rail-owned DB Schenker, followed by Freightliner, GB Railfreight, Direct Rail Services and Colas. Each has survived and developed in a genuinely competitive environment, where the main competitor is road haulage. They have invested in locomotives and wagons and built up their businesses. These are not 'franchises' but 'open access' freight operators, which pay a charge to operate across the network and stand or fall without direct subsidy.[35]

Whilst some of the freight companies have genuinely brought investment to their side of the industry, it is difficult to argue the same for many of the passenger operators. To be fair, that isn't their fault. The passenger franchising system discourages investment by the operator, whose job is to deliver the agreed specification. Where a franchise has had a long investment horizon it has been easier to justify putting money into the business. Chiltern has invested £500m into its operation, helped by a twenty year franchise – and, it must be stressed, a very dynamic management team.

SUCCESS FACTORS

The 'success factors' which emerge from an examination of current train companies are suggested below, though they need to be treated with a degree of care. The first is that it is the smaller train companies that are most popular with passengers and which command most respect in the rail industry. Staff often have a better view of their company than colleagues in some of the larger train operators. This factor chimes well with the experience of continental regional operators, where relatively small size, focusing on a clear market and geographical area, can far out-achieve larger more amorphous companies. This flies in the face of much current Department for Transport thinking, which has encouraged the merger of smaller franchises; but it is also at odds with the traditional 'left' approach of centralising rail services under one monolithic body. This question of size, with small operators often being more successful than the larger ones, is also almost counter-intuitive to railway people, who often stress the importance of a large and unified network. But with that goes the down-side of centralised control and a lack of entrepreneurial flair. By having relatively small units focused on distinct markets, it has proved possible to create a dynamic and innovative railway. This is not about public or private; the same effects have been achieved in continental Europe, notably in Switzerland and parts of Germany, where the local train operator is publicly-owned. Large, state-owned railways have been slow to innovate, particularly in local and regional services, as well as freight.

The second success factor is having a greater degree of stability. As we have seen, Chiltern and Merseyrail have long franchises (twenty and twenty-five years respectively) which give staff – management and front-line workers – a degree of long-term stability. This helps business planning processes, so that, in the all-too-rare cases where a train operating company does invest, they know they will get a return on their investment. This is much harder with, say, a seven or ten year franchise. In the case of London Overground the franchise is shorter, but it is based on a 'concession' rather than a conventional franchise. This removes commercial risk from the operator and effectively means that the contracting body (Transport for London) is in complete control, taking full risk responsibility.

The third factor is having devolved franchise management. Scotrail, London Overground and Merseyrail are the responsibilities of decentralised government, not the centralised and under-resourced Department for Transport. This brings greater accountability, an understanding of local needs and markets, and a closer relationship between operator and franchising body.

The conclusions from this are that regional services (including 'national' services in Scotland and Wales) should cover distinct (not too big) geographical communities, and that they work best when they are accountable to a devolved public body which has a close relationship with the train operator. Having a degree of long-term stability is important for both employees and passengers. The implications for a future 'social' railway are explored in chapter eleven.

A further challenge to traditional 'socialist' thinking is the role of open access operators. If they are providing a useful service to communities isolated and ignored by larger franchised companies (and government), the implications are that they should be encouraged, not discouraged, providing they do not undermine other services. Whilst the two existing open access operators are owned by the major groups (First Group in the case of Hull Trains and Arriva for Grand Central) there is a new co-operative open access operator (Go-Train) which hopes to operate services from the South-West to the West Midlands. Let's hope it succeeds. We need new models of train operator which challenge the conventional approaches, and these could include co-operatives, social enterprises of various kinds and joint public/private ventures. The options are discussed in chapter ten.

BRITAIN'S RAILWAYS TODAY

The performance of Britain's railways is showing significant improvement in terms of reliability (as well as safety), following the calamity of the Hatfield accident of 2000 when the system nose-dived. More trains are running on time, and a degree of confidence has returned to the system, across the country. Investment totalling over £9 billion was announced by the Coalition government in July 2012, which will see many routes electrified and some lines re-opened.

But all this is at a cost. Apart from the already generally high cost of running the privatised railway compared with the last year of BR ownership, the costs of many projects – like opening new stations, providing new infrastructure or procuring rolling stock – are now far greater than they were in pre-privatisation days. Part of the problem is the large number of interfaces within the industry, with each component wanting its slice of the cake – adding profit onto profit.

The 2011 McNulty Review identified some potential 'savings' – though this did not extend to a curbing of the super-profits made by the banks which own the rolling stock companies, or the plethora of supplier organisations.[36] And, whilst the profits being made by the train operator owning groups are not so extreme, nonetheless Northern Rail, for example, made £40million last year, which went back to Serco shareholders and Dutch Railways, with only a small proportion of that profit being invested back in the railway.[37] One senior railway manager commented on the huge wastage from the present structure:

> Crucially, McNulty missed the 'friction' costs of privatisation. It's not private ownership per se that is the problem, but the endless costs of bidding, bureaucracy, lawyers, regulators and other such

parasites who have been imposed on the industry by the idiots in Whitehall.[38]

One of the main outcomes of the McNulty Report was the establishment of a Rail Delivery Group comprising senior industry figures, most of whom have a vested interest in preserving the status quo. It is chaired by the chief executive of First Group.

Many parts of the UK – particularly England outside of London – are currently stuck with an ageing fleet and serious overcrowding on many routes. There is a lack of infrastructure capacity to handle any increase in traffic, be it passenger or freight. The most urgent need is new passenger rolling stock to extend existing train lengths: investing in the infrastructure to allow more trains to run will take time, and the most pressing issue is to provide seat capacity now.

Devolution has made a difference. Scotland has had rail re-openings, electrification and new trains. So has London. Even Wales, with a far less dense population, is seeing railways re-opened which would not stand a chance of getting approved in England. In the North of England, where the PTEs have seized the opportunity offered by partial devolution of powers over rail to a 'sub-national' level, a new body called 'Rail in the North Executive ' is emerging, which may take on wide responsibilities including franchising powers (see below). Looking beyond the Channel, we see the same process of investment in regional lines in Germany, France and Scandinavia.

FRANCHISE FAILURE

The franchising system foisted on us by the 1993 Railways Act has not worked. Costs have risen dramatically and the collapse of the West Coast franchising process should have been the final nail in its coffin. Short-term franchising delivers a demoralised workforce with employees who have little or no loyalty to what is likely to be a transient employer. Management is de-motivated because franchise specifications leave little room for commercial initiative and short-term franchises don't allow for investment by the franchisee unless specified in the contract. Coalition proposals to reform franchising in the wake of the West Coast fiasco will not address the fundamental issues – the underlying malaise of centralised, price-driven, franchising.

It has been argued that if you get the franchise specification right, it doesn't matter who runs it, subject to appropriate safeguards. However, the sort of company that is actually running the trains is crucial and there are a thousand and one issues which you could never enshrine in a contract which are absolutely critical to how a service is perceived by passengers, and what the company is like to work for. It's about 'culture', and getting one which combines entrepreneurial flair with social responsibility and excellent customer care. We need a new kind of rail operator that combines many of the good things achieved by the private TOCs but with an ethical approach, founded on co-operative values, one which recognises there is more to the business than the financial bottom-line.[39] There should also be a social and environmental bottom-line which ought to be of equal importance.

There are other factors as well that call into question the wisdom of the franchising model for a railway. Franchising by its nature is short-term. The Wales and Borders franchise was let for slightly longer than other franchises, at fifteen years. Even this, however, is not a long period for an industry such as rail, which relies on very long-term investment horizons. The typical life of a train might be twenty-five to thirty years; other assets last much longer. Whilst it could be argued that to some extent a strong public body in charge of the franchise can take that long-term view, the reality is that the instability of franchised train operations imposes its own, often hidden, costs, which inhibit growth. Before going on to consider alternative ways of running the railways, I now turn to the ways in which passenger groups and other campaigners have sought to improve railways and influence rail policy.

NOTES

1. John Macgregor, secretary of state for transport, in his foreword to the 1992 white paper outlining his government's plans to privatise BR, quoted in Andrew Murray, *Off the Rails*, 2001, p22.
2. There is a considerable academic literature on the effects of rail privatisation in the UK. I am indebted to Professor Richard Knowles for the following references: J. Cowie, 'The British passenger rail privatisation: conclusions on subsidy and efficiency from the first round of franchises', *Journal of Transport Economics and Policy*, 43, 2009; R. Haywood, 'Britain's National Railway Network: Fit for Purpose in the Twenty First Century?', *Journal of Transport Geography*, 15, 2007; R.D. Knowles, 'Railway franchising in Great Britain and the effects of the 2008-2009

economic recession', *Environment & Planning A*, 45(1), 2013; R.D. Knowles, 'Impacts of privatizing Britain's rail passenger services – franchising, re-franchising and Ten Year Transport Plan targets', *Environment and Planning A*, 36, 2004; R.D. Knowles, *Passenger rail privatization in Great Britain and its implications*, 1998; J. Preston, 'A review of passenger rail franchising in Britain: 1996/1997-2006/2007', *Research in Transportation Economics*, 22, 2008; J. Shaw, *Competition, Regulation and the Privatisation of British Rail*, Ashgate 2000.
3. Private communication to the author.
4. It does of course depend on how you judge 'success'. Hull Trains is just about breaking even financially, whilst GC is still running at a loss. Wrexham and Shropshire, the most popular of all, was closed down following its takeover by Arriva.
5. For a fuller outline see Harris and Godward op cit, esp. Chapter 6.
6. Personal email to the author from Chris Stokes, May 2013.
7. Personal email to the author from Andrew McNaughton, April 2013.
8. Ibid.
9. Ibid.
10. Ibid.
11. Ibid
12. Ibid
13. Co-operative Party, *The People's Rail: a mutually run, publicly accountable Network Rail*, 2008, p12.
14. I recently listened with amusement to a discussion between a rail user group and a Northern Rail manager about why a currently blocked subway which would link a new car park directly with the station it is intended to serve could not proceed more quickly. Although the cost was very small, it had to gain Department for Transport approval! Meanwhile, passengers have to put up with a half mile walk to get from the car park to the station, instead of 100 yards.
15. Senior manager, train operating company in the North of England, private email to author.
16. See Campaign for Better Transport, *Going Local*, 2013.
17. Passenger Transport Executive Group, *Rail Cities in the 21st century: the case for Devolution*, Leeds 2012.
18. A critique from the left is Andrew Murray's *Off the Rails*.
19. Ian Taylor & Lynn Sloman, *Rebuilding Rail*, 2012, p19.
20. Ibid, p19.
21. Private email to author from Andrew McNaughton, April 2013.
22. Private email to author, May 2013.
23. Taylor and Sloman, op cit, p7.
24. Christian Wolmar, *RAIL*, 1 May 2013.
25. Ian Taylor – private communication with author May 2013.
26. Ibid.

27. Ibid.
28. Report in *Daily Telegraph*, 19 February 2009.
29. Ibid.
30. 'England has the priciest train tickets in Europe', *The Independent*, 2 January 2012.
31. Nigel Harris, *RAIL*, 30 March 2013.
32. Campaign for Better Transport, *Going Local*, 2013, p16.
33. The Wrexham Shropshire and Marylebone Railway scored consistently high levels of passenger satisfaction – around 96 per cent – and was the best train operator in the NPS surveys. It was established by a group of independent railway professionals and bought by German Railways. The operation was closed down in January 2011.
34. Franchises that have proved successful and popular have included Chiltern, Merseyrail, c2c, London Overground, TransPennine Express, ScotRail and the former Wessex Trains.
35. There is an indirect subsidy to freight operators through the network grant which allows for lower than commercial track access charges, reflecting rail's environmental benefits. This is set by the Office of Rail regulation which is currently considering a substantial increase in charges, which could force traffic away from rail.
36. Sir Roy McNulty, *Rail Value for Money Study*, DfT and Office of Rail Regulation 2012.
37. See Office of Rail Regulation, op cit; and Taylor and Sloman, op cit. In the opinion of Taylor and Sloman Northern's £149 million dividend payments to Serco and NS between 2003 and 2011 represent a profit of 269 per cent (private email to author).
38. Private email to author, May 2013.
39. The Social Value Act 2012 offers some encouragement to private companies to take their social obligations more seriously

5. Passenger power: campaigns and representation

> In the current debate about the future of franchising one thing is clear – the voice of the passenger should get a boost.[1]

Rail travellers, at least a section of them, have always been vocal and assertive in condemning what they have seen as inadequate service. In the nineteenth century it was a common occupation of the upper classes to write to *The Times*, or their MP, complaining about poor service by the railway companies. In more recent times, BR was often the brunt of press and politicians' ire, often with the overt or covert assumption that this was 'typical nationalisation'! This discontent with customer service by BR was fully exploited by the Tories in the run-up to rail privatisation. This chapter explores the development of a passenger lobby, particularly since nationalisation when formal passenger representation was enshrined in legislation, and wider issues around passenger needs.

IS THERE A TYPICAL RAILWAY PASSENGER?

From the way railways have been traditionally managed, you would think there was. The passenger would be middle-aged, white, affluent middle-class and able-bodied. The reality is that rail is used by a very wide range of people, reflecting the diversity of Britain. Passenger Focus's National Passenger Survey covers a large sample of rail users, and its autumn 2012 edition gives a glimpse of the social profile of today's rail users. The data suggests a majority of female over male rail users, and a fairly balanced age profile, while the occupational profile shows that a greater proportion of users define themselves as senior or middle 'managerial', though clerical and junior management, and 'skilled manual', were also well represented. Whilst 78 per cent of respondents described themselves as 'white British' there was enormous diversity amongst the remaining sample. A total of 5 per cent of respondents had a disability or a long-term illness.[2]

So are the needs of this very diverse range of passengers being taken seriously by today's railway industry? To a certain extent. One aspect of privatisation – and BR's reducing subsidy in its last years – has been a strong commercial focus by rail managers. This in itself is no bad thing and it has led train companies to consider passenger needs with more sensitivity than BR sometimes did. This has been reinforced by legislation, for example in relation to the needs of disabled passengers. Stations and rolling stock have to comply with legislation which requires rail services to become fully accessible over an extended period of time.

Alongside the impact of legislation, there have been increasingly effective campaigns by disability rights organisations and to a lesser extent by women's organisations over issues such as personal safety at stations. The influence of the (often Labour-controlled) passenger transport executives, which have a broader social agenda, has also helped focus the industry's attention on wider social needs, which in turn has potentially helped the commercial 'bottom line'.

PASSENGER REPRESENTATION

Rail passengers in the UK (unlike bus users, until recently) have well established forms of statutory protection. The 1947 Transport Act set up the Central Transport Consultative Committee (CTCC) and a network of regional Transport Users' Consultative Committees as passenger representative bodies. The original CTCC and TUCCs were abolished by the Transport Act 1962, though they were replaced by new bodies of the same name but with extended powers; and these powers were extended further in 1968. A feature of membership of these consultative bodies was their limited social inclusivity. Retired military officers and other representatives of the great and the good who had time to spare were all too often appointed to the regional committees; regular rail travel was not a condition of appointment!

The biggest test of the committees came after the Beeching report and the avalanche of rail closures. They did attempt to resist some closures – at least in some areas – but by and large they were unsuccessful. To succeed they had to demonstrate resulting 'hardship' if a particular line closed, but even if they managed this they could then only make recommendations to the government – which were usually ignored.

The Railways Act 1993 abolished the 1962 structure and replaced it with the Rail Users' Consultative Committee (RUCC) network, comprising the Central Rail Users' Consultative Committee (CRUCC) as the national coordinating body, and eight regional committees. The new bodies were sponsored by the Office of the Rail Regulator (since renamed the Office of Rail Regulation) and their role was to speak on behalf of passengers in the new era of privatised train companies. The CRUCC and RUCCs were renamed the Rail Passengers' Council and Rail Passengers' Committees by the Transport Act 2000, and sponsorship was transferred to the newly created Strategic Rail Authority. The Rail Passengers' Council and Committees network was launched at a 'Rail Summit' in May 2000. The new bodies were well resourced, and the regional committees developed as effective voices for passenger interests. The era of line closures had long since passed, but the RPC network was able to present an independent, and often uncomfortable, critical view of the privatised railway. The RPC was never in a position to make political pronouncements such as questioning privatisation, but it was empowered to challenge the way in which the industry operated, from a passenger perspective. It was helped by having a strong chief executive, Anthony Smith, who had a background in the consumer movement.

In January 2004 the Secretary of State for Transport announced a review of the rail industry, and the resulting White Paper called for a more independent and focused rail passenger organisation, which could offer better value for money and achieve higher levels of passenger awareness. The resulting Railways Act 2005 abolished the Rail Passengers' Council and regional Rail Passengers' Committees, replacing them with a new single UK-wide organisation, Passenger Focus. In 2008 the government announced plans to widen the role of Passenger Focus to include bus passenger representation in England, outside London. It therefore now represents rail passengers in England, Scotland and Wales, bus and tram passengers in England (outside London), and passengers on scheduled domestic coach services in England.

Passenger Focus has developed serious expertise in research, which is essential in presenting a strong case to government and the railway industry. Representation on the board is based on the Nolan principles of public appointments, which ensure that the committee is free of bias. Its activities today centre around gathering research and information, including through its annual National Passenger Survey, in which over 50,000 rail passengers give their views about their rail journeys, in every aspect (station, rolling stock, customer service). Passenger Focus also prioritises working with government and the industry to ensure that the passenger voice is heard when making decisions about the future.[3] It treads a sensitive line between nurturing positive relationships with government and the rail industry whilst still having enough teeth to defend and promote passenger interests. One senior civil servant commented: 'in general I would say that both Labour and the current Coalition governments have valued Passenger Focus as a representative voice of the passenger. It has to be careful not to get political and hence the importance of the evidence base'.[4]

The organisation exists on a much-reduced budget following the Coalition government's review of all 'quangos'. The worries that Passenger Focus would be completely abolished were not realised, but around a third of its staff was shed. Its research capability was left reasonably intact, however. A key development in recent years has been a willingness to build stronger links with voluntary rail and bus user groups, leading to a series of workshops across the UK at which rail campaigners have sat down with Passenger Focus officers and board members to explore ways of joint working. The potential of the UK's extensive 'rail user movement' is explored below. By tapping in to Passenger Focus's considerable resources, the almost entirely voluntary movement may be given a significant boost. At the same time, Passenger Focus will benefit from the local knowledge and expertise of rail user groups.

The role of Passenger Focus is likely to become increasingly important in the next few years, if franchising in some form continues. Its chief executive – still Anthony Smith – has argued that rail passengers should have a say in whether a particular company should be permitted to re-bid for a franchise.[5] At the same time, the PF-sponsored National Passenger Survey has become a strong barometer of train operator performance and is likely to have an increasing influence in determining the survival of particular owning companies.

Some of the more progressive train companies have formed

passenger panels which 'advise' the company on a range of issues. There have also been more informal 'meet the manager' sessions held at stations, which offer a more accessible means for passengers to raise complaints and problems.

THE RAIL USER MOVEMENT

Britain has a large network of what can generically be called 'rail user groups'. They are invariably voluntary with no paid staff and usually cover a specific line or small group of lines. They are federated into the national organisation RailFuture (formerly the Railway Development Society), which produces a punchy and informative newsletter.

The origins of today's rail user movement lie back in the 1950s with the emergence of a number of small campaigning groups which opposed the growing number of line closures. Two national bodies emerged – the Railway Invigoration Society and the Railway Development Association. They tended to have their own geographical areas of activity, with the RDA being mostly based in the West Midlands and London, while the RIS was strongest in East Anglia. The two bodies came together to form the Railway Development Society in October 1978, with the objective of creating a strong, independent and unified voice for rail users throughout Britain. Their combined strength at that time was only around five hundred. But despite their small numbers they fought energetic campaigns, opposing post-Beeching closures and lobbying for re-openings.

In 1997 the RDS changed its name to RailFuture, as part of a push to create a more modern image for the organisation. Today's rail user movement is well established and growing, with around three hundred groups across the UK, in addition to the national RailFuture federation. Most lines have a user group or association to defend and promote the interests of passengers, and very often freight customers. They are distinct from community rail partnerships (cf chapter six) but often overlap. In many cases, where a community rail partnership (CRP) exists, the local rail user group will be a member of the CRP. Many user groups see their main role as 'promotional' rather 'campaigning'.

Many rail user groups were formed in the face of direct closure threats to particular lines. But although closures are off the agenda for the foreseeable future, there are still issues of concern for local groups.

Staff reductions, booking office closures, the worsening of local services to accommodate longer distance services, and continuing lack of disabled access at many stations, are just some of these. Each group is different, and a snapshot of a handful of groups across the UK will help to give a picture of their activities.

Friends of the Settle-Carlisle Line (FoSCL)

FoSCL was born out of the campaign to save the line from closure in the 1980s. The line had managed to survive Beeching in 1963 because of its value as a freight route, but there was an even more determined attempt to close the line in the 1980s, following the running-down of passenger services on the line and the diversion of freight onto other routes. The Friends was established in 1981, and is one of the biggest user groups in the country, with a membership of over 3000. Because of the national profile of the line, as England's 'most scenic route', it has friends and admirers across the UK and beyond. Since 1989, when the Conservative government decided that the line should remain open, FoSCL has sought to improve facilities and services for passengers, and has worked closely with the train operating companies to promote the line.

The group has a substantial bank balance, and has directly invested in better facilities, such as station refurbishment and the installation of Victorian-style lamps. It has restored and now maintains the disused signal boxes at Armathwaite and Settle Station, which are periodically open to the public. An important part of its activities is liaison with Northern Rail on passenger services and Network Rail on railway infrastructure. In addition the group do a lot of hands-on duties that help the line in practical ways. They provide 'On Train Guides' which enhance travellers' experience of the Settle-Carlisle Line, providing information 'as you go' and pointing out features of the line; and volunteers also lead guided walks from stations along the line, and help to produce and distribute promotional leaflets across the region. They also run station shops at Settle and Appleby, selling a wide variety of railway-related items and local produce. Some of these items are also sold in FoSCL's online shop. Perhaps among the most noticeable features of their activities are their work in looking after station gardens, their provision of heritage style benches, and their re-painting of woodwork, often spending money from their own funds to do so.

The group has also published its aspirations for a future Northern franchise, which would include more frequent services on the route, but also a new service using the currently mainly freight line from Hellifield to Clitheroe and beyond to Manchester. It works closely with the Settle-Carlisle Development Company, formed after the reprieve of the line, in looking at innovative ways of developing the route. Meanwhile the Settle-Carlisle Railway Heritage Trust has taken on the job of restoring and managing historic railway buildings along the line. Since March 2006 FoSCL has contributed £225,000 to the Trust, a remarkable sum for a voluntary organisation.

Richard Morris, chairman of the FoSCL, is conscious of the challenges of maintaining a voluntary organisation for the long haul.

When the Settle-Carlisle Line was under threat in the 1980s, an incredibly wide coalition of organisations, government bodies and individuals came together in a powerful and ultimately successful campaign to save the line ... But one by one they've dropped out over the years and now, like it or not, our three-way partnership of ourselves, the Development Company and the Trust is on its own. Only we can provide the leadership needed to maintain our heritage and, we hope, develop our rail services for the benefit of the local community. It's likely to be a long haul. James Towler, in his definitive book on the saving of the line, said that 'the Settle-Carlisle Line inspires a quasi-religious fervour in those connected with it'. And if that fervour sustains us in our mission, then we shall ultimately succeed.[6]

Avocet Line: Exeter to Exmouth

The Avocet Line Rail Users Group (ALRUG) must be one of the UK's most pro-active and dynamic user groups despite only having around two hundred members. This was another line Beeching wanted to close, but the proposal was stymied by strong local opposition. Today the trains struggle to cope with demand, even with four-coach trains in the rush-hour period.

The group has done a lot to raise awareness of the need for more capacity – including publishing a manifesto for the line before the last general election. Its work has been strongly supported by First Great Western, and the company's former stakeholder manager Julian Crow sees ALRUG as an excellent example of the contribution that a well-motivated user group can make. Stations are now looking their best for many years, and there has been well thought-out long-term planning and lobbying in support of Devon County Council's emerging plans for improving the local network. The group was instrumental in getting the line designated as a community rail route in 2012.[7]

The group supports plans by local authorities and First Great Western to develop a better network of services in the area. In the short term their main aim is an increase in Sunday frequency, from the current hourly service; and the additional services that they have so far achieved have run without subsidy from the start. Like many other groups, it also involves its members in tending station gardens at local stations and producing promotional leaflets, including a guide to birdlife along the route – which skirts the Exe Estuary.

The Exeter-Exmouth branch now attracts 1.6 million people per year, more passengers than ever before, and there is every prospect of further large increases, as the considerable economic development now underway in the area comes to fruition. The group has plans to make the most of this opportunity, and, according to ALRUG member Richard Giles, the only fear is that the line is too far from London to attract the attention and hence the investment they deserve. The routes proposed for inclusion in the Devon Metro plan already encompass a passenger usage of over three million annually, and such numbers elsewhere in the UK have usually been enough to prompt major investment. The group hope to show that the Exeter-Exmouth railway is not merely a country branch line, but, rather, the quickest and most efficient means of transport in a rapidly growing area. As Richard asks, 'On what other single track branch line do you get trains "full and standing" in mid-morning?'[8]

Abbey Line (Watford Junction–St Albans Abbey)

The Abbey Flyer Users' Group (better known as 'ABFLY') was created in 1995, with the aim of securing a better future for the Watford to St Albans branch line in Hertfordshire. It too had been threatened with closure by Beeching in 1963 but had survived, and it was electrified in 1994. More recently there has been discussion about using the line as a pilot for a locally managed line with community rail designated status; this would allow more flexible operation, which could involve conversion of the line to light rail operation, with a more frequent service. Ultimately, light rail could allow for extensions of the line at both the St Albans and Watford Junction ends of the line, allowing better links to the respective town centres.

The two key aims of the group are 'to watch for, and challenge, any lowering of standards', and 'to keep the branch line alive and thriving as an increasingly useful part of the public transport network in South West Hertfordshire'. The group's objectives also include smarter and cleaner stations and trains, and retention of the line as an electric railway. They also want to see better information at stations, and are lobbying for the continuation and improvement of the Sunday service, and higher frequencies during the week, as well as better integration with bus services. The group seeks to maintain good links with the train operator and community rail partnership.

Peterborough–Ely–Norwich Rail Users Association

This group is active along the Railway through the Fens in Cambridgeshire and Norfolk. Most members and all officers are individual volunteers, though local authorities are affiliated. A community rail partnership for the line was recently launched, in which the group is an active partner. It lobbies for hourly trains between Birmingham and Stansted Airport, Liverpool and Norwich, and Norwich and Cambridge, and for targeted development of bus interchange at stations, as well as car, cycle and taxi parking, and station walking and wheelchair routes. It has also been pressing for improved facilities at stations along the line.

The group is well connected with more formal organisations, both in local government and the railway industry, and they work constructively with councils, community groups, opinion-formers and the rail industry; they also carefully scrutinise new railway documents and planning applications. They work closely with the Fen Line Users Association and other local user groups, as well as Passenger Focus, Railfuture, the Campaign for Better Transport and Travel Watch East Midlands.[9]

Franchise remapping in 2007 left the group having to deal with three train operators – all with different ideas on how to engage with user groups – and a station facility operator. After the reduction of carriages on the Liverpool–Norwich route, which led to overcrowding, the group successfully campaigned for some additional trains. Capacity remains an issue on the Birmingham route, however, and other major concerns are the run-down of Thetford station and the impact of an increasingly 'five-day railway', caused by weekend engineering blockades, when replacement buses provide an extremely inadequate alternative to trains.

The group campaigns for more freight on rail as well as improved passenger services, including sufficient capacity. Some stations along the route serve very small rural communities, and the group actively encourages the introduction of extra stops, whilst also recognising that this should not disadvantage the aim of shorter end-to-end journey times. PENRUG also sees one of its roles as being to flesh out the National Passenger Survey scores with real travellers' tales, and they are always on the lookout for people's journey details for publication in their quarterly newsletter.

Friends of the Far North Line: Inverness to Thurso and Wick

The Far North Line is one of Britain's most stunning railways. According to Friends of the Far North Line:

> Not only is the scenery among the most beautiful anywhere, it is also extremely rugged and desolate and supports a very low population base. If it is surprising that a railway was built at all in such difficult and inhospitable circumstances, that it has survived into the twenty-first century, despite being under constant threat of closure, is truly remarkable.[10]

The Friends has been in existence since 1993 and has been a powerful lobby in maintaining and developing the line. Beeching proposed complete closure of all lines beyond Inverness, which would have meant closure of the Far North line to Thurso and Wick, and the 'road to the Isles' from Inverness to Kyle of Lochalsh. But today the lines are seen as a vital part of the Highland transport network, and as essential to the economic life of the region. Numbers now far exceed all forecasts.

The group's main objectives are the retention, improvement and increased use of the line and the development of services for both local users and for tourists. It also wants to see the enhancement of freight

services, including feeders into and from the line. And it works hard
to publicise the line and its attractions, including through helping to
promote heritage-based activities.

John Brandon, convener of the Friends group, is proud of its
achievements:

> We've lobbied successfully for a number of improvements, including
> getting a fourth train between Inverness and Wick which connects
> at Thurso with the Orkney Ferry. We were influential in getting the
> class 158 trains used on the route refurbished with more space for
> bikes and fewer seats, offering more leg room for what is a long
> journey. In addition, the seats are now aligned with the windows to
> allow enjoyment of the stunning scenery.[11]

The Friends of the Far North Line also work hard to ensure that the
line gets recognised in key policy debates, and make regular submis-
sions to debates on rail and planning issues in the North of Scotland.
Their most recent success was lobbying for a new station to serve
Conon Bridge, north of Inverness, a place where there has been considerable housing development. A new station opened there in February
2013, funded by Transport Scotland.

The Tarka Rail Association: Exeter to Barnstaple

This line links the growing urban centre of Exeter with North Devon,
serving a string of villages and the town of Crediton. The line was not
threatened with closure by Beeching, though most of its local stations
were. However, in the end these were saved, but the rest of the North
Devon rail network beyond Barnstaple – to Ilfracombe, Bude, and
Taunton – was closed. Today, Barnstaple railway station has become
the hub of North Devon's transport network, and it is the gateway to
the popular Tarka Trail cycleway.

The association was originally formed in 1978 as the North Devon
Rail Development Group, but changed its name to the Tarka Rail
Association following the re-branding of the line. It now works with
the Devon and Cornwall Rail Partnership to promote the line, as well
as actively lobbying for improvements. It is rightly proud of its role in
making the case for an improved timetable. John Burch is chairman
of the Association:

We've had a good number of successes in recent years, not least the improvement in the service to give us an almost hourly clock-face weekday timetable. We've also now got an additional early Sunday train and a late night Friday train, both of which are loading well. We've managed to get a number of changes to the stopping patterns and service times to better serve our users.[12]

The group is also active in promoting better integration with other transport modes. One of its officers is a bus manager, and this brings huge expertise to what is often a neglected side of rail campaigning. The association has influenced improved bus service connections at various locations, including Exeter St Davids, Crediton and Barnstaple.

The association maintains its own notice boards at all the stations, which provide a range of useful information for rail travellers; and they have also produced two award-winning 'Tarka Walks' books, which combine easy station to station walks with good maps and well-researched local history. The heritage signage at Barnstaple, and restoration of the island platform as a garden area, are also amongst their community projects.

The association has a growing membership of about three hundred. It has influenced a number of bodies and advised on detailed improvements that have provided better passenger facilities at stations. The association is probably more open and outgoing in its work than many user groups. It is involved in a range of business and consumer forums and has monthly open committee meetings held at locations along the line, allowing for as many people as possible to have their say and discuss issues of concern.

Hope Valley: Manchester–Sheffield

The Hope Valley Rail Users Group (HVRUG) is a long established rail user group covering the remaining route from Manchester to Sheffield through the Peak District. (The electrified Woodhead Route, via Hadfield and Penistone, closed in 1983.) Although the line carries frequent inter-regional passenger services and freight, it also serves many small communities in places which attract hundreds of walkers each weekend from the cities; and these are also home to a growing number of commuters into Manchester and Sheffield. All of these stations narrowly escaped closure following a death sentence in the Beeching Report.

Local train operators recognise the highly professional approach HVRUG has brought to its campaigning. As one Northern Rail manager commented, 'they make us look that much harder to see what can be achieved'. Among their successes was persuading freight operators to make changes that permitted more stopping passenger trains. As the same manager noted: 'that was real lateral thinking and everyone was a winner'.[13]

The group has campaigned for changes to the timetable, and in particular they sought to avoid the two-hour gaps between services that were occurring during some parts of the day, which meant that many people who would like to use the train could not do so. They engaged with everyone involved in the line to see if a solution could be found, and as a result the line now has an hourly evening peak stopping service in both directions.

The group has more than seventy members and includes some very young supporters. Emily, aged two and a half, helped her mother Jenni deliver 420 questionnaires in the Parish of Hope with Aston. This was part of the Rail Users Group' effort to find out from all residents of the Hope Valley how much more they would use their railway if an hourly timetable could be obtained. Jenni is parish clerk for one of the small parish councils along the line, and she got involved because she felt that trains were an important asset to the valley communities. All of the eleven parish councils in the Hope Valley helped with the survey, which involved distributing 3500 questionnaires to 6500 households. The results have provided a remarkably useful database of local needs. As well as looking at existing users, the survey has identified the needs of potential users, who might be attracted if improvements were made. In addition to achieving an hourly frequency, the group also wants to improve the quality of rolling stock, focusing particularly on over-crowding during the morning and evening peaks.

SLUG on The Saltburn–Darlington Line

This is one of Britain's most historic railways, using part of the original 1825 Stockton and Darlington Railway. Today it plays an important role in local commuting into Middlesbrough and Darlington, as well as in taking visitors to the seaside resort of Saltburn. The Saltburn

Line Users' Group, known affectionately as SLUG, was formed in 1996 with the involvement of several community activists and local business people.[14] It is a lively and positive organisation which works constructively with Northern Rail and local authorities, and it has been instrumental in making Saltburn station look absolutely magnificent. Its colourful floral displays are a particular feature, and in 2012 the station won a gold medal in the Northumbria in Bloom awards. The group has also traditionally organised an annual railtour, and it played a pivotal role in the town's celebrations of the railway's 150th anniversary in 2011.

One feature of the route is its 'ambassador' teams. The idea originated at Hartlepool, when a team of volunteers agreed to assist local operator Grand Central's passengers on Sundays, a day when the station was left unstaffed. The idea worked well, taking the idea of 'station friends' a big step further. The 'ambassadors', mostly members of SLUG, provide general assistance and advice to passengers and liaise with Grand Central's own staff if there is disruption. The volunteers are given free travel on Grand Central services as a 'thank you' for their efforts, including trips to London. Paul Stevenson, himself a volunteer, helps to co-ordinate the programme.[15]

Heart of Wales Line Travellers Association (HOWLTA)

HOWLTA is a pressure group which works to maintain and develop the Swansea–Llandovery–Llandrindod Wells–Shrewsbury railway line, currently operated by Arriva Trains Wales. Since its foundation in 1981, HOWLTA has grown to around 1000 members. In 2012 the group published a *Strategic Plan*, which set out its proposals for better passenger and freight services, arguing that if these were adopted the line could make a much greater contribution to the social, economic and environmental needs of its catchment area.[16]

The group are campaigning for improvements in frequency on the passenger service between Swansea and Shrewsbury, and for this route to be linked with an improved frequency service from Shrewsbury to Crewe; this would help reduce the need to change trains on many long-distance journeys. It also wants to see faster journeys to Cardiff and beyond. In the short term this would be achieved by running extra trains and adapting existing routes. However, as a second stage the group want the Pontarddulais to Gowerton rail route to be reopened. This is part of a wider strategy to improve connections from the Line's catchment area, including for freight routes. The aim is improve freight connections to the South Wales ports and to North West England and beyond.

The *Strategic Plan* also sets out detailed standards to be met at all stations, with appropriate enhancements to facilities at the more important stops; and it has equally developed plans for improved infrastructure on the line, one aim of which is to make higher line speeds and therefore faster journeys possible. A further area covered by the *Plan* is improvements to passenger coaches, including suggested improvements in seat capacity, air conditioning, and space available for luggage, cycles and pushchairs.[17]

The association deliberately avoids the idea that it is only for rail users, and stresses the importance of transport integration. It wants to see far better provision made for interchange between the Heart of Wales Line passenger service and other modes of transport, especially local buses and the developing *Traws Cymru* long distance bus network. The *Plan* set out the facilities that would be needed at interchange points, and argues for improved systems of inter-modal ticketing and connections.

Finally, the *Plan* advocates a more localised system of management of the line, to enable a greater focus on local needs than can be achieved by the current train operator or Network Rail.[18] HOWLTA is currently working with the Heart of Wales Line Forum, the community rail partnership for the line, to take forward its radical ideas for managing the line as a showpiece for local management.

RE-OPENING CAMPAIGNS

Several routes that were closed during (and in some cases before) the Beeching era are currently the subject of re-opening campaigns. Most groups campaigning for re-openings are part of the Railfuture network and work closely with rail user bodies. In some cases the groups that were formed with the intention of re-opening their local line have succeeded. An example is Ribble Valley Rail, covering the line from Blackburn to Clitheroe. When their efforts were crowned with success in 1994, the group decided to continue as a rail user group, and it is now a component of the local community rail partnership. But most re-opening campaigns have to be in for the long haul, and the complexities of the rail industry following privatisation have not made their task any easier. The next section of this chapter looks at a selection of re-opening campaigns around the UK to see how they have developed their case.

The Wealden Line: Lewes–Uckfield (Sussex)

The line between Lewes and Uckfield once formed part of a through route from London via Oxted to Lewes and the South Coast. It was then subject to a Beeching closure, although the route as far as Uckfield managed to survive and prosper, today serving a very affluent part of the south-east. However, the ten mile gap to Lewes limits the route's potential, and a strong campaign has developed to urge an apparently reluctant local authority to support the case for re-opening. This campaign is already backed by local Liberal Democrat MP Norman Baker, the current transport minister. Its aim is 'to secure the restoration of Uckfield line train services to Lewes and Tunbridge Wells, creating a new Wealden Line which would provide new travel opportunities across East Sussex and Kent, stimulate the local economy and benefit the environment by relieving road congestion'.[19]

The fight to reopen this section of the line was pursued by the Lewes-Uckfield Joint Railway Committee throughout the 1970s, a group that was originally set up to stop the line being closed – although its efforts were unsuccessful, it continued campaigning. The current Wealden Line Campaign was started in 1986 by Brian Hart, with the strong support of Chris Green, who was then at the helm of Network SouthEast, which actually saw public use of the railways as something to be encouraged rather than deterred. The Campaign's first objectives were to reverse the continuing degrading of the Uckfield line by reinstating main line connections to the South Coast via Lewes, and to Kent via Tunbridge Wells; and as part of this aim they campaigned for third-rail electrification. Attempts to enlist support from East Sussex County Council were rebuffed.

After years of languishing in a siding of political indifference, the campaign for what has become known as 'Brighton Main Line 2' is now developing momentum. The group argue that BML2 offers a unique opportunity to solve many of the serious problems of the over-crowded routes between London, Sussex, Surrey and Kent. In their view a strengthening of routes in this area would help maintain growth in London, particularly given that its centre of gravity is shifting eastwards.[20] It could also provide much-needed back up when the existing Brighton line is disrupted through engineering works and problems – a frequent problem for commuters and other local travellers.[21]

The Wealden Line Campaign shows that despite opposition from both local government and the rail industry, persistence and professional lobbying can pay off: they have not yet achieved their goal, but there is a growing consensus that the re-opening should happen. And if it had not been for the efforts of the campaigners, the trackbed would by now have been severed, and dozens of houses built across it.

Ashington Blyth and Tyne

If the Wealden Line serves some of the most prosperous parts of England, the former Ashington Blyth and Tyne network covers some of the most deprived. The railway forms a loop heading north from Newcastle via Blyth and Bedlington to re-join the East Coast Main Line at Morpeth, while a branch continues northwards to Ashington from Bedlington. The total population covered by the railway is considerable: this was once the heart of the Northumberland coalfield, and the popular Mining Museum is adjacent to the former railway. The railways were closed as a result of Beeching, and the last train from Newcastle to Ashington and Newbiggin ran in November 1964. At the time of the closure most people worked at local collieries within walking or cycling distance of their homes, but now that the pits have closed people are dependent on work in central Newcastle. The bus journey takes them a long hour, and is often delayed by traffic congestion. However the railway itself is still operational, but it is only used for freight and occasional diverted passenger services Newcastle and Morpeth.

The South East Northumberland Rail Users Group – SENRUG – was formed to campaign for better local services north of Newcastle on the East Coast Main Line, and also to lobby for re-opening of the Ashington Blyth and Tyne network. Its case for re-opening is based on two main arguments: it would make commuting easier and hence open up a wider range of job opportunities for people who don't have access to a car; and it would assist in the regeneration of areas served by the network through better transport links, among the benefits of which would be enabling people to commute to work but spend their money locally.[22] SENRUG has proposed a phased approach, arguing that the first section of the line could be re-opened for less than £5 million (as compared with the over-inflated figures suggested by former Railtrack). The first phase would involve the restoration of a train service to Bedlington and Ashington; the second would involve trains continuing northwards to Woodhorn, where they would serve both the mining museum and a major local hospital; and the final phase would see the full opening of the line.

SENRUG has been an effective political lobbyist. Its parliamentary campaigning has included early-day motions, an adjournment debate and meetings with ministers; and it also created an online petition which received thousands of signatures demanding that passenger services be brought back to Ashington. In 2008, with sponsorship funding from Wansbeck District Council, it chartered a special train from Northern Rail to run round the line. This was enormously popular: guests included MPs and MEPs, over forty local authority councillors, senior officers from five different authorities, and representatives from North East Assembly, Government Office North East, One North East, the Chamber of Commerce and the North East Regional TUC. A second and third trip was then made available to members of the general public, with all tickets being sold out within days. The day gave an enormous boost to the campaign, and achieved massive publicity both in the press and on TV. At time of writing the group is continuing its battle, and making regular appeals for support.

SELRAP: Skipton–Colne

The eleven-mile railway between the north-east Lancashire cotton town of Colne and the prosperous market town of Skipton, North Yorkshire, closed in January 1970. Before closure it had not just provided a link between two relatively small urban centres, it had also linked the sizeable north-east Lancashire textile centres of Blackburn, Accrington, Burnley and Nelson to Skipton and thus to West Yorkshire. The local rail network from Leeds to Ilkley, Bradford and Skipton is currently flourishing, despite Beeching's desire to destroy it, and BR electrified the network in the 1990s; modern electric trains on the Leeds–Skipton corridor are always full to capacity in the morning and evening peaks, and the route carries over 7 million passengers a year. However, the electric trains stop at Skipton. Re-opening the short link to Colne would offer the possibility of electric trains running from Leeds through to Nelson, Burnley and Blackburn, and joining the West Coast main line at Preston. But the railway from Colne to Manchester is un-electrified and suffers from lack of investment; while the line between Colne and Burnley is a run-down single track branch, joined by the re-opened line from Hebden Bridge just west of Burnley.

The Skipton East Lancashire Rail Action Partnerships (SELRAP) was formed in 2001 and has won support from a wide range of local community interests as well as famous supporters such as Ian Hislop, Joanna Lumley and Alan Bennett. It sees the track between Skipton and Colne as the missing link in what would otherwise be the lowest level trans-Pennine rail route between the Humber and West Coast ports, between Preston and the West Coast Main Line, and between Leeds and the cities of Yorkshire, and a much needed addition to current heavily used routes. It also argues that the line would connect socially deprived and depressed areas in north-east Lancashire, where car ownership is low, with the more prosperous West Yorkshire area. The group is campaigning to the keep trackbed intact so that the railway could be restored at a relatively low cost.[23]

Although SELRAP has won substantial support, formal backing from the Lancashire and North Yorkshire county councils continues to elude them. But it is going ahead with fund-raising to undertake its own study of the costs and benefits of re-opening the line (see www. selrap.org.uk).

Bere Alston-Tavistock

Devon County Council is currently promoting an exciting vision to re-open the railway between Tavistock and Bere Alston, a line that was once part of the Southern railway's main-line from Plymouth to Exeter and London Waterloo. The section between Crediton and Bere Alston was yet another victim the Beeching report, closing in 1969; but the branch from Plymouth to Bere Alston and Gunnislake was retained because of poor road links to isolated rural communities. Tavistock, a sizeable town, was isolated from the rail network, but was only three miles from the surviving branch line railway at Bere Alston.

The re-opening is interesting and innovative in its conception: it is using developer funding to pay for the construction and some of the operation of the railway. Private sector promoter Kilbride Rail is working with Devon County Council and Bovis Homes to develop a business plan that will see trains running within three years, with very little call on the public purse. The railway will provide transport for a site in Tavistock that has been identified in the West Devon Core Strategy for the development of 750 homes, together with a primary school, local shop and car park. Money raised through the development will be used to finance the costs of reinstating the rail line – estimated at £18.5 million.

The reopening of this section of line will provide a new sustainable link between Tavistock, Bere Alston and Plymouth for commuter journeys; help to minimise traffic on the busy A386; link Tavistock to the national rail network; and ensure improved options for commuting, leisure and education trips along the route. It will also deliver a sustainable link from Plymouth to the Cornish Mining World Heritage Site at Tavistock. The County Council is also planning a pedestrian and cycle trail, which will provide an attractive route between Tavistock and Bere Alston.

Kilbride Rail has studied the experience of re-openings in other parts of the UK and expects patronage to far out-strip forecast demand:

> ... passenger numbers forecast in Devon County Council's A386 report anticipate that there will be substantial growth in service from when the service begins, and this is supported by examples around the country such as Ebbw Vale, where the passenger numbers for the first year exceeded the forecast for the first 5 years of service. This experience has been mirrored by the Stirling-Alloa re-opening.[24]

They therefore have plans to increase services as demand develops. They expect that the value of the land will be realised over a three to five year period, thus ensuring full funding for the rail project.[25]

This innovative partnership approach could see trains returning to Tavistock by 2018. This perhaps might in turn lead to the reopening of the relatively short and unobstructed route over the edge of Dartmoor to Okehampton and on to Crediton and Exeter, thereby returning to the national rail network yet another line that Beeching destroyed.

The Waverley Line

The closure of the 98-miles long Waverley Line between Edinburgh, Galashiels, Hawick and Carlisle was the most controversial of all the Beeching closures. The last train ran in 1969, and the route has been a cause célèbre of rail campaigners ever since. The closure consigned the sizeable Borders towns of Galashiels and Hawick to isolation and decline; the population of Hawick in particular has declined markedly since the closure, the town's isolation from its natural 'capital' Edinburgh having been compounded by the effects of the run-down of the local textile industry. Closure of the line left Hawick and Galashiels further from the rail network than any other towns of their size in Britain, and in 2013 public transport to Edinburgh is still slower than it was in 1900. The loss of the Waverley Route also meant that the Borders became the only region of Britain without train services, an unwanted mantle which it will finally lose with the opening of the Borders Railway in 2015.

Although the closure was opposed by the local communities, resistance was too little and far too late. The campaign to save the line only began after consent for closure was announced – two years after the official proposal to close the line and *five and a half years* after the publication of the Beeching Report! As David Spaven comments, unlike the energetic response to the Beeching threats in the Highlands, 'too many people in the Borders either believed the railway would never close or were not sufficiently concerned to do anything about it'.[26]

But people in the Borders did subsequently rally 'to right the 1969 injustice'.[27] The Campaign for Borders Rail is now one of the most successful grassroots rail campaigns in Great Britain. It is also one of the most inclusive campaigns, bringing together concerned citizens from all walks of life. But reinstatement of the railway southwards has been made much more difficult by the short-term political decisions that were taken in the 1970s and 1980s by local and central government, when they allowed new roads to breach the old railway alignment. This lack of strategic vision has been estimated to have added to the capital cost of the new Borders Railway by as much as 40 per cent.

While the transport benefits which the Borders Railway will deliver are clear, its genesis was very much as an economic regeneration project, and the line's promoters have always emphasised the wider benefits that the railway will bring to the region. Their regeneration arguments share many features with other campaigns for re-opening: the goals are to mitigate social exclusion through enabling access to employment, education, health and leisure opportunities via an effective public transport link; to facilitate new housing, including affordable housing, thereby taking pressure away from a crowded urban hub; and to tackle traffic congestion.[28]

From its launch in 1999 the Campaign for Borders Rail played a key role in mobilising public and political support for what ultimately became the Borders Railway project, which will deliver a new railway from Edinburgh through Midlothian to Galashiels and Tweedbank by 2015. CBR lobbying was also crucial to securing two key enhancements to the original official railway specification. These were the inclusion of a station at Stow, which campaigners argued was essential in providing links to surrounding rural communities; and the terminus at Tweedbank being built on a scale that could accommodate special trains bringing tourists into the Borders.

Trains will come back to the Scottish Borders in 2015, but campaigners are not relaxing the pressure. The real prize will be getting trains to Hawick, the largest Borders town and a short distance beyond Tweedbank. After that, reconstruction of the entire route to Carlisle makes obvious sense, which would provide an alternative fast route from the North-West of England to Edinburgh. The group's newsletter is upbeat: 'let's not forget that the campaign is all about a complete reinstatement of the main line Waverley Route, serving new generations and old communities. So, if your appetite for reconstruction is whetted, there's still around sixty miles to go!'[29]

Bradford Cross Rail

Since the railways came to the city, Bradford's rail network has been split between services from Leeds and Halifax coming into Bradford Interchange (formerly Exchange) and services from Leeds via Shipley terminating at Forster Square. Services were originally provided by competing private companies, with the Lancashire and Yorkshire and Great Northern Railways using Exchange and the Midland having exclusive rights at Forster Square. The two termini are separated by about half a mile, across the city centre. A link between the two lines was first proposed in 1846, but never built. When the plan returned in 1898, it was given authorisation by the Midland Railway (West Riding Lines) Act, but Midland then dragged their feet and it wasn't built. Another enabling act of Parliament was passed in 1911, the Bradford Through Lines Act, but the First World War got in the way of its construction. West Yorkshire Passenger Transport executive revived the scheme in the late 1980s, but once again the scheme ran out of momentum.

Today, the Forster Square station serves Skipton, Leeds, Keighley, Saltaire and Shipley, with connections to Carlisle. The route was electrified in the early 1990s and is a busy commuter service. The Interchange station – currently un-electrified – serves Manchester Victoria, Blackpool, Halifax, Pudsey and Leeds, along the Calderdale Line. Bradford Rail Users Group has been lobbying the city council and West Yorkshire Passenger Transport Executive to see the new link as part of a much bigger development of the rail network in West Yorkshire. It argues that a through rail link between the two stations will bring major regeneration benefits, as well as creating a more efficient network that avoids costly and inconvenient reversals at the two termini.[30]

The proposals would replace the current stations with a new glass-sided four-track central station, on a new viaduct across Leeds Road, providing views of the Cathedral quarter and a link into the planned Westfield retail mall. Campaigners believe the development would encourage new investment and boost job creation, including attracting civil service jobs from London because of cheaper office space in Bradford.

The scheme is estimated to cost in the region of £100 million. As well as the rail campaigners in BRUG, the scheme is supported by a group of local business people who recognise the potential for a single city centre station's potential to stimulate economic growth. John Pennington, former owner of the city's Midland Hotel and a Conservative councillor, has been a prominent supporter. John argues that it is time to re-visit the city 'with the old blinkers removed':

> In a local economy where entrepreneurship remains, where the youth need hope and jobs, we must provide the tools to enable success. Bradford is at the bottom of its cycle and worth a punt by investors, but only if the infrastructure allows people to come and go cheaply, efficiently and conveniently. We are the sixth largest city in England

yet have a deadend motorway at the M606, two deadend stations and an inner ring road that finishes at a T-junction. We must recover from a cul-de-sac of decline.[31]

The group also includes Paul Mackie, chairman of Bradford quantity surveyors RPP Ltd, and Roger Owen, former property director of Morrisons supermarkets. Some critics have dismissed the plan as a pipe dream, but if it is considered as part of a revamped and electrified regional network it begins to make sense. If trains from Leeds to Halifax and Manchester were routed via Shipley and then through central Bradford, and services from Leeds to Skipton and Carlisle operated via New Pudsey and Bradford and then on to Shipley, a 'scissors-shaped' network would be created that would allow more trains to operate and central Bradford to be served far better.

WHAT FUTURE FOR RAIL CAMPAIGNING?

The examples outlined above show the diversity of Britain's volunteer-led rail campaigns, ranging from modest efforts to improve station facilities to full-scale re-opening campaigns. Britain has the most well-organised rail lobby in the world, though cynics might say that's because there is plenty to lobby about! The rail campaigning groups in the UK are well established and powerful, and a force to be reckoned with. Nationally, RailFuture, though without any paid staff, has an important input to policy-making. Campaign for Better Transport (formerly Transport 2000) covers all modes of transport and brings a wider environmental as well as social perspective to transport campaigning.

But what direction should transport campaigning and the rail passenger lobby take in the next ten years? Too often, rail campaigns are the preserve of the articulate male middle class who are railway enthusiasts. Speaking as one of them, I applaud their enthusiasm, but I sometimes despair at their inability to see the problems this can cause. Not a single member of the RailFuture board is female, reflecting the fact that most rail campaigners are men, though according to some data most users are women.[32] This presents a serious weakness of the rail user movement in Britain and risks creating blind spots on campaigning issues. Personal safety, for example, is a concern for many women using unstaffed stations, but appears to have low priority, whilst network expansion has high priority.

The rail lobby rightly resents being stigmatised as representing those 'rich people' who can afford rail travel, but it isn't doing enough to champion the mum struggling up station steps with her pushchair, the disabled person trying to get off the train, or the young person attempting to make sense of the fares system to get the cheapest deals. Campaigning continues to be focused on 'hardware' – electrification, new trains, re-openings. All of these issues are important, but it's easy to lose sight of why they are important: it's about connectivity to jobs, family and friends, college and school and simple pleasures.

Rail campaigners need to build strong alliances with other groups campaigning for better local facilities. Campaigns against library closures, for car restraint in town and village centres, and for access to the countryside, are all relevant here. It's about seeing the railway not as an isolated piece of infrastructure that has no relevance to people's lives other than as a means of transport, but as a vital part of community life. The railway is the link between communities, the energising spine that can make all the difference between a community which struggles and one that is vibrant and healthy.

The community rail movement, which has a greater focus on these kinds of issues, is now twenty years old and has taken root in many communities across the UK, both urban and rural. It complements and strengthens the rail user movement, whose roots go back earlier, to the 1950s. The next chapter examines how successful it has been and where it could be heading in the future.

NOTES

1. Anthony Smith, Chief Executive Passenger Focus, *Transport Times*, March 2013.
2. National Passenger Survey, autumn 2012, available on Passenger Focus website. I am grateful to David Greeno at Passenger Focus for a breakdown of the demographic profile of respondents. The total number surveyed was 31,626, across the UK.
3. See Passenger Focus website.
4. Private email to author, May 2013.
5. Anthony Smith, *Transport Times*, April 2013.
6. Friends of Settle-Carlisle Line newsletter, February 2013.
7. See Paul Salveson, 'The Avocet Line', *Today's Railways*, December 2011.

8. Richard Giles, one of the group's activists, quoted in ibid.
9. John Saunders of PENRUG, personal communication with author, March 2013.
10. Paul Salveson, 'The Far North Line', *Today's Railways*, November 2011.
11. Ibid.
12. See Paul Salveson, 'The Tarka Line', *Today's Railways*, December 2011.
13. Paul Salveson, 'The Hope Valley Line', *Today's Railways*, January 2012.
14. Paul Salveson, 'The Saltburn Line', *Today's Railways*, April 2013.
15. Ibid.
16. Heart of Wales Line Travellers Association *Strategic Plan*, 2010.
17. Ibid.
18. Ibid.
19. Wealden Line Campaign: www.wlc.org.uk.
20. Wealden Line Campaign.
21. WLC, personal communication with author February 2013.
22. Senrug website: www.senrug.org.uk.
23. Ibid, and Senrug printed newsletter.
24. Kilbride Community Rail website and personal communication from the company March 2013.
25. Ibid.
26. David Spaven, *The Waverley Line*, 2013.
27. Campaign for Borders Rail website: www.cbr.org.uk.
28. See public briefing document produced for Scottish Borders Council in 2005, quoted in Spaven, op cit.
29. Campaign for Borders Rail, *Newsletter*, February 2013.
30. Bradford Rail Users Group website: www.brug.org.uk.
31. John Pennington, quoted on Bradford Rail Users Group website: www.brug.org.uk.
32. See Passenger Focus, *National Passenger Survey*, autumn 2012.

6. THE COMMUNITY RAIL
ACHIEVEMENT

The development of a strategy for local and rural railways has shone a light on a neglected part of the network that has had little attention over the last fifteen years. What has been revealed is a group of lines and services that are important to the communities they serve, and with considerable potential for development. Both are as surprising as they are welcome.[1]

Community rail partnerships bring together train operators, Network Rail, local authorities and community groups to promote lines which were, in many cases, threatened with closure in the 1960s. Many of the routes have experienced double-digit growth thanks to imaginative promotion and community involvement, backed up by modest investment. There are about fifty community rail partnerships across the country and they generally work to the same basic principles. 'Partnership' is a much abused term, but developing a relationship of trust between train operator, local authority and wider community is fundamental. This chapter explores their achievements, but also asks 'what next?' for community rail, given that growth on many local lines has led to some services being at capacity.

Despite concerns at the time of privatisation about a possible Beeching Mark 2, major line closures have not happened since the 1970s. Following a period of uncertainty in the 1980s, secondary lines, many serving rural communities, have grown, as a result of community rail partnerships. The experience of community rail is rich and varied, offering a positive example to other railways around the world. It is a flexible tool which can be applied in many different contexts, from scenic rural lines whose main business is tourism, through to inner-city routes serving diverse and often deprived communities. It has taken off in very different parts of the country, and is far from being dependent on middle-class railway enthusiasts. Many of the station partnerships are run by community activists whose main focus is the town or village community of which they are part, rather than the railway. 'The station' is a gateway into the community which needs to be protected and enhanced. Some of the partnerships work in challenging inner-city areas of Bristol, Manchester and London; several have been able to harness the creativity of local young people.

Many community rail lines have an important role as commuter routes as well as scenic tourist lines. The Association of Community Rail Partnerships report found that CRPs achieve remarkably high value for money, with a cost benefit ratio of around 4.6 to 1 (based on funding for an officer and promotions). The study found that 93 per cent of passengers on community rail lines were 'very or fairly satisfied' with their train service, compared with 84 per cent on similar but non-CRP local lines. The national average was 81 per cent.

From a left political perspective, some have questioned whether local communities should be contributing time and effort to supporting a 'private' railway. Volunteers tending station gardens, providing art work, publicising train services – isn't that what the private train companies should be doing? In reality, the work done by community rail volunteers is additional to anything the railway industry would do, and wouldn't happen otherwise. And the railway is 'owned' not by a private shareholding company but by Network Rail, which doesn't have shareholders and pays no dividends. But there is a bigger issue here, which is about community ownership. People see the railway as being part of their community and, if it's looked after, it is a source of pride. Regardless of who legally 'owns' the railway, local communities are asserting real 'ownership' of their stations and lines, and this prefigures what a future socially owned railway might look like. They are the real railway revolutionaries.

Ironically, when the railways were under public ownership this seldom translated into people getting actively involved in their railway – it was run as a centralised state corporation for much of its existence. Only in the last twenty years have people begun to claim some kind of 'community ownership' of their railway, and the results have been transformative, with brighter and more attractive stations leading to additional use of the railway. But it hasn't just been stations – community rail partnerships have helped to improve entire routes, and to bring the railway closer to the people it should be serving.

Much of the success of community rail has been down to a combination of community enthusiasm and the support of railway managers. Despite all the pressures of privatisation and cost reduction, railway people have positively engaged with communities, with the support of their parent companies. The question is, if so much can be achieved in the less than ideal environment of a privatised railway, how much more could be done in a socially owned one?

COMMUNITY RAIL DEVELOPMENT – EARLY DAYS

Many lines that are today prospering had a lucky escape. Some local lines that had survived Beeching in the 1960s continued to have a precarious existence in the 1970s and early 1980s. Successive governments muttered about the costs of some of the more peripheral lines, with suggestions that it would be cheaper to buy all the users of particular routes their own car rather than continue subsidising little-used branch lines. The Serpell report of 1983 raised the prospect of further closures, but the ensuing public outcry gave the Thatcher government pause for thought.[2] As we have seen, that didn't stop BR from going ahead with proposals to close the famous Settle-Carlisle Line in the late 1980s. The route, originally opened, unwillingly, by the Midland Railway in 1876 to give it direct access to Scotland, had dwindled in importance during the 1970s. Only a handful of passenger services and a small number of freight trains still used the notoriously difficult and expensive to maintain route. There is strong anecdotal evidence to suggest that the British Railways Board saw the Settle-Carlisle line as a test case for further closures. If it could get away with it, other lines might be easy pickings. And in fairness to BR, it was under strong pressure from the government to save money.

With hindsight we can see that BR chose the wrong target. A massive, professionally organised campaign against closure forced the government to reverse the closure proposal. Transport minister Michael Portillo subsequently promised to look at innovative ways of developing the line, and set up the Settle-Carlisle Railway Development Company, an early example of a community-rail partnership, but without the name. Ironically, the threat of closure had led to a major increase in passengers using the line, helped by a subversive campaign to promote the line by local BR managers. The campaign had shown that determined action could work and caused members of the BR Board to re-think its attitude towards regional railways. A further boost to the survival chances of local lines came when BR introduced 'sectorisation'. Local and regional services became part of BR's 'Provincial' sector, which was blessed with a talented group of managers whose focus was firmly on the lines which in the past had been 'nobody's babies'. Alongside sectorisation, BR made the inspired decision to set up its own 'community unit' to support grassroots forms of community involvement with the railway.

At the same time, other government agencies – particularly the Rural Development Commission and the Countryside Commission – were starting to recognise the importance of railways to rural and semi-rural communities. However, clouds were appearing on the horizon as John Major's government announced plans to privatise the railways: it was unclear how lightly-used local lines would fare under privatisation but it was widely believed that it would not be a positive experience. Campaigners began to brace themselves for a possible new wave of closures, as Britain's railways were fattened up for sale to the private sector. Little money would be made out of lines like Middlesbrough-Whitby, Inverness to Kyle of Lochalsh or St Ives to St Erth – unless they were converted into seasonal tourist operations charging premium fares.

NEW FUTURES FOR RURAL RAIL

In 1992, because of concern over the future of the rural rail network, a project was developed by London-based Transnet – *New Futures for Rural Rail* – with the aim of looking at innovative ways of developing the rural rail network, considering ways of harnessing community engagement and finding examples of successful rural railways in other parts of the world. The inspiration for this came from some isolated local examples where communities were playing an active part in the upkeep of their station, and also the Devon and Cornwall Rail Initiative, which had brought local authorities, tourism agencies and BR to actively promote local rail networks.

The study was supported by BR's Provincial sector, the Rural Development Commission and the Countryside Commission. I was the manager of the project, working with a small team of researchers. Its report was published at a conference at the National Railway Museum, York, in June 1993, attended by over a hundred delegates from local authorities, rural development organisations and railway societies. There were very few railway managers in the audience.

The report had two main recommendations, based on short and longer-term approaches which were seen as complementary. The first was based around a new concept of 'community-rail partnership' that would bring together the railway industry, local authorities, businesses and community organisations to support and promote a particular route or small network. Central to the concept was the idea of stations as 'hubs' of local development; not just for transport but for community and retail services. A community rail partnership, suitably resourced with staff and a budget, would 'operationalise' the corridor approach and develop a range of initiatives which would both grow business along the line and benefit the local economy and communities on the route.

The second recommendation was more radical. Whilst 'community rail partnerships' took the existing structure of the railways – with privatisation imminent – as a given, there was a more long-term vision based on experience of some continental railways that were locally owned and managed. This became known as 'microfranchising', though the report's authors had reservations about the franchising approach.[3]

COMMUNITY RAIL GETS GOVERNMENT ENDORSEMENT

Community rail partnerships have transformed many of Britain's local railways, ranging from rural branch lines in Devon and Cornwall through to urban routes in major cities. The partnerships cover some sixty lines with over a hundred individual 'station friends' groups. They are federated in the Association of Community Rail Partnerships, which is supported by the Department for Transport, Scottish and Welsh governments, local authorities across the UK and the railway industry. Government recognition of the effectiveness of community rail came in November 2004, when Rail Minister Tony McNulty launched the Community Rail Development Strategy at an event in Huddersfield's Head of Steam, before travelling down the Penistone Line, the pioneer of community rail partnerships. This was the culmination of energetic behind-the-scenes work carried out within the SRA by senior officers such as Chris Austin and Jim Steer.

A key element of the strategy was a proposal to designate certain routes as community railways, allowing different, more flexible, approaches to be taken towards their development. Four pilot lines were selected, one of which was the Penistone Line; the others were Esk Valley, St Ives and St Albans Abbey. The objectives of the strategy were to increase revenue and reduce costs, increase community involvement, and support social and economic development. It's clear that community rail has been successful in most of these aims. It has led to increases in revenue and passenger numbers, as well as community involvement; while routes that have a community rail partnership have experienced remarkable growth levels, and have seen the emergence of a positive cycle of development, investment and increased ridership. A report commissioned by the Association of Community Rail Partnerships, with the support of the Department of Transport, found that 'an active and effective community rail partnership should reasonably expect to increase footfall and fare revenue by an additional 7 per cent over three years'.[4] In addition, the work of community rail partnerships has helped reduce car use and contributed to regeneration strategies, meeting the objective of 'supporting social and economic development'.

However, the holy grail of reducing costs whilst increasing revenue has so far eluded community rail projects. The reality is that most of the conventional savings were made by BR in the 1970s, and to achieve a step change requires a more radical approach of the sort outlined in the next chapter.

AT THE LIMITS OF CAPACITY: THE PENISTONE LINE

The Penistone Line Partnership was formed in 1993 as an experiment in railway social engineering. It was the first community rail partnership following on from the *New Futures for Rural Rail* report. A meeting was held to test out the idea, in Stocksmoor Village Hall, during Kirklees Council's Green Transport Week in June 1993. About fifty local people turned up from various community organisations, together with BR managers and PTE officers. The upshot was a decision to 'just do it', and form the Penistone Line Partnership. Officers were elected and a war chest of about £3 was established following a collection, once the village hall committee had been paid.

Though short on finance the PLP was rich with enthusiasm and ideas. A key part of the CRP philosophy was to use local talent and go 'outside' the traditional railway mentality. Two activities were started almost immediately. The first was a series of short guided walks from the line, using skilled and knowledgeable local walks leaders. These were an immediate success, sometimes attracting as many as one hundred ramblers. The second idea was more innovative. The Huddersfield area has a good network of musicians and the idea emerged to run a trial 'Folk Train' on one of the quieter evening services. To many people's surprise, BR managers were hugely supportive; they even welcomed the provision of real ale on the train! The first one ran in September 1993 and was a huge success, with about thirty people on the train leaving Huddersfield. Each station supplied more concert-goers until the train was packed-out by Denby Dale. The media loved the idea and the 'Folk Train' became a regular monthly event – followed by a Jazz Train, and a Blues Train. Over the years the music trains have proved immensely popular – and suffered hardly any anti-social behaviour. There is still a regular demand for 'special' music trains for parties. No wonder the *Guardian* described the Penistone Line in 1998 as 'Britain's Number 1 Fun Railway'! But there was serious side to it – passenger numbers started growing and growing, and so did the partnership's activities.

The breakthrough came in 1997 with a successful bid to the Lottery Fund, which allowed the Partnership to employ a full-time member of staff. The PLP is structured as not-for-profit company, with an open membership structure. It publishes a quarterly newsletter – *The Penistone Line Express* – and has a lively website.[5] Maintaining funding to staff voluntary organisations is a huge challenge, however, and after the three year period of lottery funding came to an end the staff post had to become part-time, and is now funded from other sources. Reduced professional support has meant a greater reliance on volunteers, who continue to organise music trains, guided walks and a range of special events. A special feature of the PLP is the high level of involvement of local railway staff. The chairman is a Huddersfield driver for Northern Rail, Neil Bentley, who has won several awards for his community activities. Neil has been chair for five years, and if he doesn't actually dream about the line, he certainly spends a lot of his waking hours either driving trains along it, or working on projects to support it. 'We're all intensely proud of the Penistone Line at Huddersfield depot,' says Neil. 'It's very much a community railway, with railway staff and local people working together to keep it as Britain's leading community railway.'[6]

One of the PLP's most audacious schemes was to run its own weekend rail-link bus service – 'The Holmfirth Branch Line' – providing links from trains arriving at Shepley to the popular tourist centre of Holmfirth. Using volunteer drivers, the service commenced in 1998 and survived for six years before a shortage of volunteers and a huge reduction in concessionary fare rebates forced it to end. It demonstrated that well-planned rail-link bus services can work in rural areas, with good levels of usage, providing you have the right, locally-based, organisation in place to manage it.

The PLP has done much valuable work with local schools, including an on-train poetry project which led to publication of a collection of children's writing (still available via the PLP website). The Partnership has organised arts projects involving local schoolchildren and a highly innovative project to promote rail travel to people from black and minority ethnic communities. The PLP's 'Tracking Lives' project charted the social history of the railway, with photographs and stories about the line supplied by local people and made into a superb exhibition. Its most recent project has been to encourage the formation of more station partnerships along the line, working closely with local parish councils and community groups. Funding from the LEADER Fund (an EU fund for rural projects) was obtained to employ a part-time development worker.

Northern Rail has strongly supported the PLP's efforts to market the route. Drew Haley, Northern's Stakeholder Manager for West Yorkshire, commented that 'students, ethnic minorities, walkers, shoppers and music lovers have all been targeted and this has paid dividends'.[7] Alongside the PLP, the line has its own user group – the Huddersfield–Penistone–Sheffield Rail Users Association. The two organisations are complementary, and work closely together, with many people being members of both groups.

The Penistone Line has been able to demonstrate exceptional levels of community engagement and also growth – use of the line has more than doubled since the PLP was formed. The biggest problem facing the line now is not possible closure but how to accommodate growing demand, with a route whose capacity was reduced to mainly single-line operation in the 1980s. If the line is to grow and meet its potential, major investment in capacity and rolling stock is needed.

URBAN FRINGE: SEVERNSIDE

'Community rail' can play a key role in urban regeneration, and the most outstanding example of its success in this area is in the south-west. The Severnside Community Rail Partnership, a community interest company, covers local routes in the Bristol area, including the branch to Avonmouth and Severn Beach, and runs through some of the most deprived parts of the south-west. The Partnership is working to make stations more friendly and welcoming, and to reduce crime, vandalism and anti-social behaviour.

The Severn Beach line has had a remarkable transformation. As local resident and internationally-respected tourism expert Professor Bernard Lane has commented: 'It was, until quite recently, the line the railway wished was not there. It was the line that got the bus substitution whenever they were short of trains or queues, or when a rugby match in Cardiff needed a special'. The problem was that the route was slow and not very direct. For years it was 'invisible, short of marketing, and lacking a regular interval timetable'.[8]

The transformation began in 2004, when the Severnside Community Rail Partnership was formed. The Partnership's emphasis is on working with partners and local communities to deliver quick wins and small-scale initiatives that make local rail services more attractive and bring passenger benefits. Keith Walton, the Partnership's chair since its inception, stresses the social mission of the partnership: 'We want to find ways of encouraging greater use of the Bristol local rail network but also ensure that access to stations is easy and they provide a safe and welcoming environment.'

The Partnership's principal sponsors are Bath and North East Somerset, Bristol City, North Somerset, Somerset, and South Gloucestershire Councils, Business West, First Great Western and the West of England Partnership. The sponsors fund the running costs, including the post of Partnership Officer, Heather Cullimore. Projects are funded largely through specific grants, assisted by local and community voluntary work. Uniquely for a British community rail partnership, since June 2008 it is been constituted as a Community Interest Company. (This are a relatively new company structure for not-for-profit groups that engage in commercial activities, designed to ensure strong accountability to the communities they serve.)

A key aspect of community engagement along the route is work with schools. The line has become a linear art gallery, with art work created by children in local schools on display at most stations along the line. Art work has been shown to have a positive impact on people's perception of stations, especially unstaffed facilities such as those along the Severn Beach line. British Transport Police have reported a 53 per cent reduction in crime on the line, much of which is attributable to the community projects. The partnership has also done some outstanding work with the local probation service, involving young people on community payback schemes in a number of projects. Heather Cullimore explains:

> We try to involve school pupils of all ages in art or horticultural projects at their local station. Young people who have been involved in the Severnside Schools Community Stations Programme take great pride in having ownership of the station and seeing their work on display to a wide audience. Their contribution to improving the station is generally respected by their peers; this is reflected in reduction of instances of vandalism and anti-social behaviour at stations along the line.[9]

The Partnership's work has been recognised through numerous national and regional awards. A really notable achievement was being short-listed in the 2011 national community programme awards run by the Howard League for Penal Reform, for the CRP's work with the Probation Service.

One of the most exciting projects being led by the partnership is the Portway Interchange project which will involve a new park and ride station close to the M5. This has strong Network Rail and FGW support, and will take the form of a simple modular steel-built platform that is relatively economic to produce.[10]

The Severn Beach branch ranks as one of the country's most outstanding examples of community rail in practice, reaching out to parts of the community that many fail to touch. As Keith reflected, 'the Severn Beach line success shows that community rail can work well in a challenging urban environment, far removed from its traditional rural roots'.[11]

JAZZ, BLUES AND SOCIAL INCLUSION: LANCASHIRE LINES

Engagement with ethnic minority communities has been achieved on several community rail partnerships in the North of England, with the most success being achieved in Lancashire. The county council sponsors a network of community rail partnerships, with a team of three officers headed up by Richard Watts, the county's Rail Projects Manager and Community Rail Partnership Secretary. The East Lancashire CRP was formed in 2005 following production of its report *An Agenda for Development*.[12] This referred to the route as a 'sleeping princess', and might have added that she had been slumbering for far too long. The CRP was officially launched on 20 May 2006, with every intention of awakening the dormant beauty.

One of the truly outstanding projects on the East Lancashire/ Clitheroe lines has been the CRP's work with schools. Daisyfield Infants was built in the junction of the Burnley and Hellifield lines, and is at the heart of Blackburn's Asian community. Around 95 per cent of its pupils are from Asian backgrounds. The CRP has worked with the school to raise awareness of the railway, and has developed a number of projects – including a film – to help nurture the 'rail habit' among local kids. Northern has provided travel facilities for the children and their teachers to visit the National Rail Museum in York.

The CRP is also unusual in actively involving local bus operators. Transdev, which owns bus company Burnley and Pendle, is a member of the partnership, and the 'Pendle Connect' ticket offers integrated travel between bus and rail in East Lancashire.

East Lancashire is great walking country, and the CRP has worked hard to exploit the beauty of the surrounding area; it has developed a series of self-guided walks, as well as organising short guided walks aimed at the 'beginner' market. The guided walks attract a real mix of people, some interested in railway history but most of them simply wanting to get out into the country with other people.[13]

A well-established tradition for the CRP is its sponsorship for the annual August Colne Rhythm and Blues Festival. Live blues and a real ale bar feature on an early evening departure from Blackpool South, with the sessions getting really funky by the time the train gets into the East Lancs Delta, east of Blackburn. Simon Clarke, a Northern Rail manager seconded to the CRP, loves it. 'The RnB Festival is a great East Lancashire institution bringing people from all over the North and beyond. The Blues Train has become a centrepiece of the event and helps raise awareness about using the railway to get to cultural events in the area.'[14] Northern provides additional late evening trains to take people home after a night of boogie-woogie.

MORE THAN PASTIES AND CLOTTED CREAM: DEVON AND CORNWALL

The Devon and Cornwall Rail Partnership was the first community rail partnership in the country, having been formed in 1991 in BR days. It brought BR together with local authorities and national parks, and soon expanded to serve all of the branch lines in the two counties. It is resourced by the University of Plymouth and has three staff. Team leader Richard Burningham, who was awarded an MBE in 2011 for his services to the railway industry, previously served his time as Travel Centre Manager at Barnstaple – in BR days. That job also involved active promotion of the line, and it was while he was working there that Richard produced his very first line guide.[15]

The link with the university – unique for a CRP – is extremely important and brings benefits to both sides. For the CRP it has given access to high-level research skills, and this has led to important work on the value of local rail to the south-west economy and the importance of the local lines in social, economic and environmental terms. And it has also made available a pool of student volunteers. The partnership has produced an award-winning range of line guides and other publicity, promoting each of the Devon and Cornwall branches. It organises special events and works closely with the university students' union on volunteering projects. The Rail Ale Trail has proved remarkably popular, bringing visitors into the small villages served by the line. (Richard reassures that it is not a boozers' day out! – 'most people use the trail to go out for a meal and enjoy a pleasant pint in wonderful surroundings, without the hassle of a car'.)

Concerns over the future of the Barnstaple Line led to the formation of a 'line forum' in 1988, which quickly proved an effective way of promoting local rail services and was the first real community rail partnership (though it wasn't called that at that time). While the line was not on Beeching's list, BR had tried to close it in 1965, when the bridges over the Exe at Cowley Bridge needed replacement (though fortunately the government refused permission); but the line had suffered from lack of investment for decades. It soon became clear that the approach of bringing local authorities and tourism bodies together with the railway and the wider community was to everyone's advantage, and the result was the creation of the Devon and Cornwall Rail Partnership in 1991.

Today, the main partners are First Great Western, Devon and Cornwall county councils, Network Rail and the university. Each route under the Partnership umbrella has a line working group that involves district councils, the line association and other groups and individuals. The role of Devon County Council has been crucial: 'From setting up and maintaining the Partnership, to long term support for train services and waves of station improvements, the County Council has been key to the line's development and success over the last twenty years and more'.[16]

A key aspect of the Partnership's role has been to identify good practice elsewhere. For example they organised a study visit to Norfolk to look at the success of the Bittern Line Partnership, where ridership was rocketing. Having discovered that this success was due to a combination of regular, clock-face frequencies, low fares and energetic marketing, they approached First Great Western with evidence to this effect, and FGW subsequently implemented most of their suggestions: for example the shoppers' fare from Exeter to Barnstaple was reduced and an improved timetable was introduced. As a result, there has been exponential growth on the line.

Some of the marketing effort involves grassroots work with local businesses to help drive up use of the smaller stations. At some villages along the line local shops sell carnet tickets supplied by the partnership. These give discounted travel for rail users, and the local shop gets 10 per cent of the carnet ticket's price, so everyone benefits. The timetables produced by the Partnership are widely distributed across North Devon. A total of 41,000 are sent out via a local free newspaper, with a further 4000 being distributed separately.

STATION FUN: NORTH STAFFORDSHIRE
(CREWE-STOKE-DERBY)

The North Staffordshire CRP was formed in summer 2005 and covers the railway running through the heart of the North Staffordshire potteries. Funding came from Central Trains, Stoke City Council, Staffordshire and Derbyshire County Councils and Cheshire East Council (formerly Cheshire County Council). The franchise passed to Stagecoach's East Midlands Trains in 2007 and they have continued the support. Faye Lambert, appointed

Community Rail Officer in 2006, comes from a public relations background in the health service and has used her PR skills to good effect in her current job: 'I'm not a railway expert, that's not what the work is about, but I do love the trains and the people. It's a really rewarding job to do, especially when you are supported by the very best volunteers.'[17] Faye won the prize for outstanding community rail officer at the ACoRP national awards in 2008.

The CRP is a great example of how partnerships can bring in additional funding. They won £250,000 from North Staffordshire Regeneration Zone for new shelters, Customer Information Systems and CCTV at Longton and Longport, and this led to the stations winning the 'Most Improved Community Station' award in 2008.[18] They were also instrumental in pulling together a £42,000 funding package to bring a disused waiting room at Kidsgrove back into use. And they also secured money for the installation of CIS equipment at four other stations with funds won from DfT Access for All, match-funded by partners and East Midlands Trains.

The CRP has also done a brilliant job in involving local schools, and children of all ages, in projects along the line. Thus Hannah Johnson, Oliver Watts and Charlotte Leese, all aged 5, pooled their talents to create colourful posters which were displayed at Longport station. And Year 3 pupils (7-8 years) from Excalibur Primary School took part in a poetry project following a visit to their local station at Alsager. Eva Smith contributed this poem, 'Station Fun':

> I see a train go past like a space ship
> Zooming up to the sky
> Standing on the station I hear birds
> Singing like flutes on full power,
> As a train comes I feel tense like I am
> About to go down a rollercoaster,
> The station to me is closest to my house
> And is very useful for getting somewhere quickly.[19]

Alsager station is also being used to trial a new design of 'cycle pod' which gives more protection for bikes than the conventional 'Sheffield stand' at relatively low cost. Patronage has increased by nearly 25 per cent in the last year alone.

Eight-year olds from a Longton school have also contributed art work that has been displayed at their local station; and Longton was also involved in a regeneration project with students from Sandon Business and Enterprise College, who worked with a professional artist to create colourful posters to brighten the station up, using recycled train tickets and printed rail timetables.

Kidsgrove is another station adorned with paintings by students from local schools, and their flower tubs are also planted and maintained by a group of children. Some of the older children have produced a mural that greets passengers arriving at the station. Local resident Jane Lawrence commented: 'I use the train every day to go to Alsager and it's really brightened up the place; it looks a whole lot better'.[20] Kidsgrove station is an amazing example of what community engagement can achieve. At this modest-sized station you can see most if not all the elements that make for a really outstanding example of station partnership working. Adult volunteers working alongside enthusiastic station staff; children of all ages getting involved in art work and gardening; and a supportive local town council. The work with schools has created a delightful station environment, and the children's artwork is a welcoming feature both at the entrance and inside the booking hall. A major increase in services has pushed station usage up by nearly fifty per cent. As well as the Crewe-Derby service, Kidsgrove now has an hourly London Midland train from Crewe to Euston, and another hourly service operated by Northern from Stoke to Manchester.

The problems facing the route are not dissimilar to those on the Penistone Line. Patronage on the line is growing, with a 21 per cent increase in 2010, and the biggest problem now is overcrowding at peak times. The line's single-carriage trains don't have the capacity that is needed, but there is little hope in the immediate future of getting bigger trains.[21]

COMMUNITY RAIL IN WALES

Wales has had community rail partnerships for many years, the first of them in the early 1990s. Today, community rail partnerships in Wales cover five routes: Heart of Wales (Shrewsbury–Swansea); Cambrian (Pwllheli–Aberystwyth–Shrewsbury); Conwy Valley (Llandudno–Blaenau Ffestiniog); Shrewsbury–Chester; and Borderlands (Wrexham–Bidston).

Each CRP is locally based, with its own constitution, and each has its own paid officer, though their contracted hours vary. Specific targets and priorities are locally determined but they share many core activities, and have a strong track record of working together within both Wales and England, promoting tourism by public transport. Unlike most community rail partnerships in England, they have built up strong relationships at a sub-UK level, working together on a pan-Wales basis. They have also developed and successfully launched an award-winning public transport tourism brand – *Scenic Wales by Rail and Traws Cymru*. Working on this pan-Wales basis they have built productive relationships with many organisations well beyond the rail industry, and act as a key link between transport, tourism, economic development and regeneration. The partnerships have good relationships with the Welsh government – whose existence they pre-date.

Chester–Shrewsbury

This route, linking two major English centres, runs mostly through North Wales and is hosted by Wrexham Borough Council. Other partners are Shropshire Council, Severn-Dee Travel (a social enterprise – see below) and Cheshire West and Chester Council. Arriva Trains Wales is not a funder of the CRP but is supportive of its work. The North Wales consortium of local authorities, TAITH, is another strong supporter, and has helped fund specific projects. The direction of the partnership is currently changing. There is now a much greater emphasis on linking the railway with regeneration and tourism, and using the route as a catalyst for sustainable development. Economic development and tourism officers now attend CRP meetings, and make a positive contribution to the role of the line as part of a wider strategy for the borders area.[22]

One feature of the CRP's work is the close involvement of local authority elected members. Councillor Mansel Williams, a Labour member of Shropshire Council, chairs the community rail partnership and helps ensure the railway features in a wide range of council policies, beyond purely transport. Mansel is also chair of the Shrewsbury–Aberystwyth Line Committee and the Heart of Wales Line Forum.

The CRP is quick to spot any opportunities for funding station enhancement: when partnership officer Sheila Dee realised there had been an underspend in Wrexham Council's budget she managed to get money for car park and other improvements at Chirk car park.[23] The partnership also works closely with tourism providers, encouraging 2-for-1 deals for attractions, including Chirk Castle; and they have encouraged the development of station friends, with active groups at Chirk and Gobowen. The line also has an active users association that works closely with the partnership.

The Conwy Valley initiative

The Conwy Valley Line from Llandudno to Blaenau Ffestiniog is one of the most scenic in North Wales, running along the Conwy Estuary and then climbing into the mountains of Snowdonia. As well as having been a lifeline for local people for many years, it also attracts significant numbers of visitors, both in its own right and as an attractive means of access to the mountains.

Blaenau Ffestiniog is a town built on the slate industry, some of which survives, but it has suffered from very high unemployment. The arrival of the Ffestiniog Railway from Porthmadog in 1982 – a narrow-gauge steam train service – has to some extent mitigated its economic problems by bringing thousands of visitors into the town, some of whom change on to the Conwy Valley line to continue their journeys.

The partnership started life as the Conwy Valley Rail Initiative back in 1994. This was a development of the pioneering work of the former Gwynedd County Council, which had sponsored additional Sunday services and invested in station facilities such as those at Betws-y-Coed. Today, the partnership involves Conwy and Gwynedd Councils, the pioneering tourist Ffestiniog Railway, and Arriva Trains Wales. In May 2007 a pilot scheme commenced to give concessionary pass holders free travel on the line, the Welsh government having already granted free travel on local bus services for passholders. It proved a great success and has subsequently become permanent.

Bob Saxby, Passenger Transport Officer for Conwy Council, and chair of the CRP, has responsibilities for both bus and rail. He sees the future of public transport in rural areas as being about co-operation and recognising each form of transport's strengths: 'The line brings visitors to the area in numbers that no bus service – however attractive – could achieve and thus its economic impact on bringing income to the area is very significant'.[24]

COMMUNITY RAIL IN SCOTLAND

Scotland has been less prominent in community rail initiatives than England and Wales, at least until recently. However First Group-owned ScotRail has been very active in promoting station friends groups, and the Glasgow–Stranraer Line has had an active group for some years. And in 2012 transport minister Keith Brown announced a new community rail initiative for Scotland, in collaboration with the Association of Community Rail Partnerships. ACoRP will employ two development officers in Scotland to assist with new developments. Though the project is in its early stages, it promises to develop new approaches to community rail which will be of value to other parts of the UK.

Brown is committed to encouraging and facilitating greater community engagement, and has provided financial support to ACoRP in Scotland. Transport Scotland, the transport executive arm of the Scottish government, sees an important role for CRPs in working with local organisations, businesses and the rail industry to maximise the potential benefits of locations, lines and communities. And it believes that ACoRP will play a useful role in advising CRP groups; accordingly, ACoRP will manage a project fund to be utilised for local initiatives in Scotland, designed to attract additional match funding for community based projects.[25]

The Scottish rail network is quite distinctive, and creating a community rail network north of the border will require innovative approaches. As we have seen, some routes, including the Far North route and the West Highland Line from Glasgow to Mallaig and Oban, already have active friends groups that are carrying out some of the work that a community rail partnership might undertake. Will there be an organic shift by which the voluntary friends groups take on the more formal role of a CRP?

At least one group is already constituted as a community rail partnership, on the Ayr–Stranraer Line. The line is fortunate in having one of the most active promotion groups in Scotland – SAYLSA, the Stranraer–Ayr Line Support Association, a registered charity.[26] It is headquartered at Girvan station, where it operates a community shop run by volunteers, a useful local resource that generates a modest income, and it recently increased its opening hours from just one day a week to six days. SAYLSA volunteers have adopted all the stations

along the line south of Ayr–Maybole, Girvan, Barrhill and Stranraer
itself. The volunteers have an excellent relationship with the station
staff and help with the upkeep of the station environment, including
planters and gardens. In 2010 the organisation received significant
funding, including an award from the Scottish government's Climate
Challenge Fund, which seeks to encourage a shift from road to rail
and is hoping for a 5 per cent shift from car to train along the Ayr–
Stranraer corridor; it also received local community grants that have
enabled the purchase of a community minibus that, among other
things, will provide links from the railway to local attractions.

STATION PARTNERSHIPS

At a more local level, there are dozens of station-based groups that are
purely volunteer-run. Many station partnerships are on routes without
a formal community rail partnership, though they sometimes link up
with neighbouring station groups to organise special events, such as
the Christmas station carol-singing evening on the Caldervale Line in
Yorkshire, when singers stop off at each station along the line to
welcome home-coming commuters with carols and mince pies.

Though many station partnerships exist as standalone bodies,
most community rail partnerships also sponsor some of them. In
East Lancashire, the CRP actively promotes station friends along
the line, including at Brierfield, where they have been carrying out
some innovative work with young people who have been placed
on Community Reparation Orders: members have held a 'dig-in'
alongside the young people, to develop the station's garden areas.
Community reparation is unpaid work that benefits charities and the
community as a whole with the aim of giving young people a chance
to put something back to the community. Ideally, the young people
should be involved in activities from which they can take pride in a
job well done, so station gardening is an ideal task.

The last few years have seen a push to bring unused station buildings
back into use for a range of purposes, including ticket sales. Station
partnerships have been at the fore of this. Gobowen is only one of
many examples where historic buildings have been restored to their
former glory, often with help from the Rail Heritage Trust. Wakefield
Kirkgate will be the next, through a scheme led by Groundwork,

the national environmental charity. In nearby Moorthorpe the local town council stepped in and led the regeneration of station buildings that had been derelict for many years; the £400k scheme was a huge risk, but support was received from the Railway Heritage Trust and Wakefield Council's Green Corridor Initiative. Part of the building is now occupied by the Backstage Academy, which runs courses in theatre management and design; while the Mallard Coffee Lounge and Café provides nourishing food for rail passengers and the local community.

Several other stations have come back to life when local entrepreneurs (social or individual) have decided to take a risk and provide a good facility for passengers. Chester-le-Street has a private business trading as Chester-le-Track, and recently opened a new outlet at Eaglescliffe station. Millom and Gobowen are run as social enterprises. Lancashire County Council staffs Carnforth and Clitheroe stations. All these developments go against received wisdom in the railway industry and DfT, which wants to see fewer, not more, staffed booking offices. We are sagely informed that everyone will soon be buying their tickets on the internet. But many of us think this will only happen if passengers are not given any other choice: plenty of people still like to talk to a real person and have options explained to them.

A typical example of a larger station partnership is Todmorden, on the Lancashire-Yorkshire border in the Pennine hills. The station serves a small market town which has become famous for its promotion of local food growing – the Incredible Edible Todmorden project, started by the local wholefood store and then taken up by a wide cross-section of the community. The station partnership agreed with the train operator, Northern Rail, to take over some vacant land by the station to grow vegetables. On the platform itself there is a herb garden. Local artists use some of the station buildings. Each year the group organises a festival in the station car park, attracting local bands, artists, stalls from community groups and other displays.

Gobowen, served by the Shrewsbury-Chester CRP, is a once-unstaffed station that is now run by a local social enterprise, Severn Dee Travel, with friendly and well-trained staff who can sell you a ticket to anywhere from Penzance to Plockton. And there's also a nice warm area to sit and wait, with the added attraction of a café run by the local school for children with learning difficulties. One of the directors of Severn Dee Travel is Sheila Dee, the CRP officer.[27]

Crediton, on the Tarka Line between Exeter and Barnstaple, has a fine Brunelian building which now houses an excellent award-winning café, run by local businesswoman Linda Brown. The Friends of Crediton have been active since 2002 and their achievements are little short of miraculous: the entire station is a monument to community partnership working. First Great Western have supported the Friends in their efforts to re-create a station with the ambience of the London and South Western Railway circa 1900, and it is now one of the most outstanding small stations in the country, with superb gardens, well-kept buildings and not a hint of vandalism. The visionary behind Crediton's magnificent revival is the Station Friends' David Gosling, who persuaded and cajoled funders to help with the transformation, including local authorities, First Great Western and the Railway Heritage Trust.[28]

Millom is another model of how community engagement can transform a run-down unstaffed station. The town, which is on the Barrow–Carlisle Line, was once the location of a major ironworks, but it has suffered since the works closed in 1968 with the loss of thousands of jobs. It was also home to the poet Norman Nicholson, whose memory is celebrated in the town museum that is located inside the station buildings. Today, the station is staffed by a community group and is a hive of activity. A few years ago it was an unstaffed and unwelcoming gateway to a town that has been through hard times. Its revival was initiated by the community rail partnership officer for the line, working closely with the line operator Northern Rail. Having staff at the station has encouraged more growth, and the Trackside Café run by the CRP opened in 2012. It's now a popular venue for community groups and shoppers.

Slaithwaite station, between Huddersfield and Manchester, is a busy commuter station handling around 250,000 passengers a year. It was closed as part of the Beeching cuts in 1968 but re-opened in 1982. It has a dynamic and innovative Friends of Slaithwaite Station group (FOSLS), which is unusual in being mainly run by women. In 2013 the FOSLS celebrated International Women's Day with a leaflet for women commuters, applauding the contribution of women railway workers. Another event – a less auspicious occasion – was their commemoration of the fiftieth anniversary of the publication of the Beeching report, on 27 March 2013. In driving snow members of the group, suitably clad with 'Beeching Axes', gave out 'Beeching Cookies' to shivering commuters.

Betws-y-Coed station, in the Snowdonia National Park, is another superb example of how station development can lead local sustainable development. The old station building was derelict for many years, but, thanks to the efforts of the local community council and the Northern Development Agency, the building has slowly been brought back to life. It now houses several cafés and shops and is the focus of the popular tourist resort. It even has a railway museum with a functioning miniature railway! The station is on the scenic Conwy Valley railway, and is supported by the Conwy Valley Community Rail Partnership (see above).

At Lympstone, Devon, village organisations and individuals have worked together to transform the station area and have also provided small gardens for local people. Volunteers from Friends of Lympstone Village Station, including the chair of the parish council, have signed up to adopt different areas of planting, and Lympstone Garden Club now manages a planting scheme on the platform, and has a rota of volunteers to water planters and hanging baskets; and five Lympstone families – most of whom do not have a garden of their own – now tend small patches at the station.[29] At the 2009 ACoRP awards Friends of Lympstone Station won a prize in the Best Station Garden competition.[30]

Two stations on the Manchester–Buxton Line in the Peak District have brilliant examples of station adoption: Furness Vale and Whaley Bridge. Furness Vale, serving a small village along the busy A6, has an active station friends group which keeps the small station looking attractive and welcoming. Its first secretary Ann Picot, a keen garden designer, led the development of the delightful station gardens, but she died of cancer in 2011. Her work has been commemorated by the creation of 'Ann's Meadow' on the station platform. Whaley Bridge has one of the North's most active station friends groups, who have worked with Northern Rail and Network Rail to make many small but important improvements to the station. In 2011 the station was 'highly commended' in the Network Rail Partnership Award in the National Rail Heritage Awards, for its sympathetic restoration of the 1857 station building and provision of improvements in accessibility; and they were also cited as 'a good example of partners and stakeholders working together'.[31]

Across the Derbyshire hills, Glossop station vies with Whaley Bridge to win accolades for community involvement. Friends of

Glossop Station (FOGS) has transformed the humdrum terminus of
the commuter line from Manchester into a thriving cultural hub, with
an art gallery, poetry board and gardens. It has worked closely with
local schools on educational projects. The historic but once-neglected
station buildings now look magnificent and attractive.

But what if there are no buildings? BR demolished hundreds of
station booking offices and rooms in the 1960s and 1970s, as part of
an understandable drive to bring costs down: many of the buildings
would have cost a fortune to bring up to a decent standard for future
use – although others might have been salvaged with external help.
As a result, many locations that today might benefit from a staffed
booking office have no suitable building in which to house it, and
the knee-jerk reaction tends to be that it would be too expensive to
provide one. But this is not necessarily the case. Thus, for example, in
2012 Lancashire County Council realised that it would be far cheaper
to demolish the old station building at Burnley Manchester Road and
build a new fit-for-purpose eco-friendly building than to restore the
derelict shell. And Network Rail has now provided modular station
buildings in a number of places, including Uckfield and Chorley
Buckshaw Village (in partnership with Lancashire County Council).
Friends of Handforth Station, in Cheshire, have also persuaded
Network Rail to provide a new booking office, which is staffed by
Northern Rail.

Accrington offers an outstanding example of what can be done
when starting from scratch at a small to medium-sized station. When
the original station was swept away in the late 1960s, its replacement
hardly did justice to the needs of a substantial town of some 80,000
people: a modest brick booking office was provided, with a few shelters
scattered along the two remaining platforms. Then in 2005 an idea
emerged for creating a really transformational station, based on best
environmental practice, and a partnership was set underway between
Lancashire County Council's community rail team, Hyndburn
Borough Council, Northern Rail and bus operator Transdev, supported
by consultants Transport Regeneration. Their vision was to clear the
1960s dross and build an entirely new building on the town-centre
side, on publicly owned land. The building would combine a range
of environmental features with much-improved passenger facilities, as
well as space for community events. Funding came from the European
Union and was matched with cash from Lancashire County Council

and other sources, and a new Sustainable Stations project was created with partners in Germany and the Netherlands. Manchester-based architects SBS were commissioned, and the new station opened in autumn 2011. Its education room is enormously popular with school groups, and there are an average of five school visits each week.

The building features the use of locally recycled materials, including stone both for the new station building and the paved areas around it, and recycled plastic for the kerbs in the car park; it also has twenty-eight photovoltaic panels, solar hot water, and rain-water harvesting to supply the station toilets; and there are improved cycle facilities and car parking, and better links to local bus services. Community facilities are provided underneath the main building. The Eco Station shows the way forward for new small to medium sized stations.[32]

A RECORD OF SUCCESS

Community rail partnerships and local station partnerships have had a transformative effect on local railways. They have directly led to increased patronage, improved services and facilities and less anti-social behaviour. They have been good for local communities and for the thousands of individuals whose lives have been changed by getting involved with friends and neighbours in making their local station an attractive and vibrant part of the community. Conservatives might call this a perfect example of the 'the big society' in action, but, equally, a socialist would see it as an example of socialist co-operation and community action par excellence. It is people co-operating for the benefit of their own community, with no expectation of personal financial benefit.

If community rail did nothing more than it is already doing, the approach would be of continuing value to railways and the communities they serve. But there is potential for building on these successes. The Community Rail Development Strategy has achieved most of its objectives – there's no doubt that the trains are often full, and community rail is making a great contribution to community involvement and regeneration. But it could do more. For example, the designation process could be used to drive much more radical approaches, which, although they would not be appropriate on a busy, high-speed main line, would make great sense on some of the UK's more lightly-used and lower speed routes.

There is one big challenge on the horizon which is both a threat and an opportunity: the loss of funding through local government cuts. Most CRPs are funded by their local authority and the rail industry, and at least two CRPs have run into serious difficulties as a result of funding problems: one had to be wound up altogether, while another was able to continue but with much-reduced resources. It would be highly optimistic to think that these are isolated examples, given the current climate. If community rail is to survive it needs to move forward and occupy new territory without abandoning its community development work.

The succeeding chapter explores ways in which the community rail achievement can be developed further, using the potential of the Community Rail Development Strategy to transform local railways. In particular it argues that local railways could form the core of sustainable communities, along a railway corridor – 'the sustainable branch line'. Using the railway as the core for development plans, locating housing, retail space and offices around a railway hub, makes sense economically, socially and environmentally. And we can also do much more on rail-bus co-ordination. But all this requires political will.

NOTES

1. David Quarmby, then chairman, Strategic Rail Authority, in his rather cautious foreword to the *Community Rail Development Strategy*, SRA, November 2004.
2. See Chapter three.
3. Paul Salveson, *New Futures for Rural Rail*, 1993. See also Paul Salveson, *Microfranchising: community control of local railways*, 1994.
4. Association of Community Rail Partnerships, *The Value of Community Rail Partnerships*, Huddersfield 2008.
5. www.penline.org.uk.
6. In Paul Salveson, 'The Penistone Line', *Today's Railways*, January 2011.
7. Ibid
8. Paul Salveson, 'The Severn Beach Line', *Today's Railways*, June 2012.
9. Ibid.
10. Ibid.
11. Information from Keith Walton, quoted in ibid.
12. Available on the CRP website: www.eastlancashirecrp.co.uk.
13. Information from Brian Haworth, quoted in Paul Salveson, 'The East Lancashire Line', *Today's Railways*, November 2010.

14. Ibid.
15. Richard Burningham, quoted in Paul Salveson 'The Tarka Line', op cit.
16. Ibid.
17. Paul Salveson, 'The North Staffordshire Line', *Today's Railways*, May 2011.
18. Ibid.
19. Ibid.
20. Ibid.
21. Ibid.
22. Information from Shropshire's former rail officer Dave Koring, private email to author, February 2013,
23. Private email to author March 2013. See also Paul Salveson, 'The Chester–Shrewsbury Line', *Today's Railways*, July 2011.
24. Paul Salveson, 'The Conwy Valley Line', *Today's Railways*, June 2011.
25. Ministerial statement from the Scottish Government, January 2013.
26. See Paul Salveson, 'The Stranraer Line', *Today's Railways*, February 2011; also www.saylsa.org.uk.
27. See Salveson, op cit, 'The Shrewsbury-Chester Line'.
28. See Salveson, op cit, 'The Tarka Line'.
29. See Salveson, op cit, 'The Avocet Line'.
30. Ibid.
31. See Paul Salveson, 'The Buxton Line', *Today's Railways*, July 2012.
32. See Paul Salveson, 'The East Lancashire Line', *Today's Railways*, November 2010; and Lancashire County Council 'community rail partnerships' page on www.lancashire.gov.uk.

7. THE SUSTAINABLE BRANCH LINE

Community rail development has become an established part of the UK rail scene, and is supported by both government – local, national and devolved – and industry. Few would deny that the approach has been successful in generating new business for local railways and attracting external investment to traditionally neglected routes. But there is clear potential to go further. For example a new approach to stations could be developed, bringing the dreary unstaffed halt back to life. But this kind of initiative needs to be part of a wider and holistic vision for local lines. It is time to revisit the radical vision of *New Futures for Rural Rail*, and explore new ways for the local railway to place itself at the heart of local sustainable development. The future should involve people having a more direct stake in their local railway, with railways forming the core of a community transport network. The government's *Community Rail Development Strategy* has been enormously helpful in raising awareness and ambition, but the potential of creating a flourishing local rail network comparable to the Swiss, German and Swedish lines (see chapter nine) has yet to be fulfilled. Community rail needs to refresh itself, through a combination of renewed national and regional support (and political will), and strengthened grassroots creativity and determination.

There is a need to go beyond the narrow confines of the railway, or even transport, and to look at the relationship with the wider community, whilst at the same time ensuring that the railway and its complementary transport modes operate in the most sustainable way. This is where the concept of the sustainable branch line comes into its own.

The sustainable branch line should integrate with wider local development and act as a motor for growth. It is based on an integrated vision of a railway forming the core of a transport network that is fully integrated with the local economy and society – an energising spine based along the rail corridor, which provides high-quality, community-focused transport services that are safe, environmentally benign and socially responsible – and support a diverse and complementary range of economic activities.

In continental Europe and in the United States there are many examples of development that is closely integrated with rail, in which stations act as community hubs. And a new organisation, Smart Growth UK, is now aiming to learn the lessons of this experience for the UK. It aims to promote a sustainable approach to planning that emphasises compact and accessible urban communities, and opposes urban sprawl and car dependency. It also seeks 'traditional ways of planning towns based around local services, ease of walking and cycling and good public transport, especially rail-based', and it is looking for ways to rebuild 'our lost sense of community'.[1] This fits perfectly with the concept of the sustainable branch line.

Whilst the optimal organisational structure for managing sustainable branch lines may be a completely locally-owned and run community railway such as we see in Switzerland, the approach could also be implemented without any legislative change in the UK – through an existing train operator and Network Rail working together with a community-rail partnership, but transformed into a more developmental body. This could be a 'local sustainable transport company', which could manage or directly provide a wide range of activities (though not the most safety-critical roles, which would be left to a licensed train operator and Network Rail).

Much of this strategy depends on having the right people on board, with enthusiasm and knowledge, but this is more likely if there is a supportive framework in place. The community rail partnership can offer an over-arching body that drives forward new ideas and approaches. It can ensure a form of governance that brings the railway right into the community, with a route manager who works with a partnership board that includes employees, volunteers, local businesses, and municipal and community representatives.

Not all of these ideas are new. In the nineteenth century some railways developed as genuinely community-owned businesses, for example the tiny Killin Railway that operated in the Scottish Highlands. The company was funded and owned by the local community, and this included not just the inevitable laird but also local businesspeople and farmers. It was 'their' railway in every sense![2] I'm not suggesting we go back to that degree of local independence – local railways need a sensitive balance between local focus and economies of scale – but for many years we have tended to over-emphasise the latter while giving insufficient weight to the former.

Achieving the vision of the sustainable branch line will require determination and leadership. It will be faced with the reality of an existing service pattern that is often resource-led rather than customer-led. To change this focus will be expensive in the short-term, but any initial investment will be justified in the long term by the growth in revenue that will develop through more people travelling, as well as by the savings that will be made through doing things differently. It will be important to focus on immediate improvements that can bring rapid results, but to also have a longer-term vision that flows on from the early benefits. Developing a virtuous spiral of modest improvements, better marketing and publicity and a real sense that the railway is part of the community is the way forward for many local lines, or small networks of lines. This will require start-up funding to establish that virtuous spiral. Possible sources for pilot projects could include local and regional support, foundations and government sources.

The main features of a sustainable branch line are outlined below. (It should be emphasised here that this is likely to result from an evolutionary process rather than being something that happens all at once in a single 'big bang'.)

People

The 'sustainable branch line' should be founded on its staff; it should be an outstanding employer, offering good salaries and conditions, high levels of employee involvement, and direct participation in how the business is run. Train operating companies and Network Rail employees need to be brought into the partnership. Staff are absolutely crucial – including front-line workers as much as managers – but there is also an important role for volunteers.

Service

The train service should be run to meet the needs of local communities along its route, as well as serving the needs of visitors – and this includes evening services and all-year round Sunday operation. It should be accessible and affordable, with feeder buses and taxis, and easy access for walkers and cyclists.

Stations

Station buildings should be built and operated on sustainable principles, and should be welcoming and full of life, with good passenger facilities at stations, and excellent staff.

Trains

There is a need for modern, technically standardised rolling stock that is high-quality, light-weight, with low (or nil) emissions, and plenty of space for luggage and cycles; this should be serviced and maintained locally, and internally/externally reflect the culture of the area.

Information

There should be good quality information – both on transport facilities and on all other local facilities, and activities/attractions for visitors arriving at stations; similar information should be available online and by phone, and the rail service should be linked to a wide range of local business and tourism websites.

Management

The railway should be managed locally and based locally, and it should support the local economy both by providing employment and by supporting other local businesses through local purchasing; there should be a high level of community governance, and it should be operated at least in part by a locally-based social enterprise that is an active player in the local economy.

Partnership with the local economy

Locally produced goods should be on sale at stations and on trains, including local food and drink, local crafts, guides, etc. There should be partnerships with local businesses, including hotels and B&Bs, cycle hire companies and holiday companies, and station buildings should be used to assist small business development.

Community involvement

There should be active involvement of the local community through an enhanced community rail partnership and through station friends schemes; and the railway should be at the heart of local social and cultural life, and play an active part in festivals and events, from 'Britain in Bloom' to cultural events, schools projects and celebrations, food fairs and music.

Value for money

The railway should offer good value to the community in return for the financial support it receives, including through the development of innovative low-cost forms of operation, from staffing to signalling, and through making the most of community-rail designation. There should be discounted fares to socially-excluded groups

Environment

The railway operation should be committed to sustainable principles, including energy use, recycling of materials, and making best use of existing resources.

Local planning

The railway should be linked into local planning strategies and provide suitable locations for sustainable development, be it housing or employment-related. Station areas should be hubs of social and industrial activity, as they were originally. Communities should be encouraged to develop around station hubs, avoiding sprawl, which encourages car use, and promoting walking and cycling access.

Applying principles of localism to local railway services often runs up against ingrained railway operating practice, not least in terms of staff policy. Having conductors, drivers and station staff who feel that they have a stake in the community makes a huge difference to services. Customers and staff get to know each other, and conductors become familiar with the route and what is on offer along it – and they can act as real ambassadors for the service.

Patterns of implementation may vary from line to line. Thus it may not at first be appropriate for a local company to take over employment of on-train staff, whether conductors or drivers, owing to the complexities of modern train crew's railway and safety-critical tasks. There are, however, very strong arguments for drivers and conductors to feel part of the local operation, rather than working through a complex route system. The best option is for a dedicated link of drivers and conductors for a particular route, employed by the parent train operator, and possibly based along the route itself, instead of in a large central depot.

One of the exciting challenges of running local railways differently is looking at how people could best be deployed. Some jobs, such as that of the driver, seem to have a very specific remit, but there may be scope for drivers becoming multi-skilled in relevant areas, for example in engineering. Many drivers are already adept at sorting out technical problems, and to an extent this is already part of their training and competence, but this could be developed. Similarly, conductors do much more than sell tickets – they can also be ambassadors and guides.

A frequent mistake in the past has been the imposition of top-down solutions to the ways in which employees' duties are defined. The right way to do this is to bring together employees based on a particular route and ask them to come up with the best solution for the deployment of current resources in a way that ensures that their jobs are well-rewarded, fulfilling and creative. This will be challenging for management, and also for the trades unions to which most of the employees belong. But it may come up with solutions that are innovative and positive. There is need for a different approach to salaries and job description, but taking that forward requires the direct involvement of the employees themselves, as well as their union representatives.

Finding appropriate mechanisms to involve staff at a local level should be an important part of the sustainable branch line. And this should not be confined to having one or two representatives sitting on some consultative body. For what would be a relatively small number of staff, finding ways of involving all employees should not be a difficult task.

Running a railway is a highly professional job, whether it is a high-speed main line or a rural branch. But volunteers can contribute greatly on the margins, as we have already seen with station friends groups. However, even for heritage railways, getting the right mix of professional staff and volunteers can be an issue, with some railways opting for more paid staff for core tasks. The general principle should be that core jobs, including bus driving, on-train conducting and track or station maintenance, should be the responsibility of paid staff. Volunteers can then provide important back-up through 'additionality' – looking after station gardens, acting as couriers on trains aimed at the tourist market, and assisting with catering services. But they must be trained to the appropriate standard, have a strong safety awareness, and be subject to the same discipline as paid staff.

AN INTEGRATED LOCAL NETWORK

Currently, many services on local railways are inadequate and infrequent, and this inhibits growth. Some routes have no Sunday service, and the last train home from many large towns is often much too early to allow people to attend concerts, visit friends or just have an evening out. It is also depressingly common to find that the train arrives at a station just as the bus is departing. If local railways are to get out of the vicious circle of poor services, lack of co-ordination with other transport and low demand, there needs to be a commitment to extending and enhancing services, either as part of the franchise specification, or through a contract between the train operator and transport authority.

Ensuring high levels of integration between bus and rail is crucial, yet Britain is still way behind other European countries in this field. Ensuring good connections between trains and buses needs to be written into contracts, with incentives put in place to encourage rail and bus operators to co-operate; the current lack of co-operation is often excused on the grounds of competition legislation, but it should be made clear that this a paper tiger. It is particularly ironic given that very often train and bus operations are owned by the same parent company.

Having a local operator running both buses and trains could be a very attractive solution in many rural areas. This is the situation in many areas of Germany, Switzerland and the Netherlands, and there is no doubt that single ownership and unified local management does lead to very high standards of integration and quality; and that, as a result, ridership increases. But to get to that situation will be a long journey: a gradualist approach therefore makes sense in the UK context. A first step would be to tackle the currently deregulated bus environment, which is completely at odds with this approach. Local integrated transport zones (see chapter ten) would allow for a far better use of scarce resources than the current system.

Cycling and walking should be seen as important complementary modes for rail. Every station should have well-signed and safe routes to and from town and village centres, places of employment and education. A locally based railway operator would be well placed to work with bodies like Sustrans and the highway authority to develop a range of initiatives to assist cycle users, including safe storage for bikes at stations. Cycle hire at stations, for both leisure and irregular commuting journeys, could also be developed as a subsidiary business for the local sustainable transport company.

Taxis are another vital community resource in many rural areas, and the railway should work with local taxi firms to develop good integration. Train-taxi schemes have particular relevance to rural areas where population densities are low. This area is currently relatively unexplored, and there is scope for much more development, in particular through drawing on the experience of train-taxis in the Netherlands: integration is not just about integration between transport modes.

For many people in both rural and outer urban areas, the car will continue to be an essential means of getting to the train. This means that if stations do not have sufficient car parking there is a risk that people will drive the entire journey. Here we should be looking at innovative solutions that help to avoid over-dependence, such as community car clubs, car-sharing and lift-sharing to stations. Commuter lift-sharing has taken off in a big way in many countries, and would be relatively easy to organise through a community rail partnership or the local sustainable transport company.

ACCESS FOR ALL

Rail is the most accessible form of public transport, and most modern trains have reasonable standards of accessibility – though there is still much to be done with older trains such as the Pacer fleet, whose derogation for disability legislation expires in 2019. The biggest problem is stations, and access to stations: many local stations remain inaccessible, with footbridges often providing the only means of access to platforms. This is not just an issue for disabled people, but is also a major problem for people with prams, and elderly people who may not see themselves as disabled.

Here the 'Harrington Hump' has been one simple and affordable solution to raising platform heights at many lightly-used stations. Other solutions include re-opening disused entrances, or looking at alternatives where costly, fully-accessible ramped bridges are likely to be seldom used. In the case of low-speed lines with good sight-lines, traditional 'barrow crossings' offer a basically safe, low-cost means of accessing platforms, providing they are subject to a full risk assessment.

Developing easily accessible links to stations – including footpaths and cycleways, as well as accessible bus and taxi services – is a key issue that should be the concern of the railway company. This includes ensuring that the street environment is safe and accessible – through the provision of pavements with dropped kerbs, good street lighting and safe crossing points.

Personal security is also part of the accessibility issue. People will not wait at stations that are dark, threatening and unwelcoming. But the best solution to the security problem is to change stations into places of human activity. The concept of the secure station should be dumped and replaced by the idea of the sociable station – where security isn't an issue.

Affordability remains one of the major disincentives to use rail, and Britain has the highest fares in Europe. This is the issue that comes up with monotonous regularity when people are asked what puts them off using trains. A local railway company could do more to develop special deals with job centres and local authorities, for example, aimed at people going to job interviews, or offering half-price travel for their first month of employment. Local residents' railcards, offering discounts of up to 50 per cent on local rail fares, have also been shown to bring in substantial new business and encourage train travel. These work well on a line or local network basis, and help generate new business for local lines. But they need strong local promotion – and this takes us back to the need for local, not remote, management, which knows the local scene in detail.

A SUSTAINABLE STATION

Stations are the gateway *to* the railway but also gateways *from* the railway into the wider community. The station partnership approach, as we have seen in chapter six, has been hugely successful, and has reversed the decline of the unstaffed station. Why can't more stations be warm, welcoming and convivial places, operated along eco-friendly lines? We have to move away from lonely, unloved and unstaffed stations that people use only as a last resort, and instead make them vibrant centres of community life, in the evening as well as the daytime.

The aim of the sustainable branch line should be to have as many stations staffed as possible in some way; this would not necessarily be a railway employee, but could be someone doing something that adds value to the railway service and fills a gap in the community, be it a shop, service or other facility. Such services could either be provided by local sustainable transport companies, or by individual small businesses. The alternative for very small stations is to use a local shop, pub or café as a source of information and sales point for selected tickets (for example rover tickets aimed at the leisure market).

In appropriate locations stations can be developed as business centres, with low-rent starter units available for small businesses. A central, easily-accessible location where there is a cluster of enterprises would stimulate local economic development and provide quality, accessible jobs. A good example of this approach is Redcar, where the former station buildings have been converted into a business centre. More recently, Moorthorpe has been redeveloped by the local town council to provide space for small businesses and an arts training centre. Millom, an outstanding example of integrated community enterprise, was discussed in the previous chapter. Bargoed was another early pioneer: here the train company persuaded a local taxi company to relocate to the previously defunct station building, which has helped breathe life back into the station: vandalism stopped overnight and passenger numbers grew.

An advantage of local authorities leasing the station is that they can locate within them a range of public services, including libraries, nurseries and tourist information centres. This is something that happens in Sweden (for example at Nassjo), and in other countries. Not only does it make sense in transport terms; it also helps ensure that local services in smaller communities are protected. Bringing a mix of facilities under one roof, with easy access by train, bus, bike and car, would help sustain the local economy, and services that could disappear if seen as stand-alone facilities.

The staffing of smaller stations is often not commercially viable for a conventional train operator because of high overheads. But a community-run facility (possibly organised through a route-based co-op or partnership) could form part of a greater whole and might have more chance of success, whilst still being able to offer good salaries and conditions. Location is 99 per cent of the battle in such cases, and some very small rural stations, miles from the nearest settlement, may never qualify for such special treatment. But in many cases there is enormous scope for transforming the unwelcoming, unstaffed and dismal places we call stations into something much better.

A small sustainable station should be just that.[3] Solar-powered heating and lighting would reduce initial setting-up costs as well as ongoing charges, and water could be provided by rain-water harvesting with chemical toilets, or through shared use of an adjoining facility. And economic sustainability, as we have seen, could include independent retailers running the station, selling much more than rail tickets – including drinks, light snacks, newspapers and magazines – while cycle hire and repair could be another side-line.

This would help with another important part of the sustainable station concept – convivial space: 'I'd like comfy seats and tables inside where people can wait for their train during the long Pennine winter, with local art work displayed on the walls, and space outside for a tea garden in the summer'.[4] Utopian? It shouldn't be.

The enemy of progress in the railway industry can sometimes be an understandable desire to be 'different'. But if Network Rail could agree a simple design for what would basically be a well-insulated secure box with doors and a retractable window, costs could be kept down to a sensible level. It would need to be fitted inside with retail space, an area in which to sit and read the paper whilst enjoying a cup of freshly-brewed coffee and chat with your fellow travellers, and a toilet. In the evening the space could be used for community meetings. Such a 'box' could be produced by Network Rail, and then could either remain within their ownership, be leased to a local group, or be sold outright. The best solution would probably be for Network Rail to retain ownership and offer the building at a low rent, though one which ensures that their direct costs are covered.

For this the active support of the railway company (whether a local operator or a larger franchise) would be essential, as well as that of Network Rail and the Office of Rail Regulation. A rail industry contribution might well be leasing ticket machines at attractive rates (i.e. free) and providing staff training for their operation. The role of the local authority (or PTE) is also important here: being part of a PTE-managed ticketing system would be vital for the viability of a booking office. Ultimately, everyone would then benefit. The community would get a facility that it could be really proud of, and the train operator and Network Rail would get a well managed, safe and cared-for station. And more people would then start using the trains.

SUSTAINABLE LOCAL PLANNING

Instead of seeing growing pressure to decentralise planning decisions as a threat, promoters of the sustainable branch line should see it as an opportunity, and seek to mould it in a democratic and inclusive direction. Neighbourhood plans should have the station as the core of local development, with housing and business located within easy reach of the station. While care needs to be exercised not to build on land that may be needed for railway use, including car and cycle parking, developing former railway land for sustainable housing makes planning sense, and will be commercially attractive to developers.

Devon County Council's *Structure Plan* zones new housing development along rail corridors, which brings a major upsurge of use to small stations. Copplestone, for example, has developed into one of the busier small stations along the Tarka line following some enlightened planning by the local authorities. The village has tripled in size with quality housing development located around the station, offering an example of truly sustainable development.[5] Some of the growth in rail travel was driven by planning policy guidance that encouraged development around transport hubs.[6] That guidance has now been abolished, but there is still a commitment to integrated transport in the *National Planning Policy Framework* – though arguably it has been weakened.

Where major development is planned the local railway should benefit from planning agreements and the Community Infrastructure Levy, which has already been used to fund new station development. The same process could be used for enhancements of existing facilities. Too often, opportunities are missed because planners don't understand how the railway works, and the railway doesn't understand the planning framework. Every community rail partnership should have a planning and development specialist. As we have seen, directing development along rail corridors, with stations becoming hubs of transport, commercial and residential activity, is an important way of developing communities that are sustainable both economically and economically.

SUSTAINABLE LOCAL TRAINS

Together with stations, trains are the most important physical element of the passenger's travel experience. They need to be clean, comfortable and accessible. The interiors should be welcoming and bright, and with some local branding so that passengers feel they are travelling on *their* line, something special. People should also be able to see out of the window – enjoying the view is an important part of train travel, something many rolling stock designers seem to have forgotten about. And there should be adequate space for prams, bikes and luggage.

Getting suitable rolling stock for local rail services is becoming an increasingly difficult problem in the UK. There are two really big challenges: cost and the availability of suitable designs. The issue of cost of trains is dealt with elsewhere in this book (see chapter ten). Here we deal briefly with the current lack of suitable modern diesel designs for local railways in the UK, and the problem of the approaching end of diesel and consequent urgent need to think about its replacement – though there may be scope for low-emission diesel engines in the short to medium term. The option of electrification is an attractive and realistic one for some routes, but longer-distance and relatively lightly-used local railways – that is, the typical sustainable branch line – need a different approach. The initial capital costs of electrification are high, and the programme of electrification work facing Network Rail over the next twenty years is huge, and this means that management resources will be in short supply.

The Parry People Mover has been operating successfully on the short branch from Stourbridge Junction to Stourbridge Town. It uses zero-emission flywheel technology and is suitable for very short distance lines, and it has potential for longer routes if a viable design with greater capacity could be developed. Network Rail has been in discussions with manufacturer Bombardier on alternative motive power for some time, and a battery-operated vehicle should be trialled very soon; the concept is that the batteries are charged from the overhead line equipment, so that the train can then run over a non-electrified branch and come back for recharging when necessary. The company is looking at branch lines like Colne Valley in Essex or the Matlock line, which are relatively short-distance, and where there is difficulty in making the case for full electrification. To its credit the Railway Industry Association is doing its best to promote innovation, and a number of energy storage systems for trains are about to be trialled. There is also potential for tram-train on some routes – explored further in chapter ten. However, this is not a cheap option, and it works best in more urban areas.

In Hungary, an independent narrow-gauge railway company has designed a solar-powered train with a modest top speed of 25 km/h (the line's maximum speed in any case). This experimental train is called *Vili* (William), and is at time of writing undergoing more tests. The single carriage vehicle has 9.9 square metres of solar panels on the carriage roof, which feed batteries underneath the seats, while regenerative braking also feeds the storage units.[7]

There is clearly a need for a greater focus on rolling stock that is suitable for sustainable local transport. Developing designs for an eco-friendly train is certainly an area where partnerships with universities could bring great benefits.

THE GREEN BRANCH LINE

Environmental sustainability has a number of dimensions in the local railway context. Rail is accepted as one of the more environment-friendly forms of transport; it has substantially lower emissions than road traffic and a less damaging impact on land. New railways are few, but the land they take is generally less than that of a new road. Rail can provide a quality alternative to using the car, as well as taking freight off the roads. But this needs to be constantly demonstrated and fought for, not simply asserted. People will rarely choose rail simply because it is more green – they need to be convinced that it's a better quality product. And it has to be remembered that an empty train is far from green.

Rail must not rest on its green laurels, but should strive to maintain and improve its position. As we have noted, new trains are needed and low or nil emission trains will be necessary; and stations also need to be environmentally sustainable. There needs to be a focus on getting appropriate standards for a wide range of railway activities, which may involve getting derogations from standards which are designed more with a busy high-speed railway in mind: for a while, several stations on the Heart of Wales Line had their modest lighting requirements met by solar power. Ironically, Network Rail had these removed and replaced them with cable-supplied electricity from the National Grid in order to confirm to group standards.

INFRASTRUCTURE

Infrastructure is, by a very large margin, the biggest driver of costs on the railway, be it a high-speed main line or a rural branch. We're talking here not just about track but about signalling, bridges, viaducts, tunnels and stations. Getting an appropriate level of infrastructure that can safely and efficiently handle the traffic expected is a critical issue for the sustainable branch line.

Most rural railways in the UK have been reduced to the bare minimum necessary for them to function, with single line operation, removal of 'surplus' crossing loops, and limited facilities at terminal stations. This often means that useful extra traffic, such as locomotive-hauled charter trains, finds it difficult if not impossible to use the lines. The potential for enhancing frequencies is also reduced because of lack of capacity – mainly a lack of crossing loops along the line and additional track capacity at the terminus. The costs of enhancing existing infrastructure are very high.

However, a locally managed railway, if it had some degree of control over track maintenance and renewals, could ultimately undertake such trackwork to appropriate industry group standards, which would allow the railway to be more responsive to needs. In the short term, however, a route or small network of routes could have dedicated multi-skilled maintenance gangs, employed by Network Rail.

This does not mean taking infrastructure ownership away from Network Rail; rather, it involves a restructuring of responsibilities. In time, the local sustainable transport company could become infrastructure controller, employing its own staff, or using qualified locally-based sub-contractors where appropriate. Track maintenance could be taken over by those local railway companies that have access to the right skills – which might include a heritage railway based nearby. It has to be stressed that today's railway is both a very tightly regulated and an increasingly specialised industry, and letting loose untrained workers, whether paid or volunteer, even on a low-speed and lightly-used railway, is not recommended. Yet if trained and fully skilled staff can be available locally, costs could be reduced and efficiency improved.

There are also more innovative opportunities for rail re-openings where the track-bed is not owned by Network Rail (although the experience of the Borders Railway project, when the Scottish government attempted such an arrangement but eventually gave the project to Network Rail, suggests that caution is required). A regional not-for-dividend company could be established, to take ownership of the formation and act as a developer for sites along the rail corridor. Most UK tram infrastructure is owned by public sector bodies such as passenger transport executives, so there are many precedents. Such a body would charge track access either to an established TOC, or to a local operator. Alternatively, it could run the trains itself, along the lines adopted by several independent railways in continental Europe.[8]

MANAGEMENT

Whatever the company structure or ownership, the management of the sustainable branch line should be locally based, with – as a minimum – a manager who is based on the route and has responsibilities for all employees concerned with the line. Here Network Rail and the train operators have already developed some innovative joint working arrangements – known as 'alliancing' – and with some success. This approach should be taken forward for local lines or small networks, with one person having overall management responsibilities for operations and infrastructure. This could work both under the current structure and with a more integrated (and possibly publicly owned) regional operation.

Currently, many local lines are resourced from a large central depot. This seems sensible in traditional railway terms, but in fact it is far from the right way to run a local railway. Most journeys on local lines start from the periphery and go into a centre – a large town or city – with people returning home in the evening. The logical place to have a train depot, with train crew, is therefore at or towards the peripheral end of the line, not in the centre: otherwise you have trains running out from the main depot, empty, in the morning and returning back in the evening once more carrying nothing more than fresh air. Locating depots in peripheral locations makes operational and financial sense and gives a huge boost to local economies. It also nurtures a strong sense of local ownership and camaraderie by small teams of dedicated workers. Again, a balance is needed between big depot and tiny sub-depot. What would work well is a number of smallish depots at nodal points, providing overnight stabling for perhaps seven to twelve trains and fifteen to twenty crews. With modern rolling stock trains having extended intervals between servicing and examinations, this is increasingly possible, and indeed a number of operators have already adopted this approach.

A further advantage of remote depots is the potential for local purchasing, discussed below. Managers could be freed up to make decisions within a specified budget to buy in local services and – where appropriate – expertise. Currently, there is huge wastage involved when maintenance workers based scores of miles away at 'central' depots are called out for relatively small jobs, which might very well be within the competence of a local electrician, painter or joiner.

AN ENTERPRISING RAILWAY SUPPORTING THE LOCAL ECONOMY

However it is managed or structured, a local railway operation is in a position to take on increasing levels of peripheral commercial activities, and to build up strong commercial expertise in providing a range of services to meet local needs. A local sustainable transport company could develop commercial activities alongside its parent CRP that might include rail-link bus services and other community transport; on-train and station catering; marketing; station cleaning and maintenance; offering tourism packages; cycle and electric car/bike hire; and lift-sharing schemes. The initial focus would depend on location and demand. For example, the Settle-Carlisle Railway Development Co, a company limited by guarantee, provides trolley services on trains and runs the station café at Skipton. Using this approach, a rail-based social enterprise could develop as a focus for rural enterprise, with the railway becoming the heart of a range of commercial activities, and stations the hubs of business activity.

Some community-rail partnerships have the potential to become social enterprises undertaking the sort of duties suggested above; and some could also go beyond the useful but peripheral mix of marketing and community development to provide direct services that complement the core railway service. Indeed, having a commercial arm might be one way of safeguarding important community activities while also freeing up local entrepreneurial talent. Local railways bring visitors into the area, who spend money – not just on the railway, but in shops, pubs, and visitor attractions. A community rail partnership with its own commercial manager would be an exciting immediate step forward in developing this kind of activity.

An economically sustainable railway isn't simply one that pays its bills – though that is important. Winning new passengers through offering improved and good quality services is also an essential part of what the sustainable branch line should aim for. Additional business can also be won through peripheral – but important – business activities, as we have seen above. The community-rail partnership could become less a local marketing operation and more a local development agency.

The railway could have a very direct local economic impact as an employer of local labour – with locally based train crew, track maintenance staff, administration and management. At present, with centralised operation of local lines being the norm, direct employment benefits, particularly in the more rural railways, are negligible. That should change, with more railway employment being based along the route.

A further important economic benefit of a local railway operation is through its purchasing power. A locally managed railway should purchase goods that are available locally for its catering, office services and equipment, a well as a wide range of other goods and services. This tends to happen more or less spontaneously, through business networking and informal social contacts. But it does not happen now, because railway managers are often hundreds of miles away. The local railway should also be proud to offer local produce for sale at its stations and on its trains, rather than mass-produced, anonymously-sourced goods.

Lateral thinking is also a useful tool in making best use of resources, and recycling and re-engineering equipment where possible; while profit can be made from the re-use or sale of surplus materials. One heritage railway earns around £10,000 each year from the sale of timber it fells along the line side; whereas commercial main line railway contractors often just leave cut timber to rot. Other local railways make money from hosting film crews wanting a railway back-drop. Having a local focus means that you can spot business opportunities of a multitude of different kinds. Many local railways, through CRPs, are also linking up with community food projects that provide healthy and cheap food for the local community. The 'Incredible Edible Todmorden' scheme began with some herbs being grown on the station platform; and Accrington has its 'Accrington growers' project. There is also great scope for developing food projects on stations, with station shops selling the produce.

VALUE FOR MONEY AND FUNDING: THE AFFORDABLE BRANCH LINE

The ideas behind the sustainable branch line require some initial investment, in rolling stock, infrastructure and stations. If the maximum benefits are to be extracted this will require some risk-taking – which is something the UK rail industry is not good at doing. However, time after time, we have seen investment in local railways not only as completely justified but also far exceeding expected returns, whether it has been in new lines (Ebbw Vale, Alloa) or in enhancements to existing services (Chester-Shrewsbury).

It is now high time for a pilot sustainable branch line to get funding, whether from the Department for Transport, Transport Scotland, the Welsh Government or from an English regional consortium. Only through a well-funded pilot project, involving at least three lines with different characteristics, and starting from a blank sheet of paper, can we really get out of the current impasse about how local railways are run.

To get out of the vicious circle of under-investment and stagnation there is a need for a number of complementary investments, but the most important, as outlined above, is rolling stock. Local services need more trains now, and in many cases that will mean old, inadequate stock. However, experience shows that increased frequencies, regardless of how poor the rolling stock is, generate big increases in passengers;[9] and that should lay the foundations for achieving something better in the future. In the short term, rolling stock leasing companies need to be persuaded or compelled to offer their bottom-end products (e.g. Pacer trains) as an initial contribution to the sustainable branch line concept. They, and colleagues in the railway industry, have the expertise to come up with something much better, but we know that takes time.

The Department for Transport's Community Rail Development Strategy has bringing down costs as a main objective. In reality, this has proved difficult to do. It is a myth that local lines have a lot of fat that can be trimmed. As we have seen, BR stripped out most of the remaining fat in the 1980s. The challenge is rather to look at cost-effective ways of running local lines, thereby providing a springboard for further growth and investment. If the scope for conventional economies is very limited, are there options for more unconventional approaches? Signalling is one of the biggest infrastructure costs, and conversion of some lines to tram-style 'on-sight' driving has been suggested. However, the down-side here is reduced speeds (even with improved 'track' brakes) and public concern about safety. Having said that, the technology exists to signal single-line branch lines with passing loops simply and relatively cheaply, once the initial investment is made: the entire Highland line network is controlled by two signallers based at Inverness.

Network Rail has track engineers who have a very clear understanding of infrastructure maintenance, and they argue, convincingly, that if you provide modern track and it is used by lightweight trains, it will last a very long time with minimal maintenance. The disadvantage is that you can't permit heavy, track-wearing locomotives. This means that the occasional charter special, or freight train, can't operate on your line. But the gains in terms of cost savings and potential improved frequencies are vast.

INFORMATION: THE WIRED-UP BRANCH LINE

Getting accurate and up to date information about a transport service is critical, and people have increasingly high expectations of their train or bus service in this regard. Several community rail partnerships have developed websites that include timetable information but also other news and information about what is happening in the area served by the train. An inclusive website that uses the railway as the main structure but has much wider business, tourist, cultural and social information can help bind the railway and the community together. Each community served by a specific station could have a click-on page that has very local information. Each sustainable branch line should have all the relevant social media infrastructure – twitter, face-book and other emergent means. At the same time, local railways must be fully integrated with the national rail enquiries website

A good transport service needs also to have up to date paper-based information – timetables, line guides and posters, and available beyond the railway station itself. CRPs have been successful here, in getting transport information into guest houses, pubs, hotels and tourist information centres. Estate agents could also be targeted, with proximity to a railway station seen as a major selling point. Public transport information should also be available in publications from a wide range of local organisations, from the local press to church newsletters, tourist guides and community magazines. It's easy to do if you have the resources to do it in the community.

Information at stations is of course crucial, and this should take the form of a mix of display information on poster boards, real-time electronic information and aural announcements; while staff need deep knowledge and access to up to the minute information in order to advise potential passengers. Staff at the sustainable station must be knowledgeable about their local community and be able to advise arriving passengers on places to eat, drink, visit and stay – with tourism information readily available at the station.

Information on trains themselves is equally important: trains should have visual and aural information about destinations and the next stop. This is by now well established technology. Even more traditional, but of vital importance, are announcements by the train crew whenever there is a problem or delay.

On the Far North Line in Scotland, several stations have customer information displays that are solar-powered. They also have an automated speech facility for the visually impaired, and at some sites the displays are also fitted with the RNIB's 'React' system, which visually impaired passengers can trigger using a small personal radio fob. The screens use a combination of solar power and large batteries; storing excess summer energy supports the systems in leaner winter months.[10]

THE ROUTE TO THE SUSTAINABLE BRANCH LINE

Most aspects of the sustainable branch line can be seen in operation in some part of Europe, including in the UK, but there are few examples where one can see everything brought together in one branch line. As with community rail in the 1990s, the concept brings together into one whole a range of disparate but potentially complementary activities and concepts.

The idea needs champions at local, regional and national level. A well-resourced community rail partnership could, with the right people on board, be the driving force behind it; the way forward could be through a combination of grassroots, bottom-up involvement and support from a national or regional agency or local authority. If some of the radical alternatives outlined in chapter ten are adopted, a sustainable branch line could easily sit within a socially owned parent company.

The idea will not suddenly happen: it will come about through an evolving process, possibly eventually leading to completely locally owned and managed railways on the Swiss model. There are, however, disadvantages as well advantages in that model, and the UK does not have a complementary system of devolved governance as in the Swiss case. Making a judgement about the right level and scale of operation is critical. These issues are explored in chapter ten.

NOTES

1. Smart Growth UK website: www.smartgrowthuk.org.
2. See John Thomas, *The Callander and Oban Railway*, 1968.
3. See Chapter six for the example of Accrington eco-station.
4. Conversation with a passenger at Slaithwaite station, April 2013.
5. For a detailed overview of post-war railways and planning see Russell Haywood, *Railways, Urban Development and Town Planning in Britain 1948-2008*, 2009.
6. Planning Policy Guidance Note 13 Transportation. It was abolished in 2012.
7. See *Today's Railways Europe*, May 2013, p209.
8. Se Chapter nine for several examples, e.g. Hohenzollern, Inlandsbanan, etc.
9. Cf Matlock Line – a 25 per cent increase in number of trains brought a 90 per cent increase in number of passengers – not least because trains ran at times when people wanted to travel, and connections became much better.
10. See Paul Salveson, 'The Far North Line', op cit.

8. THE NATIONAL NETWORK: IS HIGH SPEED THE ANSWER?

As we have noted, the rail network has been relatively stable since the aftermath of the Beeching cuts in the 1970s. Very few lines have closed and a small number have re-opened. But there is scope for doing much more work on building new lines or re-opening closed ones, and this would help to strengthen the network as a whole. The government's answer to increasing capacity has been the 'HS2' project, a new 'Y' shaped route from London to Leeds and Manchester, and this has been widely welcomed by all the main political parties, the TUC and business organisations. The few voices raised publicly in opposition have come, understandably, from people whose land or homes would be affected by the proposal. However, a number of respected academics and rail professionals have challenged several of the assumptions behind the project, as well as its supposed benefits.[1] The best way of judging HS2 is to assess whether it has the best answer to the problems currently facing the national network, and this chapter accordingly explores how high-speed rail fits into a wider strategy for rail in the UK.

HIGH-SPEED SOLUTION – BUT WHAT'S THE PROBLEM?

Undoubtedly one factor in support for HS2 is politicians' love of grand projects. Words like 'game-changing', 'transformational' and 'visionary' are all part of the politicians' lexicon of favoured words, and HS2 fits nicely into this. But even the government's own assessment suggests that the project's 'value for money' – based on cost-benefit analysis – is quite weak, at about 2:1 (for every £1 you invest you get £2 back in terms of wider benefits).[2] And even this figure is based on skewed methodology, because conventional transport appraisal models put an undue emphasis on time savings.

The benefits of high-speed rail have been summed up as follows: (a) it will bring substantial regeneration benefits to regions; (b) it will bring environmental benefits by reducing dependence on aviation and the private car for longer journeys; and (c) it will provide much-needed extra capacity on the rail network. However, the National Audit Office report on HS2, published in May 2013, was highly critical of Department for Transport's evidence for these proposed benefits. Amyas Morse, head of the NAO, said:

It's too early in the High Speed 2 programme to conclude on the likelihood of its achieving value for money. Our concern at this point is the lack of clarity around the Department's objectives. The strategic case for the network should be better developed at this stage of the programme. It is intended to demonstrate the need for the line but so far presents limited evidence on forecast passenger demand and expected capacity shortages on existing lines. It is also unclear how High Speed 2 will transform regional economies by delivering jobs and growth. The Department is trying against a challenging timetable to strengthen its evidence and analysis, which at present provide a weak foundation for securing and demonstrating success in the programme in future.[3]

Another issue is the actual feasibility of the HS2 project. According to Andrew McNaughton (former Chief Engineer with Network Rail):

there is no credible way to add tracks to the main line trunk routes which pass through the cities, towns and villages which have been built up around the existing stations. I studied this at great length in my Railtrack and Network Rail days and concluded beyond doubt that this was not possible. There are some open country bits where it's no big deal – the dynamic loops on the Great Western Main Line or the Trent Valley four-tracking, but the core lengths – where capacity matters most – are through the conurbations and beyond, where the combination of long distance, regional, commuter and freight growth create huge capacity problems, and these are hitting us now.[4]

A further issue is the length of time the project is taking. Part of the reason for this is that the railway is being over-specified, but probably the biggest reason is Treasury reluctance to allow spending much more than £1 billion each year on the scheme. This is related to another nagging worry about the scheme. It will be complete – we're told – in 2032. What will our travel patterns be like in twenty years? Will we be travelling more, or possibly less? For example, we have yet to see the full effects of the digital revolution. Will this have effects on travel patterns? The HS2 forecasts are based on very optimistic passenger growth forecasts (just as the failed West Coast franchise bid was), but the truth is that nobody really knows what demand for travel will be like in 2032 – whatever our economic modellers tell us. The conventional wisdom in the 1960s was that demand for rail travel would continue to fall. Experts could just as easily be mistaken in assuming that demand for rail travel will continue to grow over the next two decades.

In the end I find it difficult to disagree with Christian Wolmar's assessment:

> Ultimately, this whole scheme is a finger-in-the-air job. The Victorians built their railways on that basis, not really aware of the huge impact they would have or, indeed, whether they would ever pay for themselves. However, in the nineteenth century, the railways were a monopoly and it took almost a hundred years before the car and the lorry made inroads into the railways' market. Today we have the internet, broadband, mobile telephony and even the possibility of driverless cars, let alone more mundane exogenous factors such as oil prices and planning policies that ultimately could all affect demand for rail travel. The variables and what Donald Rumsfeld would call the 'unknown unknowns' over a 20-year period are so great that in effect, despite all the pseudo-scientific business case methodology, this is all one big punt by the politicians. Yet, despite the lack of evidence to support the case for the line, it has now become part of the political consensus supported by all three main political parties – rather like the idea in the noughties that Britain's wealth would be sustained by allowing bankers free rein. And we all know what happened next.[5]

The regional development case

Professor John Tomaney, an economic development specialist who is a strong supporter of rail, has cast considerable doubt on the supposed economic benefits of the plans for the North, suggesting that the effects might at best be 'neutral'. In his evidence to the Transport Select Committee's enquiry into High-Speed Rail, he outlined conclusions from an extensive review of available literature on the impact of high-speed rail:

> The clear balance of this literature suggests that these impacts are ambiguous at best and negative at worst. It is very difficult to find unambiguous evidence in support of the contentions that are being made about the potential impacts of HS2 on the cities and regions of the UK. We noted the theoretical and empirical evidence that suggests investments in intra-urban and intra-regional transport systems may provide more local benefits than high-speed North-South links.[6]

Here it is important to remember that a railway, just like a road, takes people in two directions. There is evidence from other high-speed lines elsewhere in Europe that the capital city benefits more than the outlying regions. The Italian geographer Puga has noted:

> Road and rail tracks can be used to travel both ways. A better connection between two regions with different development levels not only gives firms in a less developed region better access to the inputs and markets of more developed regions, it also makes it easier for firms in richer regions to supply poorer regions at a distance, and can thus harm the industrialisation prospects of less developed areas.[7]

The English regions have always struggled to get their fair share of investment, and there is a danger that politicians will grasp the current HS2 scheme as showing their commitment to regional development, without in fact being committed enough to find out if the project is the best solution. And there are a number of worries about whether good connectivity will in fact be delivered, and about the length of time that may elapse before the project reaches Leeds and Manchester and then Scotland. There is also anxiety that, instead of being part of the national fares system, fares will carry excessive premiums, leading to disappointing usage.

Britain isn't Germany or France: it is actually quite small and compact, with many large centres situated quite near each other. These centres need good connectivity with each other and rail is well placed to do that; yet the current scheme will miss out lots of potential stops in the interest of getting from Leeds or Manchester to London in less time than it takes to finish your cup of coffee. (However there are also some welcome commitments in the proposed route. The plan to go right into the city centres of Leeds and Manchester, with good links to the local and regional networks, is very welcome. Even making Meadowhall, a few miles out of Sheffield city centre, the station for South Yorkshire is not as bad as it might sound: the existing Sheffield station is poorly linked to the city centre and Meadowhall is on both Supertram and conventional rail routes serving South Yorkshire and the East Midlands.)

But there are better options for regional development than those offered by this scheme. For example, immediate implementation of a scaled-down scheme but with wider geographical coverage would have a huge impact on the economy now, when we need it, with jobs in construction and manufacturing.

Liam Robinson, chair of Merseytravel and on the whole a supporter of HS2, has argued that high-speed rail must be complemented by parallel measures to ensure that the regions have a growing economic base supported by devolved political powers, so that the railway doesn't simply suck growth towards London. Devolution to the regions, cities and localities would mean that 'we have the power to shape our own destiny (and local economies) so that we don't become satellite suburbs of the capital'.[8] This is a key point: part of the success of high-speed rail in Germany and France has been the strength of regional governments, which have provided a counter-weight to their capital cities. We lack those alternative centres of power in England; and this absence of a strong regional government structure will limit the benefits of rail investment in and to the regions, and tend to benefit London. But that is less an argument against high-speed rail and more an argument *for* regional devolution.

The environmental case

The environmental case for HS2 has also been challenged. As railway writer Christian Wolmar observed:

> When HS2 was first announced, it was presented as not only having enormous economic benefits but also as environmentally sustainable because of people transferring from road and air to rail. In fact,

subsequently the environmental case has all but collapsed since the effect of the line would be pretty much carbon neutral according to the study by HS2 Ltd, the government body charged with taking forward the scheme, if the impact of its construction were taken into account. The environmental case was fatally weakened by the realisation that few high-speed train passengers would transfer from air. Again, HS2 Ltd found that most users would otherwise have taken conventional train services or simply not made the trip.[9]

Furthermore, the logic of high speed means that it misses out important stops that would benefit from an improved train service, and that stations are sometimes placed at locations remote from a city centre (as with the proposal for Derby/Nottingham); this often means that they do not have good connectivity with the rest of the rail network. In these cases, people will simply drive to the high-speed rail station and negate the supposed environmental benefits – which are quite small as it is.

And the emphasis on very high-speed – 400km/h – both increases the costs and makes the environmental benefits weaker.[10] Whilst the one-off cost of building a 'very high-speed railway' engineered to 400 km/h is only marginally more expensive than one built to 250 km/h, there will be additional costs in terms of energy consumption, through the ongoing running of the trains in the future. As far as I'm aware these have not been quantified. But a well-engineered railway that could average at about 250 km/h would bring all the supposed benefits – and more – of the current scheme, and would also be easier to extend northwards to Scotland.[11]

Improving capacity

Overall, there is a real danger that HS2 will soak up cash that could otherwise be used to invest in the wider rail network. This has been denied by the pro-HS2 lobby, but high-speed rail is undoubtedly going to take a very large chunk of transport's allocation in the cash-strapped decade ahead. My argument is that it would be far more cost effective – and would better address Britain's transport needs – to opt for a more integrated high-speed network of around 250 km/h, with selective new infrastructure.

There is certainly a case for building new, faster, stretches of railway to solve capacity problems and shorten journey times. It's clear, for instance, that parts of the West Coast Main Line, from Euston to the West Midlands, North-West and Scotland, are approaching capacity. There is a need to ensure that there is capacity to accommodate growth over the next twenty to thirty years. But a number of rail experts have suggested ways of achieving this without any need for HS2. For example, Chris Stokes, formerly a senior manager in BR, is one of a number of experts who have suggested infrastructure improvements at key pinch points on the West Coast Main Line south of Crewe: these would bring a much quicker gain in terms of capacity on the route.[12]

In my view the best way of delivering increased capacity is through the adoption of a UK-wide InterCity strategy – and one that can be delivered within ten, not twenty, years. The logical approach would be to develop a high-speed network which really does connect the UK, with a 250-200km/h route to central Scotland. Rail already has the lion's share of the Birmingham–London, and Leeds and Manchester to London market, which means that any shift from car or plane to train would be proportionately greater for a properly thought-through high speed rail route to Scotland, and would therefore bring a greater environmental benefit. Transport Scotland, supported by a wide cross-section of interests, stresses the potential of significant shift from air to rail in such a case: 'the inclusion of Scotland in the UK's high speed rail network is essential for realising significant reductions in UK carbon emissions and is vitally important in achieving major levels of modal shift from air to high speed rail'.[13] A route that makes use of the faster stretches of the West Coast Main Line north of Preston, but uses some new alignments in places where speeds are slower, makes a lot of sense, and could bring journey times from Glasgow and Edinburgh to London within 3h 30 mins.

Lack of capacity on the West Coast Main Line, particularly south of Manchester and Crewe, could be addressed by re-opening the former Midland route through the Peak District to Derby, which would provide a fast alternative route from Manchester to London and also give much-improved connectivity between the North-West and the East Midlands (see below). This line would run straight into St Pancras, and would allow either easy interchange to Eurostar or direct journeys on to continental Europe. Current plans have Northern high-speed trains terminating at Euston, an unpleasant fifteen minutes' walk from St Pancras. What's more, the London to Birmingham market, which will get high-speed rail well before anyone else, also has other options for improvement, including an upgrade of the Chiltern route via Banbury. The West Midlands already has a huge lead over aviation for journeys between the two cities. The route needs more capacity, not 'high speed', and improved northward links, particularly to Manchester.

All these improvements – a high-speed line to Scotland using a mix of new and existing infrastructure; Peak route re-opening and improving the existing Midland route south of Derby to 250 km/h; and upgrades to the Chiltern route – would cost considerably less than the £33 billion we're being asked to pay for HS2; they could also be completed more quickly, and would bring more benefits to the regional economy.

There are also additional cost benefits in adopting a strategy based on a 250km/h speeds. A genuinely UK-wide InterCity network that includes high-speed infrastructure on some key routes needs not only to connect up major centres but also larger towns that are distant from the major cities (Inverness, Aberdeen, Penzance, Truro, etc). And it also needs to have a baseline of standards covering speed, quality and comfort. It therefore makes sense to standardise rolling stock – to ensure both economical operation and a high standard of comfort – and this would be no problem with a 250 km/h maximum speed network. But a 'very high-speed' fleet capable of 400 km/h would be based on different trains from those running on the rest of the network.

Another necessary improvement to the national network that risks being denied funds if the HS2 project absorbs the lion's share of the transport budget is electrification. A future InterCity UK should also be a fully electrified railway, with the existing diesel fleet being redeployed to longer-distance regional lines. Although much of the UK's InterCity network is either already electrified or in the process of so becoming under current government plans, there are significant gaps, including from Glasgow/Edinburgh northwards to Aberdeen and Inverness; while in the south-west, electrification needs to be extended to Plymouth and Penzance.

Less glamorous but still important investment is also needed in other areas to increase capacity. For example, 'flat' junctions where trains have to block oncoming traffic cause delay and limit the number of trains on a route. 'Flying' junctions avoid this problem and are required at several locations on the West and East Coast Main Lines. And on some routes there is a need to quadruple the track (or even for six-tracking on very busy routes).

There are also a number of locations – many of which once had London services – that should be brought back into the InterCity network, including Blackpool, Scarborough and Middlesbrough. Open access operators have demonstrated that these kinds of services can be operated commercially.

RE-BUILDING THE NETWORK

There are a number of other ways of developing the UK's national rail network that would more useful than a single focus on HS2. These are discussed below.

New lines and re-openings

There are a number of routes which should either be re-opened or developed anew to meet expanding demand and new journey patterns. As we saw in chapter five, there are several well-organised re-opening campaigns across the UK that have strong support in the community. However, community-based re-openings usually focus on very local journeys and leave out the strategic network dimension (the Wealden Line campaign being a notable exception). For example, there is no well-organised campaign arguing for the re-opening of the Woodhead Line between Manchester and Sheffield, because its benefits would be strategic and inter-regional rather than local. Similarly, there is no well-organised lobby arguing to re-open Midland Main Line through the Peak District.

In fact there are a number of very short stretches of railway which, if re-connected, would offer new journey opportunities at relatively low cost. These include the Todmorden Curve in West Yorkshire, planned for re-opening in 2014 and involving about 250 yards of new track. Once re-instated this will allow for direct trains from Burnley to Manchester. Equally, opening short stretches of unobstructed disused railway in West Lancashire would allow significant new journey opportunities for through trains on Merseyrail's Liverpool to Ormskirk route.

Connecting the regions

There is a need for better connectivity between the main centres of the English regions, as well as to the south, Scotland and Wales. Thus, for example, the Caldervale route via Hebden Bridge urgently needs major investment. There are also limitations on the current electrification scheme for the TransPennine main line: major centres such as Hull, Middlesbrough and Barrow are being left in the cold. Even more worrying, the opportunity to provide additional track capacity on the core Leeds–Manchester route is being ignored on the dubious assumption that electrification in itself will provide all the extra capacity required. In addition, the programme of North West electrification needs to be generally cranked up and accelerated, with key strategic routes across the Pennines given greater priority. Finally, the major English city-region networks outside London above all need new trains. Even with electrification the regions are being offered nothing better than elderly trains displaced from the Thameslink franchise. Overall, a major programme of investment that combined network electrification, complementary enhancement (e.g. four-tracking on certain corridors) and a selective re-opening programme could be achieved quickly and would have a far greater economic impact than HS2.

The suggested Strategic Rail Agency (cf chapter ten) would take a lead in promoting re-openings that are inter-regional and of genuine strategic importance to the UK as a whole; while regional agencies and the devolved governments for Scotland and Wales should have the powers and resources to progress local or regional schemes (both Scotland and Wales have already undertaken new initiatives but would benefit from greater flexibility). Local or regional projects should be largely funded through funds ear-marked for devolved transport authorities, whereas strategic national projects should be funded centrally. We need to develop more innovative approaches to funding rail projects, including learning from continental experience (e.g. funding from fuel taxes).

The railway industry also needs to be much more pro-active in influencing development proposals, with a presumption that major development should be concentrated around rail hubs. The loss of Regional Spatial Strategies has been a problem here, and these need to be restored under any new regional governance, but more is needed. One idea is that railway interests – both infrastructure providers and service operators – should be statutory consultees in all planning applications that at the moment are referred to the National Infrastructure Commission and the Planning Inspectorate, including major developments such as new or expanded airports, power generators, major waste disposal and harbour facilities or major or trunk road schemes. This would help ensure better integration with rail (or indeed, opposition to proposals if warranted). At a more local level it might also be useful if rail interests were made statutory consultees for local authority major applications (e.g. new large-scale housing, warehousing, industrial and retail applications) within a certain distance from an operational rail line.[14]

NOTES

1. See Simon Jenkins, *Guardian*, 16 May 2013: 'When I asked a transport economist why the BBC couldn't find a member of his profession to defend HS2 on air he said "because there aren't any"'.
2. Ibid.
3. Amyas Morse, National Audit Office press release, 16 May 2013.
4. McNaughton, op cit.
5. Christian Wolmar, 'HS2 is one big punt', *Guardian*, 23 January 2013.
6. Written evidence from Professor John Tomaney to Transport Select Committee (HSR 14) on 'The Local and Regional Impacts of High Speed Rail in the UK: A Review of the Evidence', 31 May 2011.
7. D. Puga, 'European regional policies in light of recent location theories', *Journal of Economic Geography*, 2 (1) quoted in Tomaney, op cit.
8. Liam Robinson, chair of Merseytravel, personal email to author.
9. Wolmar, op cit.
10. I'm grateful to Andrew McNaughton for his comments in a personal communication to author: 'The cost of engineering an alignment for 360km/h (with passive provision for 400km/h at some future point) was worked out very carefully in 2009/10 and compared with a "classic speed" route alternative of, notionally 200km/h. The difference was 9 per cent. In other words, a new classic railway would cost 91 per cent of a 400 km/h one.
11. See Transport Scotland, *Fast Track Scotland: making the case for high-speed rail to Scotland*, 2013.
12. Chris Stokes, 'Do We really Need HS2?', *Modern Railways*, October 2012.
13. Ibid.
14. Email to author from longstanding politician David Walsh, who is particularly interested in planning, 10 May 2013.

9. RAILWAYS IN THE TWENTY-FIRST CENTURY: BEYOND BRITAIN

... models of municipal socialism in practice, providing high quality integrated rail and bus services[1]

We can learn much from the experience of other European countries, both good and bad.[2] The management of railways in many European countries has changed dramatically over the last twenty years. The traditional model of a single, state-owned operator providing a mix of inter-city, regional and freight services has been transformed in all but a handful of countries. Whilst some of the traditional state-owned operators, like Deutsche Bahn in Germany, Nederlands Spoorwegen in the Netherlands and SNCF in France remain, their roles have changed substantially.

The transformations in these companies have taken several forms, but a common factor has been the separation of infrastructure from operations, in large part driven by EU policy and a series of rail directives from the European Commission. Train operating companies tend now to be responsible solely for operations, with infrastructure usually coming under a separate, state-owned, body broadly similar to our Network Rail (which of course is not, theoretically, state-owned). Alongside this, the large state operators in most countries (with the exception of France) have faced competition from other private operators, particularly for regional franchises. Some of these competitors are foreign state-owned rail operators.

It has to be said that change was essential. Local and regional rail services were being inefficiently run, with little attempt made by the state operators to attract new business. InterCity trains were the main focus of investment – and the pioneering TGV operations in France and Germany's ICE are the stuff of legend. But these projects were often, particularly in France, at the expense of local services, which

continued to decline. Services in many countries across Europe were
operated by ancient trains running to erratic timetables that made no
attempt to reflect local needs, while stations had seen no investment
for decades and were staffed by people with rather a lot of spare time
on their hands. Something had to change: otherwise a massive round
of rail closures was inevitable.

Change did come. It's useful therefore to look at the experience of
a selection of European countries that have grasped the nettle of the
regional rail problem and started a virtuous spiral of re-structuring
and investment. The Netherlands, Sweden, Denmark, France, Italy
and Germany all offer useful insights, and I have also included some
brief comments on the situation in parts of central and Eastern
Europe. Those countries have taken reform of regional rail further
than most other European countries, though the models are, in every
case, significantly different from the UK approach.[3]

FROM STATE OWNERSHIP TO LIBERALISED MARKET

The changes that have taken place across many of Europe's regional
railways have not happened at a uniform rate. The 'high speed' revolution began in France, with its first TGV service starting in 1981
between Paris and Lyon. Germany followed shortly after with its ICE
network, along with Sweden's X2000 and Italy's 'Direttissima', which
opened with conventional traction as early as 1978. Spain's 'AVE'
service from Madrid to Seville opened in 1992. All of these projects
were state-funded and state-managed. The French TGV was seen as
symbolic of French national pride and technological excellence. This
was very much a state-led revolution, and it would have been very
difficult, given the huge investment involved, for it to have been
anything else. Even now, private sector involvement in high-speed rail
across Europe is the exception to the norm.

It was in the regional sector that some of the main reforms began
to take place. Sweden and Germany were the first to 'regionalise'
some rail operations, though it should be pointed out that in several
countries, notably Germany, Denmark and Italy, independent, usually
publicly-owned, regional rail operations had existed for decades. One
example is the Hohenzollern Regional Railway, which operates local
passenger services in parts of southern Germany. This is a vertically-
integrated railway, owned by the local communities which it serves.

Similar operations, such as the 'Lokalbanen' (Local Railways), have existed and flourished in Denmark for decades.

The traditional model for regional railway operations has been highly centralised. Local and regional services were provided by the state operator (be it Deutsche Bahn, SNCF, Nederlands Spoorwegen, etc). Regional rail services were usually treated as just another part of the network, without any specific management attention, other than inasmuch as they were part of a geographically-based management unit (region, division, area, etc) that had responsibilities for other operations such as freight and express passenger. Traditionally, there was little contact between the railway company and local or regional governments, with relationships confined usually to a very senior level of railway and national government.

From the 1960s onwards, regional rail services began to suffer from competition from the private car and bus, and service reductions were common across Europe. However, the realisation that local and regional rail could form part of an overall strategy to reduce car dependence began to find favour during the 1990s. This rise in regional focus was also fuelled by concerns over the rising costs of maintaining regional rail services and the political difficulties in closing any more of the networks. It was realised that managing regional rail as part of the overall network, whilst making for operational integration, meant that services had little or no marketing. Community involvement in regional rail was an unknown concept across Europe at this time, other than on a very ad hoc basis.

On a more strategic level, the 'liberalisation' ethos within the European Union began to have an effect. The assumption that there should be only one state rail operator began to weaken, as European legislation provided for a degree of separation between operations and infrastructure, opening the way for further legislation to enable 'open access' operations on the state owned network.

Change came first in the Scandinavian countries, notably Sweden, which was the first country to separate operations from infrastructure. As Ingemar Lundin, former managing director of Jönköping Transport Authority put it, those were the days 'when the wind shifted and regional rail become an attractive mode of transport again'.[4]

Germany, Denmark, the Netherlands and France followed. In some central and eastern European countries, particularly the Czech Republic and Poland, experiments were made in devolving responsibility for local and regional rail to a more local level, but these were initially fraught with problems and political controversy, reflecting the cost-driven agenda which lay behind the policy. It would seem that Poland and the Czech Republic now have some degree of stability, with considerable regional devolution.

The reforms in western European countries were also partly driven by cost considerations, but equally by a concern to provide a more responsive and co-ordinated approach to public transport as a whole. The Swedish ambition to develop local railways through using regional devolution, franchising and cost reductions, coupled with investment in new stations, services and rolling stock, has led to a positive cycle of growth and reduced subsidy per passenger.

There are a number of elements which the successful regional rail projects have in common. All are promoted by strong, elected regional authorities through their passenger transport (or sometimes specifically rail) authorities. The transfer to regional control has usually come with what can only be described as a seismic shift in how rail is managed. Traditional working practices have been abandoned in favour of slimmed-down operations, with trains typically becoming driver-only, serving unstaffed stations. Investment has provided for re-signalling, taking out expensive and inefficient mechanical signalling systems.

Whilst the number of staff per train operated has drastically declined, more staff are now employed in directly productive roles, notably driving, because of the investment that has taken place in new, modern rolling stock, improved integration between bus and rail, higher frequencies, and attractive, localised, marketing. The informal evidence suggests that staff like the new arrangements and enjoy being part of a much smaller and less hierarchical team.

Another feature of most regional railways – with significant exceptions – is that the separation of infrastructure from operations, in accordance with European law, generally applies. Exceptions are long-standing independent railways such as those in Germany and Denmark, the more recent pilot scheme in Düren, and the Basque metre-gauge 'Euskotren' network. In each of these cases, results have been impressive, but there has been a reluctance amongst many regional transport authorities to pursue vertical integration further, on largely legal grounds.

There has been a presumption in favour of franchising, again partly based on European law. Forms of franchising vary, but the key difference is between 'net' and 'gross' cost contracts. An increasing number of transport authorities favour gross contracts, allowing them a greater degree of control, with the operator purely providing a service for an agreed price and all revenue going to the public body. This is, of course, quite different from the UK model which is based on net cost franchises with the operator having a greater degree of risk.

THE EUROPEAN UNION DIMENSION

The European Commission has had an increasingly direct involvement in railways since the early 2000s and this is likely to increase. The core European legislation affecting railways is in the EC's 'First Railway Package', but that has been added to in recent years. Transport academic Professor Chris Nash has summarised the position:

> In brief, these required: separation of the management of infrastructure, freight and passenger services, at least into separate divisions with their own profit and loss accounts and balance sheets; non-discriminatory setting of access charges and allocation of paths (as a safeguard, if the infrastructure manager was also involved in train operation then these functions had to be undertaken by an independent body); the establishment of a rail regulator, independent of the infrastructure manager and any train operator, to whom appeal could be made in the case of dispute; a performance regime to incentivise the infrastructure manager; and financial equilibrium of the infrastructure manager to be ensured – either through the regulatory system or by means of a multi-annual contract lasting at least 3 years – whilst maintaining pressure for cost reductions.[5]

Two further packages have introduced important measures regarding safety and inter-operability, but most crucially have completely opened up the market for both domestic and international freight traffic, and will increasingly open the market for passenger service. However, implementation of these Directives has been very variable. Nash makes the point that EC proposals to make competitive tendering compulsory for unprofitable local services were shelved following major political disagreements. However, the EC's Fourth Railway Package, published in draft form in January 2013, revives the proposal.

The process of reform has not been uniform across Europe, however, and some countries, notably Belgium, have continued with the traditional model of a state operator providing all passenger services without any significant separation into market segments or business units. Meanwhile some smaller countries or regions have developed as self-contained entities. A notable example is Mallorca Railways, which passed from central to regional government control in 1994, since when it has trebled in size.[6]

SWEDEN

Sweden was the first European country to institute radical reforms to its rail network, though this was sometimes through a slightly ad hoc process.[7] It was the first country to separate infrastructure from operations. Initially, the infrastructure company was called Banverket (now Trafikverket) whilst most rail operations continued to be provided by SJ (Swedish State Railways), which remains state-owned.

One Swedish authority commented:

> The 1988 reform, part of a comprehensive Transport Policy Act of that year, was given three motives. One was to put railways on an equal footing with roads by organisationally separating infrastructure from service operations. This is one reason why Banverket was made a government agency, operated in the same way as the National Road Administration (later the two authorities merged). Secondly, since railways were considered a uniquely safe and environmentally friendly means of transport, the Parliament also voted for continued financial support so that these special benefits could be fully realized. The third given reason for the reforms was to arrange for subsidies to secondary, low-density lines, by way of transferring the responsibility for commercially unviable traffic over these lines to regional transport authorities. This would then be a means of carrying on with operations for regional policy reasons.[8]

The reform of the regional rail network began in earnest in the early 1990s, with responsibility for local and regional rail services being transferred to 21 regional transport authorities (RTAs), responsible to regional councils. The involvement of the RTAs developed over the following decade in a process that was far from being uniform. The picture today remains complex, with the RTAs having responsibilities for franchising local and regional services and also owning the rolling stock used. Some of the RTAs have joined together to create a rolling stock provider, and the RTAs are major investors in stations, in some cases owning station buildings. The RTAs and transport operators (rail, bus, ferry) have also created a not-for-profit company called Samtrafiken which co-ordinates ticketing and information services.

The RTAs have responsibilities for all modes of transport, and are able to ensure a very high level of integration between bus and rail, with buses providing feeder services to rail station hubs. They finance regional rail, with their parent regional councils being responsible for raising most of the finance through local and regional taxation. The central state provides very little funding.[9] The introduction of tendering for regional services was far from being a smooth process, as Jan-Eric Nilsson observes:

> ... in 1989, the first competitive procurement of regional train services resulted in a four-year contract being awarded to a private company. BK Tåg, at that time a coach operator, submitted the lowest bid and could start its services in 1990, using previous SJ drivers that were now given higher salaries. Although the contractor in reality only has control over a few parameters – rolling stock is owned by the regional authority that also controls ticket prices and takes care of all revenue – BK Tåg acquired a reputation to deal with the operations in an un-orthodox and largely successful way. This is the first example of competition *for* the tracks, where an entrant is in charge of a certain service for a pre-determined period of time. When this particular contract was up for renewal in 1993, SJ won it back. BK Tåg filed a complaint against SJ with the Swedish Competition Authority, claiming abuse of dominant position, asserting that SJ had submitted a bid below costs in order to get rid of the entrant. The complaint was approved and SJ was fined SEK 8 million for its bid.[10]

BK Tåg brought a very distinct approach to local train operations. Under the aegis of the country transport authority, staffing was reduced and the driver became responsible for ticket sales (a practice that no longer applies). Station staff were removed from smaller locations and ticket machines installed, as well as smart-card readers on trains.

From these modest beginnings, with small domestically owned train companies like BK winning some RTA contracts, today's picture has become one of Danish domination. Various Danish State Railways (DSB) subsidiaries have won contracts to operate Swedish RTA services, though these may not continue following DSB's recent experiences (see below). The new regional operation in the north of the country – 'Norrtåg' – is a mixture of gross and net cost contract, and is run by a joint venture owned by Arriva (60 per cent) and SJ (40 per cent).

An interesting exception to the general Swedish pattern is the 1089km Inlandsbanan ('Inland Railway'), which opened in 1937 and runs up to the far north of Sweden. Banverket divested itself of the line in the 1990s to a consortium of local authorities along the route, which formed Inlandsbanan AB to manage the infrastructure. Separate companies owned by the authorities have been formed to run freight and passenger (tourist) trains. The experiment has been highly successful, for both freight and passenger services. The tourist trains, using a fleet of old but comfortable diesel railcars, has helped boost the tourist economy in isolated rural areas.[11]

Trafikverket (originally Banverket) now covers both rail and road infrastructure. It has the overall responsibility for the planning, development and functioning of the rail sector and has a much stronger role than most other European infrastructure bodies. Most rail traffic is controlled from Trafikverket's seven operation centres.

Swedish railways are now highly liberalised. Since October 2009 international services have been open to competition, and from summer 2010 all domestic services have been open to licensed operators. The assumption is that long distance train services will operate without subsidy, though one route to Northern Sweden does require state support and services are tendered via national transport body Rikstrafiken. Track access charges in Sweden are low, and reflect a policy which aims to encourage rail on account of its environmental benefits.

The overall result of Sweden's rail reforms is positive. Regional rail services have been transformed and costs have come down by about 25 per cent compared with the pre-1988 SJ costs. Ridership has increased dramatically, and investment has gone into station facilities, ticketing systems and new rolling stock.

DENMARK

Denmark, with a population of 5.5 million, is comparable to Scotland. As well as having a similar size of population, that population is also concentrated in one area, Copenhagen. DSB (Danish State Railways) has been the main operator for many years. It is structured as 'an independent public company owned by the Ministry of Transport'. In recent years it has come under considerable pressure by politicians to become more market oriented. It has responded to these challenges with some alacrity, forming partnerships with the private sector, stripping out inefficiencies, and bidding for work abroad – with stunning success in neighbouring Sweden. The main railway infrastructure is managed by Banedanmark, a state-owned body. It is interesting to note that Denmark also has about twenty long-established independent railways which are owned by municipalities. These are usually vertically-integrated operations, largely separate (though not entirely) from the main DSB network.

Competitive tendering is not universal and so far only about 22 per cent of the regional network has been put out to tender by the Danish Transport Authority (Trafikstyrelsen). Some local services have been won by Arriva, which initially established a base in the Silkeborg area. Part of that package included complete fleet replacement, with Angel Trains acting as rolling stock supplier. Arriva's main area of operation is now in the Arhus area.

The Danish experience with competitive tendering and public-private partnerships has been difficult, to say the least. DSB teamed up with UK-based First Group, as DSB First, to win some contracts, particularly the Oresund operation, which was let on a 'net cost' basis. In mid-2011 the situation went dramatically wrong and was described by one expert as 'hell'. This led to a political crisis that resulted in DSB deciding to withdraw from further foreign bids and to concentrate on its home 'core' business.

The network of Danish local railways is very well established, with about twenty lines that tend to be owned by the local authorities. 'Lokalbanen' in Zealand, for example, has a 138km network and a fleet of 29 modern trains. It carries 6 million passengers a year and is a good example of a modern, community-owned railway. But it isn't all good news. Where Denmark has been a disaster is in freight operations. Since DSB's freight arm was sold to the Deutsche Bahn subsidiary DB Schenker, the emphasis has been entirely on bridge traffic between Sweden and Germany, and almost all internal freight traffic and terminals have been discarded.

SWITZERLAND

Switzerland, with a population of around 8 million, has long enjoyed a highly reliable, attractive and 100 per cent electrified (since 1960) passenger rail system.[12] The country is a confederation of 26 autonomous cantons, each with its own parliament and internal administration. Along with defence, foreign affairs, economic policy and a few other areas, an overview of transport is one of the few fields in which the central government has any direct involvement. This has resulted in a country with a high degree of decentralisation in all aspects of life. Rail transport provision involves around sixty different operators, mostly vertically integrated small private companies that serve individual, or groups of, cantons. Some are standard gauge operations, but many of the local lines run on the metre-gauge. At the extreme some of these simply serve one community.

By far the biggest operator, with over 50 per cent of the route network, and a much higher proportion of passenger-miles-travelled, is the central-government-owned (since 1902) standard-gauge Swiss Federal Railways (SBB); Bern-Lotschberg-Simplon (BLS), a semi-private company, is the next largest. As Switzerland is not in the EU there is no requirement to separate the infrastructure from operations, and the railways are 'vertically integrated'. However, the government requires that the SBB has a clear internal financial and operational internal separation, and the BLS has the same procedures for its own network through the Alps. Both SBB and BLS have semi-autonomous freight divisions, with Deutsche Bahn partially owning the BLS operation. The entire public and private network works to an integrated national timetable, which also indicates the types of service provision required, and is determined by the Federal Transport Office. This ensures a basic minimum of hourly interconnecting trains on virtually all routes, along with a similar basic provision of bus services to non-rail served destinations. Many services operate more frequently, either because of a commercial decision by the operators, or due to the cantons and communes requesting and funding the enhanced operations (communes are equivalent to our parish councils, but with far more powers and their own locally determined tax-base).

There is a clear distinction made within Switzerland between long distance, regional and local passenger services. The long-distance InterCity network, along with the major regional services, are provided by the SBB and the BLS, some on a commercial basis, most subsidised by the federal government. Both organisations operate some regional express services, in the financing of which the cantons have some say. In addition to operating some local services, they also operate the majority of the S-Bahn services around the major conurbations, in association with the local authorities who heavily subsidise them. Some of the regional express services are provided by the small private railways who provide many of the local services. These locally owned, 'arms-length', railway companies are all vertically integrated, operating their own rolling stock on their own tracks to their own timetables and service standards. A contract (normally a service level agreement) between the canton and the local railway (and with SBB and BLS where appropriate) is generally negotiated every four years, with 'net cost' contracts awarded. In other words, the operator is given a baseline of funding and any extra revenue goes to the company, whilst it has to bear any loss.

Many of the smaller operators (often described as 'private') are actually publicly owned – generally by the cantonal authorities and some communes, although some private capital is also present in some cases. Malcolm Bulpitt, of the Swiss Railway Society, has described them as 'models of municipal socialism in practice, providing high quality integrated rail and bus services':

> This is a paradox given that Switzerland, centre-right politically, has probably one of the most market-oriented economies in Europe, if not the world. The pragmatic Swiss reason is that public transport's main competitor is the private vehicle so why waste money (and subsidies) competing within the same area of operation. This means that all bus services complement the rail network and there is no public transport competition, except perhaps on a very small scale in some conurbations where routes run parallel.[13]

Towns and cities control their own tram and bus operations, whilst in the rural areas all bus service licences are held by the Swiss Post, who either operate their own vehicles on the routes, or put them out to tender as a service contract with operators running their vehicles in the yellow 'PostAuto' livery.

Regionalverkehr Bern-Solothurn (RBS – Regional Transport Bern-Solothurn) is a good example of a medium-sized Swiss transport operation. It runs a local network of metre-gauge trains, as well as connecting bus services, between its namesake cities and out to Worb, now a Bern suburb. It also has a tram route to this town that is operated in association with Bernmobil, the Bern municipal transport operator. The RBS is vertically integrated, owning the track and operating its own trains. The company is the result of a 1985 merger of several organisations that started life in the 1890s. Shares are owned by the Confederation (31 per cent), cantons (43 per cent), the communes en-route (5 per cent), Bernmobil (15 per cent) and the private sector (6 per cent). In its striking orange livery, it operates forty-three electric trains plus some one hundred and thirty road vehicles, on 69.7km of rail routes (three of which are as part of the local S-Bahn, and one of which is a regional express route), and ten bus routes. It is a major player in Bern's transport system, carrying over 23 million passengers annually, including a significant percentage of Bern's S-Bahn passengers. The RBS's 1964-built terminal station in Bern is located beneath the SBB's main station, and in its own right is Switzerland's eighth-largest in terms of passenger usage. It was built to handle 16,000 passengers daily but now has to cope with 60,000 at peak times, and is currently undergoing a £400-million reconstruction, on a new, also underground, alignment. Between 2009 and 2013 RBS introduced a fleet of 14 new, 120kph capable, trains from Swiss manufacturer Stadler both to boost performance on its 'mainline' regional express service between its namesake cities, and to allow its inner-suburban lines to offer a 15-minute headway through more intensive use of the whole fleet.

Swiss 'private' railways (i.e. independent of the state) vary enormously in size. The biggest is the Rhätische Bahn, which is effectively the 'State Railway' of the Graubünden, Switzerland's largest canton, located in the mountainous southeast of the country. Its 384km metre-gauge network carries 11 million passengers and 800,000 tonnes of freight annually, using over three hundred powered vehicles, almost four hundred coaches and over five hundred freight wagons, all run by 1,400 employees. It has hourly services on its main network running regional express and local services, and around Chur it has an S-Bahn network that operates more frequently. The aim of the canton is to move to a half-hourly frequency on all lines (even up remote alpine valleys) in the next few years and it is in the middle of a multi-billion franc investment programme in new rolling stock.

At the other extreme is the unusual 1200mm-gauge, 1.9km long, Rheineck Walzenhausen Bahn, with just one four-wheel, 28-seat, rack and adhesion railcar, linking the 2000 inhabitants of the village resort of Walzenhausen, high above the Bodensee, with the SBB main line. It is now managed by the Appenzeller Bahnen, a local grouping. It has been described as 'the ultimate community railway'.

Another example of a locally-based railway operation is the electrified 16km metre-gauge line between La Chaux-de-Fonds and Les Ponts-de-Martel, a small town of some 1300 people in the Jura, Switzerland's other mountain range. The line serves the very rural Vallée de la Sagne with a total population of less than 5000, yet it runs an hourly service, with peak hour and school extras, to cope with local needs. It also runs 'Night Owl' trains very late on Friday and Saturday nights to allow locals to enjoy an evening-out in La Chaux-de-Fonds. Being Switzerland, there is not a parallel bus service along the valley. The operation, run by Transports Régionaux Neuchâtelois, is based in the station at Les Ponts-de-Martel. Trains have adequate space for cycles and buggies and also carry ticket machines, as none of the ten intermediate stops are staffed. To encourage tourist traffic the line has invested in a 44-seat panoramic driving trailer that is complete with a galley and toilet and is attached to trains at the request of tour companies, giving their clients a 25-minute glimpse of the local scenery.

Unlike the UK where thirty-year-old four wheel 'Pacers' still struggle to serve long-suffering passengers on many busy routes, Swiss operators from the SBB to the smaller private railways have consistently invested in modern rolling stock, often phasing-out equipment that is far younger than that seen on British railways. Community-owned lines understand that it is not only schedules designed to deal with local demand that are important; in the twenty-first century, their local customers (and part owners) demand twenty-first-century standards of comfort and reliability.

The only real downside of this remarkable transport organisation is that its own efficiency, together with a fare structure that is very cost-effective for the comparatively highly paid Swiss, is threatening to overwhelm the system, especially the SBB's main lines. Swiss incomes are on average far higher than in the UK, but across the system the normal point-to-point fares are generally comparable with the basic fare structure in the UK, meaning that they are much more affordable.

There is also no market pricing, which can lead to very high fares on certain routes at certain peak times. Almost 5 per cent of the population hold an annual pass for the whole system (all trains, buses, trams, many funiculars and mountain lines, ships, etc), which costs around £3000, or less that a thirty-mile annual season ticket in the UK. This means people travel a lot and often commute long distances. Another 50 per cent of Swiss have an annual £60 half-fare discount card, many have season tickets, and many others have local discount tickets. This is all good in environmental terms, but the system does need major on-going investment. And although Switzerland missed out on the worst of the financial crisis, even here funding is not as easy to access as it once was. New lines, reconstructed tunnels, station enhancements and the removal of bottlenecks are all urgently needed.

Transport is high on the Swiss political agenda, and the country has a unique system of public initiatives, whereby 100,000 signatures can force a national referendum on a proposal. If it is carried it has to be implemented – the people really do have the final say on policy. It was a referendum in the 1990s that required the government to fund the two new base railway tunnels under the Alps, in order to provide a rail-borne alternative route for the HGV traffic that was threatening the eco-systems on the mountain road routes. This can work both ways though, as SBB found in 2012 when proposing a new direct rail tunnel in canton Neuchatel. A local referendum was called and the proposal was defeated, due to concerns over the state of the canton's finances, that would have had to be drawn on to part-fund the proposal. There is no right of appeal.

GERMANY

Germany has the largest national railway market in Europe, with a burgeoning network that combines high-speed with conventional inter-city and high-quality regional and local services. German Rail AG is a wholly-owned state company which has a separate subsidiary company responsible for infrastructure.

The country has to a large extent led the liberalisation process for regional passenger traffic over the past fifteen years, and today there are some four hundred separate operators, including freight companies, although many of them are very small. Within the regional passenger sector there are some seventy different companies operating – a mix of public and privately-owned. Deutsche Bahn (DB) remains the colossus bestriding both operations and infrastructure, although it has separated infrastructure management into a separate body, DB Netz. Most of its regional passenger services are provided by its subsidiary DB Regio, which owns Arriva and has several UK operations (Chiltern Railways, Tyne and Wear Metro, Cross Country, Grand Central).

Prior to liberalisation in 1994, Germany already had much experience of local, publicly-owned railways, such as the successful 'Hohenzollern Regional Railway' in the south of the country, for example, whose history stretches back to the nineteenth century. In the early 1990s, a pilot scheme in northern Germany saw the re-organisation of two 'failing' branch lines into a local authority-managed railway called 'The Dürener Kreisbahn' (DKB – or 'Düren County Railway'). The lines were taken out of DB control, whose only interest in the railway had been to shut it down as quickly as possible. Over the next few years a positive dynamic of improved frequencies, investment in new rolling stock, station modernisation and re-signalling took place. From a handful of trains a day, hauled by over-powered diesel locomotives with a couple of carriages, modern 'Regiosprinter' trains now operate a half-hourly service to rural communities in the area. Trains are operated by one person – the driver – with back-up from roving revenue control teams. (Ticket machines are very common at German stations, and tickets are usually valid for travel in a zone, i.e. if you buy a ticket on a bus you can continue by train without even showing the ticket.) Unlike many 'new generation' local railways, the operation is vertically integrated with operations and infrastructure under single control. Ridership has leapt from a couple of hundred a day to thousands, with growth of 500 per cent. The railway is now owned jointly by the county council and a private company, and operates as 'Rurtalbahn AG' (Rur Valley Railway).[14]

The success of the Düren project encouraged the German Federal government to go ahead with a more general regionalisation of services. Germany has a well-established system of regional government, based on 'Länder' (or 'regions') which cover large areas, and these were now given powers to take over franchising of local services. This led to a flowering of innovation in local rail services and some outstanding successes. In many parts of the country, neglected branch lines suddenly found they were getting much-needed investment, with new management, station refurbishment and new rolling stock. The

German rolling stock manufacturers found themselves with orders for hundreds of new trains, mostly diesel railcars, which have provided a huge leap in ride quality and passenger comfort – and reduced running costs. Many other small networks of lines have been franchised, with DB Regio and other larger groups tending to win most of the contracts. The 1994 rail reform was aimed at attracting more traffic to the railways; limiting support to the sector from the public purse; promoting competition on the tracks; and restoring the state railways' operation according to business principles.[15]

Funding for regional rail was transferred to the Länder in 1996. Today, the total provision is around 7 billion euros. The Länder run services either through direct procurement or through competitive tendering. DB provides most of the contracts, but around 12 per cent (measured in passenger-km – 20 per cent measured in train-km) is delivered by other operators. Over 60 million train/km of services are now tendered out.

DB itself has the lion's share of contracts, and Veolia (formerly Connex) is the next largest contractor. State-owned Dutch company Abellio also has a number of contracts. At one time Arriva had a number of regional rail contracts in Germany (as 'Arriva Deutschland'), but when it was bought by DB in 2010 it was forced to divest its contracts. These were purchased by Italian Railways, which now markets the services as 'Netinera'. Many of the smaller operators are owned by local authorities; one of the biggest of these is Karlsruhe's AVG, which operates an extensive network using tram-train technology. The Regiobahn network, based on two connecting routes into Düsseldorf, is owned by a consortium of local authorities, and has been immensely successful in revitalising the two decrepit routes.

There is considerable diversity in approach. Bayern, for example, with a sixth of Germany's total train-km in regional traffic, has only one procurement body, while others have divided responsibility over several smaller bodies. All in all, there are about thirty procurement bodies in the sixteen regions, known as 'Rail Passenger Transport Authorities'. These are represented by their federal association BAG-SPNV.

DB has also established five 'regionetze' – vertically integrated operations in more rural areas. One example is the Usedom Railway, which is almost a self-contained operation in the north of the country. The Rail Public Transport Authorities normally require bidders to provide rolling stock to precise specifications in the tender document, and this has sometimes led to difficulties during the transfer of contracts. Exceptions are Niedersachsen and parts of Hessen, which have 'rolling stock pools' owned by the Rail PTAs in a similar way to the Swedish PTAs. Rail PTAs have chosen different solutions regarding fare structures, timetable design, vehicle design, etc. Net agreements are the most common type but mixes of net and gross agreements also exist, where the revenue risk is shared by the operator and the Rail PTA.

Germany still has a mix of both direct procurement and competitive tendering – policies vary between the federal states. In 2007, 50 per cent of total train-km was tendered out in Schleswig-Holstein, and more is planned, but only 5 per cent is offered for tender in Bayern.

Controversy continues over franchising versus direct procurement. In 2002 German courts decreed that Rail PTAs must procure services through competition and not through direct procurement with a single favoured provider. This was reinforced by a ruling of the Federal Court of Justice in February 2011. Bertil Hylén suggests that the courts based their 2002 decision on competition legislation:

> The decision led to intense discussions and lobbying by DB Regio who would really have liked to see that direct procurement continued. DB Regio appealed both to higher authorities in Germany and to the European Commission. A gradual phasing-in over 13 years was discussed and a compromise was eventually agreed where the federal states are forced to show greater transparency in their procurements, while legal proceedings concerning the forms of procurement care are still on-going.[16]

As Hylén adds, it should be noted that EU Regulation 1370/2007 permits direct procurement of train traffic.

DB remains a firm supporter of vertical integration, arguing that there is no firm evidence that a separation will benefit the development of rail services, the customer, or the development of competition. Instead, it argues, an integrated railway under strict regulation may show positive results. Hylén's view is that experience in other countries shows that vertical separation has led to little development of competition, and to an increase in demand for public funding.[17]

The independent German operators (including public as well as privately owned companies) in BAG-SPNV commented that their preferred model would be based on a regional infrastructure manager for regional networks, as for example with the Thüringer Eisenbahn GmbH, a private railway infrastructure that manages 116km of tracks in Thuringia. In this model the Länder would define regional networks and tender the managing of the network, and, alongside municipalities, would have more influence on the local infrastructure. They argue that in experience this kind of system is much more efficient than the centralised DB.[18]

The German example has been explored in some depth because it has seen by far the most comprehensive overhaul of regional rail services in Europe (together with Sweden). The results are certainly impressive, with lines having been transformed through major investment. New fleets of trains, both diesel and electric, have been ordered, stations upgraded and frequencies drastically improved. Some regional lines have experienced growth in four figures – (e.g. Regiobahn in the Düsseldorf area, operated by Veolia). This all comes at a cost (€7 billion), but clearly the federal government and the Länder see this as good value for money.

A down side of the German situation has been the loss of through ticketing between some operators. And another area of worry has been the growing concern over punctuality and reliability. There have been criticisms in the German press about the decline in DB's once famous efficiency, and some railway commentators have suggested that part of the problem is DB's focus on foreign markets.

THE NETHERLANDS

The Netherlands is a relatively small country with a population of 16.5m compared to the UK's 61 million. However, it has a more dense population, which makes it good terrain for public transport, particularly in its most densely-populated area, the Randstad, which covers Rotterdam, Amsterdam and The Hague. Rail in the Netherlands is a popular means of transport, and is responsible for nearly 10 per cent of surface passenger transport (compared with 6.8 per cent in the UK).

The state operator is the long-established Nederlands Spoorwegen (NS) which, up until 1995, was a vertically integrated operator. The situation now is that NS operates 'main line' services with exclusive rights from the Dutch government, whilst Pro-Rail has responsibilities for infrastructure. NS's subsidiary Abellio has several contracts for both rail and bus services in the UK. It owns the Greater Anglia franchise (let in 2012), and shares the Northern Rail and Merseyrail franchises with Serco. It has acquired a number of rail and bus contracts in mainland Europe.

The reform of regional rail services began in 2000 with the Passenger Transport Act. The aim of the legislation was to drive forward improvements to local passenger transport and also to recoup a greater share of costs (increasing the proportion from 35 per cent to 50 per cent of total costs). The Act provided a framework for the regionalisation of local ('branch line') rail services, bus and metro systems. A total of eighteen regional transport authorities were formed, based on the provinces (in more rural areas) and on seven 'city-regions' in more urban parts of the country. The Dutch state was treated as the 'nineteenth transport authority', as it retained control of main line rail services – including local rail services operating over the main line routes.

The regional transport authorities formed part of the elected authorities, be they provincial councils or the city-region bodies. Funding of passenger transport was (and is) primarily based on a transfer of funds from central government to the provincial councils and city regions, with very little coming from local municipalities, which tend to be very small and without access to large funds. Not all of the provincial councils have responsibilities for rail, reflecting the nature of the local rail network. In one case (Groningen/Drenthe), two provincial councils co-operate to manage local rail services in their areas.

A pioneer of the new approach, used as a pilot prior to the 2000 Act, was the 'Syntus' operation in the east of the Netherlands. Here a joint venture company comprising a local bus operator and NS was formed in order to promote a highly integrated local transport network. Competing bus routes were re-organised to feed into local station hubs, and the company had responsibility for both bus and rail services. Staff, including drivers, were multi-skilled in both bus and rail.

The experiment proved highly successful, and the 2000 Act enabled the regional transport authorities to take over responsibility for local 'branch line' services in their areas. In some cases the transport authorities specified integrated franchises that included both rail and bus services, ensuring very high levels of integration. Several companies then entered the rail market, including Arriva (now owned by DB), which already had extensive bus contracts in the Netherlands. Connexxion, a bus company now owned by Transdev, won some contracts as did Veolia, which itself recently took over Transdev. The Syntus operation is now owned jointly by NS and French-owned Keolis, although the company has recently lost a number of its branch line contracts to Arriva.

The Dutch experience has been largely positive, though there have been some problems because of the size of the provincial councils, which has resulted in some overlapping of services. The partnership between Groningen and Drenthe suggests that this need not be a major barrier if authorities are willing to co-operate. The relatively short franchise length (up to eight years) means that there is a degree of instability in the network. The loss of a large part of the Syntus network to rival operator Arriva has been seen by some commentators as risking a decline in the high quality service currently provided. Time will tell, but what is clear is that the instability which is part of the franchising process does have a negative impact on both staff and passengers.

ITALY

The pace of rail reform in Italy has been slow, to the frustration of the European Commission, which has taken the Italian government to the European Court of Justice for its failure to implement the first package of rail reforms (though Italy was not on its own, sharing the same fate as Germany, Spain and France). The bulk of train services, both long distance and regional, are operated by state-owned Trenitalia (formerly FS, Ferrovie dello Stato or 'State Railways'). The infrastructure is owned and managed by RFI, established in 2001 following EU legislation to separate infrastructure from operations.

Italy's twenty regions do have a degree of autonomy, and are responsible for regional public transport, including rail. Each region has a contract (normally net cost, with the exception of Bolzano) with Trenitalia for the provision of regional rail services. Trenitalia itself has regional business units that correspond to the twenty regional councils, each having considerable commercial autonomy.

The only region to experiment with tendering has been Emilia-Romagna which put out some services to tender, which were won by Trenitalia. Italy also has a number of independent, publicly owned railways which operate in mostly rural areas. Typically these will be vertically integrated, with the regional council owning the rolling stock.

In April 2012, NTV, Europe's first private high-speed operator began operating 300km/h services on an 'open access' basis on Italy's high-speed routes (Turin–Milano–Rome–Napoli–Salerno). French state-owned operator SNCF has a 20 per cent share in the business.

SPAIN

Spain's railways are going through considerable changes following the election of a right-wing government in 2011. The state railway company, Renfe, is facing possible privatisation, and the operation is being divided into four sectors, covering passenger, freight, infrastructure and rolling stock. The reforms are scheduled for completion by summer 2013. Spain was a relative late-comer to the high-speed rail market, but has since pushed forward an ambitious programme of new lines that complement the original AVE (high speed train) Madrid to Seville route, which started in 1992 with lines to Malaga, Barcelona, Toledo and Albacete. Its 2,665km network of dedicated high-speed infrastructure is currently the largest in Europe, and second largest in the world (after China). Several new lines, including the controversial 'Y' shaped route to the Basque country, are currently under construction. By 2020 it is hoped to have a network of 9000km.

Regional rail services in Spain are only partly operated by Renfe, reflecting the asymmetric pattern of devolution within the country. Following the end of the highly centralised Franco regime, a process of devolution began which created self-governing regions in some parts of Spain, notably Catalonia and the Basque Country. However, Renfe continues to provide the overwhelming number of local and regional passenger services, as well as longer distance and AVE services.

In the Basque Country, partly on account of railway geography and politics, the Basque government has progressively taken over responsibility for the extensive metre-gauge network which centres on Bilbao and San Sebastian – the 'Euskotren' network. (This is different from the state-owned FEVE narrow-gauge network which also serves Bilbao but extends well beyond the Basque border.) Euskotren is a vertically integrated operation wholly owned by the Basque government, and it has invested heavily in upgrading what was formerly a decrepit network, with track doubling, new stations and new rolling stock (built by Basque manufacturer CAF). Euskotren also owns a fleet of buses which provide connections into the rail network. Several local rail services operated by Renfe, including the FEVE network, are now threatened with cuts by the Madrid government, but Euskotren is protected because it is completely owned by the devolved Basque government.[19]

In Catalonia the regional government contracts with Renfe for the provision of regional services, but it has also transferred some moribund Renfe local lines to regional control. Like the Basque government (and Valencia), it now owns the formerly independent (of Renfe) narrow-gauge lines; these are fully vertically integrated railways and are now doing very well.

FRANCE

Railways in France have been at the heart of political debate over liberalisation of the rail sector and everything else. Election of the Hollande Government in 2011 halted the process of liberalisation that had been gathering pace under the previous right-wing government.

The state-owned operator SNCF (formed from five private companies in 1938) has 1,850 km of designated high-speed track that accommodates more than eight hundred high-speed services per day. The SNCF's TGV trains carry more than 100 million passengers a year. Since 1997 the tracks and signalling have belonged to a separate government body, Réseau Ferré de France. RFF contracts all track maintenance and the operation of signalling to the SNCF, which also retains ownership of all the stations.

Since the early 2000s France has moved a considerable distance away from its highly centralised past. The emergence of regional councils as powerful devolved governments has had a major impact on regional rail, though the process has a long way to run. A total of twenty metropolitan regions (excluding Ile de France and Corsica, where separate arrangements apply) have responsibilities for regional passenger services (the TER network). They are federated into the association of regional transport authorities, GART. Currently, SNCF is the sole supplier of train services, contracted to each of the regional councils. The minimum length of contract is five years. Regional funding for rail – some 2 billion euros – mostly comes via central government sources devolved to regional councils. Infrastructure is managed by RFF. A feature of the French regional scene has been a significant investment in new rolling stock (built by Alstom). However, the quality of local and regional services remains very patchy.

During autumn 2011 a 'rail summit' (or 'Assises Ferroviares') took place in France, involving regional and local authorities, user groups, unions and operators. The objective was to look at the various problems facing the railway network, including future financing, freight, deregulation and the future of loss-making long distance services. One result of the summit, announced by the transport minister in December 2011, was that the loss-making longer distance services, currently operated by SNCF, would be opened up to competition. However in October 2012 the incoming socialist government announced a complete change of direction: according to transport minister Cuvillier, the system was dysfunctional and financially unsustainable.

SNCF and Deutsche Bahn have both pressed European policymakers not to force companies to separate rail infrastructure and operations, citing the spotty record of such efforts in the past twenty years. In 2012 the two companies released a report questioning the efficiency of separate operations, arguing that in countries with integrated rail operations – including the United States, Canada and Japan – there has been steady growth in investment and passenger or cargo traffic, in contrast to the sluggish European market: 'The results show that integrated management of infrastructure and train operations is not an obstacle to improving a railroad's efficiency and performance'.[20]

CENTRAL AND EASTERN EUROPE

The picture further east is if anything more complex, with some states retaining a traditional highly centralised approach with a single operator, whilst others have experimented with different models. In several countries lines have closed, as governments faced up to chronic under-investment in rail infrastructure during the 'socialist' era, or succumbed to a new-found faith in the private car.

In Poland, responsibility for local and regional passenger services now lies with sixteen regional councils (voivodships). Whilst the state operator PKP remains dominant in longer distance traffic, the regions jointly own their own railway company – PR ('Regional Railway'), which provides many of the local and regional services using the 'REGIO' brand. It also provides some longer distance services as InterREGIO and short distance international services as REGIOEkspress, with DB Regio. Funding for regional services comes partly via the state-run National Rail Fund as well as from local and regional taxation. In addition to PR, some foreign operators including Arriva have won some concessions, notably in the Kujarska-Pomorskie region. It is likely that more regional services will be opened up to external competition.

In the Czech Republic the reform of local and regional rail began in 2005, when fourteen regions were given extensive powers to support regional rail services. National operator České Dráhy (CD) remains predominant, providing services on a contract basis to the regional authorities. However in the Liberec region some services were put out to tender, with CD winning one and German independent Vogtlandbahn winning the other. Meanwhile Hungary is considering opening up some of its routes to private competition, following closure of some lines operated by state-owned MAV.

LESSONS FOR THE UK

The experience of reforming regional rail across Europe is enormously varied and it is clear that there is no single model that could be applied to the UK. We can learn from both the negative and positive features that exist.

Separation of infrastructure from operations is common to nearly all the examples outlined above, though this has happened to varying degrees. The policy of the EU continues to be strongly in favour of this separation, but many observers (and not necessarily those with a vested commercial interest) in Germany, France and the Netherlands (as well as the UK) are opposed to the process, arguing that it has introduced additional costs and inefficiencies to the rail network.

Chris Nash has argued that overall the results have been largely positive, but adds a note of caution:

> Further liberalisation of passenger services remains a controversial issue. As we have seen, the experience to date of both competition in the market and competition for the market is not entirely posi-

tive. Competitive tendering seems generally to have worked well as a way of delivering services tightly prescribed by franchising bodies on gross cost contracts, but has had more difficulties where – as in Britain and Australia – operators are expected to bear revenue risk and to take at least some of the initiatives in developing services. On the other hand, simple open access for commercial services is also found to have disadvantages. A cautious approach is therefore justified, but further research to identify the best way of opening up the rail passenger market to competitive pressure is urgently needed.[22]

The experience in the UK would suggest that if there is to be separation, it is of vital importance that train operators and infrastructure management work together closely, with shared control centres and other integrated networks. To an extent this already happens in the UK, and the devolved arrangements have worked reasonably well. Network Rail in Scotland, for example, provides a degree of synergy with the main operator, ScotRail. However, there is scope for further integration and this is discussed below.

A very clear feature of most of the railways studied is the separation of regional from longer distance services. This is a quite rigid separation in countries such as Sweden, France, Denmark and Germany, and this has brought considerable benefits particularly though the consequent strong management focus on regional rail services, and capability of working closely with regional and local authorities. The alternative, where all rail operations come under a single command (e.g. Belgium, and, in an earlier period, Germany, France, Sweden) suggests that in a centralised system regional rail suffers from a lack of both management and political attention.

A significant down-side of European railway liberalisation, seen in a number of countries, has been the inability of different operators to collaborate on through ticketing, with many smaller operators offering tickets that are only valid on their own networks. One of the sensible decisions of the architects of BR privatisation was to create the Rail Settlement Plan, which underpins the current system of inter-available tickets.

Some European countries – notably Sweden, Netherlands and Germany – have tendered quite small networks with some positive results, particularly in respect of transport integration. However, some commentators have suggested that this can lead to inefficiencies and duplication, particularly where what are essentially regional passenger services cross regional boundaries. Starting from scratch, the aim should be to identify sensible boundaries that have a political, economic and even 'cultural' meaning.

Whilst Switzerland is an outstanding example of how a decentralised railway can deliver excellent, integrated services, it is based on a very different political system.

Malcolm Bulpitt argues that the UK's top-down system of government, whereby Westminster basically controls every aspect of local government expenditure, means that major local investment in railways such as seen in the Swiss system will probably never get off the ground. He also believes that the arcane systems set up under UK rail privatisation work against most local initiatives to upgrade services, especially rolling-stock provision:

> The combination of the dead hand of the Treasury, and the apparent unwillingness of the leasing companies to countenance new equipment, means that under the current system we will probably never see the sort of investment in modern trains for local routes that is common in Switzerland. Our system depends upon the sort of local services that the Swiss see as essential to invest in having to make-do with hand-me-down units from other operations.[23]

I wouldn't be quite so pessimistic, but there is clearly a direct relationship between strong regional and local democracy and good public transport, which the Swiss have taken to dizzy heights.

Europe's obsession with franchising has not been universal. Apart from non-EU Switzerland, several German authorities prefer the system of direct procurement with a favoured operator, similar to the position in France, although in the German case there is only one provider. If the procurement authority understands the market, and the costs of providing rail services, this approach can work. However, it raises the question of why, if a regional authority is to have a preferred operator, it should not set up its own arms-length operating company, where it will enjoy complete control and accountability. This is the model used in the Basque Country, which owns its operator Euskotren.

A further problem with franchising, in both the UK and other

European countries, is the inherent instability of the system. Railways – at every level, including customers and employees – need long-term stability. Investment horizons are long, with the life of a typical train being up to thirty years. Franchising, whilst it may offer some degree of accountability, does not deliver stability, and can lead to serious problems in the hand-over from one operator to another – as in the experience with DSB First in Denmark. (In the UK this has tended not to happen.)

However, the much-vaunted advantages of franchising in bringing costs down have yet to be demonstrated in Britain, in contrast to Germany and Sweden. Why is this? Possibly the strongest argument would be that BR had already radically pruned its operations in the 1990s, driving out many of the inefficiencies which continued in the continental railways well into the 2000s. When privatisation came to the UK in 1994, there were very few inefficiencies to be addressed, as BR had largely successfully eliminated them.

Germany, France, Italy and Spain have developed strong and expanding state-owned inter-city businesses, which have trounced domestic airlines. Regional services in Germany are excellent, but they are patchy in France, Italy and Spain. Meanwhile, the debate over vertical separation continues and is likely to intensify. Hylén claims that for on-track competition on fully commercial terms you need a big country *and* a big population. We find this in the UK, France, Italy, Germany, Poland and perhaps Spain. Belgium, the Netherlands, Switzerland, Denmark and Sweden do not meet these criteria.

A report for the Community of European Railway and Infrastructure Companies (CER) concluded:

We find no evidence that vertical separation increases competition compared with a holding company model and likewise none that such increased competition would reduce costs. Nor do we find any evidence that vertical separation improves rail's modal share compared with a holding company model (although it does improve passenger market share when combined with market opening compared with vertical integration). For freight, there is no evidence that if it did increase competition, this would improve market share. A decision to impose vertical separation throughout Europe would raise costs by at least €5.8 billion [per] year for no accompanying benefits … Our overall conclusion must therefore be that there is no evidence to support implementation of a single structure on all railways regardless of their circumstances.[24]

There is a final irony to this story of European rail development. We have seen successful bids for UK franchises by several European state-owned operators (DB, SNCF and NS) and expressions of interest from Renfe (Spain) and DSB (Denmark). However, many of these 'foreign adventures' have been sharply criticised at home, with both DB and NS being accused of taking their eye off the ball, and giving excessive management attention to winning lucrative foreign bids whilst neglecting services at home. Further, it has been suggested that some of the state-owned operators are abusing their dominant position at home by putting in very low bids for competitive tenders. The reality is that however you structure a competitive framework for delivering rail services you run the risk of unintended consequences, some of which could be the very opposite of what its promoters intended.

NOTES

1. Malcolm Bulpitt, Swiss Railway Society, private email to author April 2013.
2. Part of this chapter is based on Paul Salveson, *Regional Rail in Europe*, study for HITRANS, 2012.
3. A particularly useful source for information on regional rail across Europe is *Regional Rail Passenger Transport in Europe*, edited by L. Sippel and T. Mayer and published with the assistance of the German association of passenger rail authorities (BAG-SPNV) and the Inter-Regio project.
4. I. Lundin, communication to author, January 2013.
5. C. Nash, *European Rail Reform – The Next Steps*, 2011. The legislation comprising the First Railway Package is contained within three directives – Directives 2001/12; 2001/13; and 2001/14.
6. Local historian Martin Bairstow, author of *Mallorca Railways*, has pointed out that there have also been some fiascos on the way. 'Devolved government may be quite good at lobbying central government for funds but it is no good at project management. If they don't employ anyone with industry experience, they are just putty in the hands of manufacturers and contractors'. Private email to author, 29.1.13.
7. See Gunnar Alexandersson, *The Accidental Deregulation*, 2010.
8. J-E Nilsson, 'Re-shaping Sweden's Railways – The Unintentional Deregulation', *Swedish Economic Policy Review*, no. 9, 2002.

9. See Bertil Hylen, *Public Transport in Sweden – Deregulation and Intermodal Integration*, VTI (Sweden) 2011.
10. Nilsson, op cit.
11. See Philip Groves, 'The Inlandsbanan', *Today's Railways Europe*, May 2013.
12. I am indebted to Malcolm Bulpitt of the Swiss Railway Society for much of the information in this section.
13. Ibid.
14. See Paul Salveson, *Getting the best from bus and rail in rural communities*, Huddersfield 1999.
15. Bertil Hylen, *Germany and De-regulation of its Railways*, Stockholm 2011.
16. Ibid.
17. Ibid.
18. Private email to author January 2012.
19. See *Today's Railways Europe*, May 2013 news report.
20. Andreas Schwilling, a partner at the Roland Berger Strategy Consultants in Munich, which conducted the study. Other railway observers have commented 'they would say that, wouldn't they?'!
21. Private email to author, January 2013.
22. C. Nash, op cit.
23. Private email to author, January 2013.
24. Community of European Railways, Brussels 2013. CER is in effect the mouthpiece of the major state-owned railways in Europe.

10. RADICAL ALTERNATIVES

I believe that there are alternatives to the current system that could help deliver some of the initiatives suggested in previous chapters. A centre-left government could develop a radical but deliverable policy for rail that would be electorally popular, deliver a better transport system and save money. Furthermore, this would not involve a total revolution in structure; it would be more a case of substantial reform. This chapter explores a number of feasible options that could deliver a growing railway and offer value for money alongside quality.

Currently, there are far too many centres of power, and too many overlapping and ill-defined areas of responsibility, and these lead to an inability to progress projects, a demotivated workforce, and higher costs. It has become abundantly clear that the franchising system has not delivered a better railway and has added to costs.

Though forms of franchising are common on the regional networks of other European countries, they are in general contracted to regional governments on a concession basis: the public body simply pays an operator to deliver a service at an agreed price, itself taking on the commercial risk. And in many cases, it is the regional authority, not a profit-hungry leasing company, that owns the rolling stock. This makes for a more accountable and efficient process. But even this approach can be costly: the private operator, typically one of the big multi-national transport groups, still wants a profit; and passengers – as well as employees – still live with the consequences of instability because of short-term franchises; while concessions need managing as much as any other franchise, thereby pushing up costs, and there is no incentive for the operator to generate new traffic.

Public opinion polls about the desirability of re-nationalising the railways show a consistently high level of support. This demonstrates not so much a desire for a particular model of public ownership, more a wish to see a railway that is better integrated, more affordable, and run primarily to meet the needs of the country rather than shareholders.

CREATING STABILITY, GROWTH AND INVESTMENT

Experience in Britain and continental Europe suggests that railway services flourish best with relatively small and focused management units – possibly sharing some overheads with others – within a framework of long-term stability and democratic accountability. Furthermore, public or socially-owned train companies can be every bit as enterprising (possibly more so) as wholly private companies. The challenge is to find an approach which fits with the existing UK rail industry structure, so that a costly and disruptive re-organisation is avoided. The starting point is getting the right objectives for rail in the UK, not an ideological fixation on private versus public. We need a railway which:

underpins economic regeneration and supports a growing economy based on the principles of sustainable development, while offering quality services (passenger and freight) at an affordable cost to the nation

meets the needs of all sections of the community, providing an affordable and accessible form of transport across the UK

is accountable and responsive to the wider community, including its customers and funders

forms the core of a co-ordinated transport network and is fully integrated with local, regional and national spatial planning policies

provides quality employment and maximises opportunities to involve its work force at all levels

supports an expanding manufacturing industry backed up by high-quality research and development expertise

is able to innovate and to both drive and respond to market opportunities and technical change.

THE ALTERNATIVES

Few would argue that the present arrangements in the UK are ideal: the present system is costly, confusing and inefficient. As we have seen in previous chapters, there are a number of alternative ways to run the railways. Drawing on these examples and experiences, it is possible to draw up a range of possibilities for an alternative system – many of which are capable of delivering the objectives outlined above. These are discussed and evaluated below.

Modest reform of franchising through implementation of the 'Brown Review' recommendations

Many people within the railway industry take a pragmatic view that reforming the existing system is the most sensible way forward, offering minimal disruption; they argue that any re-organisation, however well-intentioned, can have negative impacts and costs. The review of rail franchising undertaken by Richard Brown in 2012 ('the Brown Review') suggested a modest tweaking of the system, involving short and simpler franchises that are easier to manage and monitor.[1] However, this does not address some of the deep-seated problems with franchising, including high overall cost, both in evaluating franchise bids and the cost of the contracts; inherent instability; short-termism; and lack of buy-in from staff – amongst several other issues.

The British system of franchising, with notable exceptions, gives a level of risk to the franchisee: in return they can make a lot of money if they win new business. However some franchises have collapsed – because of the economic downturn, or because they got their sums wrong (notably East Coast). Some have suggested having longer franchises, to give greater stability and make investment more likely, but this exposes the fundamental contradiction of franchising: the disadvantage of long franchises is that there is a real risk of a franchisee getting into financial trouble and having to be bailed out by the state; while the disadvantage of short-term franchises – which are back in favour and to some extent avoid that problem – are lack of stability and all the negative aspects of short-termism.

Furthermore, the 'modest reform' approach does nothing to address the outflow of profits to shareholders, of whom an increasing number are state-owned railways operating abroad. And existing franchisees have shown little or no interest in co-ordinating their services with those of bus operators – though there are some notable exceptions. And they have also proved reluctant to involve their employees in any meaningful way: pay rates tend to be based on market conditions, with well-paid workers in some sectors and very poorly-paid staff in others.

This approach therefore is too timid, and entirely fails to address some of the major problems with the current system.

Reforming franchising to make them into concessions

The London model of management contracts (see chapter four, p61) has much to recommend it; it has a clear allocation of responsibilities between public specifier and private provider. In essence the public body specifies the outputs it wants from the railway company, and private (or for that matter socially-owned) operators bid for the right to run the services to this clearly-defined specification. Within the tender price for the contract each bidder will include an element for the profit they want to make. The duration of the franchise becomes less of an issue, as the risk is clearly 'owned' by the public body, so that whether revenues rise or fall, the operator is still paid to provide the service, while all revenue goes back to the public body once their contractual obligations have been satisfied. This is also broadly the model for Merseyrail.

However there are still problems. The franchise, or concession, still needs careful monitoring, and even with a long contract (as with Merseyrail) there has been a degree of instability in the system. Moreover, the economic success of Merseyrail has resulted in profits going to Serco and its Dutch Rail co-shareholders. (One Dutch Railways senior manager told me that he found the British system of franchising 'crazy': he couldn't understand how we tolerated a system which basically handed over large profits to Dutch Railways.[2])

This system is in general better suited to a highly concentrated network such as London. And while management contracts offer some improvements over the existing system, they do not bring sufficient benefits to address some of the more deep-seated problems facing the industry

The 'back to BR option' – a vertically-integrated railway (either state or private)

There would be some advantages in going back to the old British Rail system of a single organisation with a much greater degree of vertical integration between operations and infrastructure. There are also many ways of achieving this: one approach would be to re-constitute the current Network Rail organisation as the new BR, with operations as well as infrastructure coming under its wing. Network Rail is already structured as a not-for-dividend company, and it would be possible to maintain this role as an arms-length company without shareholders, but effectively controlled by government through a mix of funding and regulation. The question of rolling stock would remain but could be resolved by placing a cap on leasing companies' profits – or by outright nationalisation.

However, a return to a British Rail model would be immensely difficult and complicated, and could risk losing the positive momentum that rail has now achieved. It would also require a degree of political radicalism – something that is missing in the current main political parties. In the immortal words of Gerry Fiennes, one-time general manager of BR's Western Region: 'When we re-organise, we bleed'.[3] The BR option would be likely to be a bloodbath.

One of the achievements of privatisation in some areas has been to bring a degree of dynamism and market focus, especially in relatively small franchise areas; and going back to a centralised BR, with a bureaucratic management subject to the constraints of the Treasury, would risk losing those gains. It would certainly be possible to create devolved management units within a national system, on a functional or geographical basis, but these would always be subject to re-organisation and the centre taking back control. This is what happened to BR after its early days with strong semi-autonomous regions, and it has happened more recently with Railtrack.

There are other major issues. BR was the creature of a unified United Kingdom, and was based at a central headquarters in London. The UK of today looks very different, with Scotland and Wales having devolved governments. Scotland has substantial control over its domestic rail services and Wales is moving in a similar direction. It is unlikely that governments in either Edinburgh or Cardiff would be willing to cede power back to a central railway administration in London.

In addition, the separation of infrastructure from operations – and the creation of Network Rail as infrastructure manager – has led, albeit more slowly than anyone would have liked, to a welcome focus on the investment needs of the network. This is helped by Network

Rail not being directly subject to the whims of the Treasury, and thus able to plan for the long-term.

In conclusion, although the structure is far from perfect, it would be a massive risk to throw the whole thing up into the air and start again from scratch – as this option would involve.

A single state-owned operator providing contracted services

This model is essentially the arrangement in France today (see chapter nine, p176). SNCF is, with some very minor local exceptions, the only train operator, and the – increasingly powerful – provincial councils contract with it to provide services at a negotiated price. Whilst the absence of competition may seem to give SNCF a major advantage, the reality is that the regions have been able to negotiate mutually acceptable prices for good quality services. This model was the direction in which BR was heading prior to privatisation, with increasingly close co-operation with the metropolitan passenger transport executives. It would encourage economies of scale, including for depot facilities, general overheads and other resources, whilst allowing for a management unit to have considerable autonomy in terms of running the regional operation. However, the big disadvantage would be that it would probably lead to the creation of an unwieldy central bureaucracy, which would run the risk of inertia and/or being too closely tied to Treasury constraints.

The conversion of existing franchises into publicly owned and accountable 'arms-length' businesses

One approach that would avoid the turmoil involved in a re-integration of the industry under single unified control would be either to progressively take the existing franchises back into public ownership, or to re-constitute them as arms-length social enterprises. Network Rail would continue as infrastructure owner and manager, with co-operation continuing to develop with operators. Train operators could be managed or owned by the devolved governments of Scotland, Wales, London and other English regional consortia (such as the embryonic Rail in the North Executive). The Department for Transport would have responsibility for InterCity services.

However, it should be noted that the financial gains to franchisees would not be very big. As we have seen, the really big money is being earned by the rolling stock leasing companies. Having said that, capping ROSCO profits, or taking them into public ownership, is compatible with this option, as with others.

The German model

This is a development of the preceding option, and would involve a single national InterCity service, while regional networks would be run on behalf of devolved governments and regional consortia of local authorities as well as regional networks (see chapter nine, p168 for more on the German system). This model allows the devolution of regional and local services to localities, while recognising that the InterCity network needs a degree of centralised management and marketing.

The structure for this model already exists in the UK, in the form of the state-owned Directly Operated Railways, which are basically shell public companies with a minimal core staffing; these could be expanded to take on the running of a failed franchise. This is what has happened with East Coast, which is being managed by DOR prior to being handed back to the private sector at the behest of the Coalition government. A further 'sub-option' would be for 'InterCity UK' to be a 50-50 public/private venture, which might bring in additional investment if the partnership was for a sufficiently long period (a minimum of twenty years).

In either of these scenarios, as franchises came up for renewal they would not be re-tendered but would be re-integrated into a single InterCity UK. Local and regional services (including those currently within combined InterCity and local franchises, e.g. Great Western) would be constituted into regional operations with a high degree of local input.

Here it should be noted that there is no fundamental reason why regional franchises should not be re-structured as licences. These would be subject to periodic review but not necessarily to a compulsory tendering competition at specified intervals. If performance is good, why have to go through the turmoil and cost of a new competition? This system is not good for passengers, employees or the wider public interest.

This option is not far from the German approach, where there is a single state-owned InterCity operation and a large number (possibly too many) of regional networks that are the responsibility of the Länd governments. Some are publicly owned, some are private concessions. The German approach is quite liberalised, though not as much as in the UK: there are clear lines of responsibility, with the federal government having responsibility for developing the national InterCity/high-speed network and the regions having lead responsibility for local and regional networks. One major disadvantage of this approach in Germany, as noted in chapter nine, is the lack of joint ticketing arrangements between operators.

The Japanese model

This was a late addition to the options being considered for this book, and was suggested by colleagues in the railway industry who have seen the success of the privatised Japanese railways. In Japan, a number of vertically integrated, privately owned passenger railways operate in a given area for both local and intercity trains, with nationwide track access rights for freight, plus some locally managed commuter lines. In addition to the main railways, there is a network of small independent railways that are locally owned and in many cases financed by Japan's network of regional banks.

The system has some attractions, but a key problem in the UK context would be its lack of public accountability, and the risk that some of the secondary lines that are part of the core railway could suffer from lack of management attention. The evolving political structure of the UK also militates against the Japanese model, narrowly interpreted: it would not be able to encompass devolution and the current development of regional rail bodies.

However, in some areas, particularly Scotland, there could be scope for a different approach, with a largely vertically integrated ScotRail taking on infrastructure as well as operational responsibilities for the domestic rail network. This could be either wholly public, private or a joint venture.

A MUTUAL APPROACH

A further principle – and one that is central to my thinking on the way forward – is the development of a new model of social enterprise for the railway industry, based on mutual principles. This is a business model that has worked in many other sectors, and could deliver a high-quality, value-for-money rail service. Stuart Cole has argued that a co-operative train company would have many advantages over a conventional for-dividend company:

> A co-operative business could be expected to give a greater sense of collective ethos, which would help the industry through difficult times.
>
> Staff absences could be expected to be lower than other forms of business structures, as is claimed by the John Lewis Partnership.
>
> Many of the complaints about rail companies might disappear if the passenger felt a direct ownership. Of course, the last time the railways were in public ownership that didn't happen, though that might have been because, in effect, the British Rail model was no different from a conventional private company.
>
> It would help persuade travellers that the railway really was being run for their benefit and might remove the 'them and us' perception'.[4]

Such a mutual approach, building on the existing structure of the railways but bringing a more co-ordinated model, offers the best way forward for the industry. Several bus companies in the UK are already run as arms-length not-for-dividend companies, including Swindon-based Thamesdown Transport, which recently won the award for 'Britain's best bus operator'. Cardiff Bus is owned by the local authorities, and Hackney Community Transport is now running TfL bus routes and operations as widespread as Yorkshire and the Channel Islands.

The most appropriate model could be the simplest – the company limited by guarantee. This involves active involvement of both workers and users of a service, with clear lines of accountability to a board of directors. Any profit (surplus) is channelled back into the company. Most community transport operations are set up on this basis, some now having a turnover in excess of £1 million per annum. They are highly successful enterprises and have not been unduly hamstrung by their not-for-profit status. They are motivated by ethical and social rather than commercial goals – those of providing a valued public service that is accessible for all. There is absolutely no reason why the same approach could not work with a railway company, large or small.

THE WAY FORWARD

Drawing on these examples and principles, I believe that the way forward lies in retaining the current separation of track and operations, while gradually reforming the organisational structure of Network Rail, and taking franchised mainline operations back into public ownership as they come up for renewal. A new InterCity organisation would be responsible for the major routes and be run from a national centre, while regional railways would be increasingly subject to the control of local democratic bodies. And in order to co-ordinate all the different elements within the industry a Strategic Rail Agency should be set up. I develop these proposals in more detail below.

Creating a 'guiding mind' – a Strategic Rail Agency

A problem with the existing rail industry in the UK is that it lacks a strategic body that can steer Britain's railways in a clear direction with a long-term planning horizon. Currently, the Department for Transport, Office of Rail Regulation, Railway Safety and Standards Board, devolved governments and Network Rail often pull against each other, with the result that progress is stymied. There is a need for a new, over-arching body that would provide strategic direction to the industry as a whole, taking over most of the rail responsibilities of the Department for Transport plus the functions of The Railway Safety and Standards Board and Office of Rail Regulation. A Strategic Rail Agency should take over the role of the existing, operator-based Railway Development Group, and should be at a distance from ministers. A key part of its role would be to translate government strategic objectives into effective industry strategies and plans.

The proposed agency should have a number of divisions, including research (involving universities with specialist expertise), high-speed rail development, safety, standards and licensing, rolling stock, intercity (currently Directly Operated Railways), freight development and regional passenger. The culture of the SRA would be such as to encourage innovation and fresh thinking, co-operative working, crossing departmental boundaries and partnerships with external bodies.

The Strategic Rail Agency's governance should be based on a board with a small number of representatives from the Department for

Transport, Scottish and Welsh governments and English regional consortia, and an executive board of highly experienced railway specialists who understand rail's wider social and environmental context. It should also include a stakeholder board to give a strong input to passengers, employees and the wider community, whilst keeping Passenger Focus as an independent consumer watch-dog.

The SRA should manage franchises until they come up for renewal, at which point they would be transferred into social ownership. In this scenario, the agency would develop, via its Intercity division, a strategic network of routes, but would leave regional services to devolved governments (Scotland, Wales and the English regions). However, it could also have an equivalent of DB's 'Regio' management unit, which could offer directly-operated regional rail services to those regions that prefer that approach (similar to the French model).

The agency should encourage freight development through research, grants and infrastructure facilities, as well as providing a more favourable playing field in terms of tax incentives to rail or 'inter-modal' freight operators.

Network Rail

Whilst Network Rail already owns and manages the national rail infrastructure, and is set up as a not-for-dividend company, it has little direct accountability either to government or the public – let alone its employees. It also has a huge debt – around £28 billion – which is an enormous risk to the future stability of the rail network.[5] Whilst there are strong arguments for bringing it back into the public sector as a division of the SRA, there are even more compelling arguments for keeping it at arms-length from government, though with a better form of governance, as discussed below. It would work best as a mutually owned company with a remit to work even more closely with industry partners, and with clear lines of responsibility to replace the current chaotic mess. Network Rail's job should be to deliver the outputs, not to decide what they should be.

Network Rail's role should be to ensure high standards of efficiency and bring more activities in-house, so that excess profits are no longer funnelled into sub-contractors' pockets. Surpluses and savings made by the infrastructure body would go back into the industry, in order to deliver ever-higher maintenance and safety standards. It needs to concentrate on what it does well, which is managing and developing the infrastructure, over a long investment horizon. It should also work closely with train operators who have a shared vision of a railway that is run to meet wider social and economic objectives, rather than the narrow interests of shareholders.

There is a need to incentivise the employees who are currently part of Network Rail, and to give them a real say in how the industry is run, while ensuring that senior managers and directors are accountable and are not paid huge bonuses. We need to get away from the idea you only get good leaders if you have large bonus incentives. You don't. You get people who are in it solely for the money. The existing directors should be given the option of leaving or taking a salary which is based on top rates of pay in the public sector. Lord Berkeley, a public member of Network Rail, has already argued for a mutual option: 'I think it is time to consider a new governance structure as a mutual, with members (or governors) elected by groups of people who are stakeholders – such as passengers and employees – in a similar manner to hospital foundation trusts'.[6]

The Co-operative Party's proposals for Network Rail, which would involve turning it into a consumer-mutual, build on Lord Berkeley's comments. However, the suggestion that all passengers should be able to become members of a Network Rail mutual miss the point about what Network Rail is for, which is to manage and develop the railway infrastructure. It is essentially an engineering company, carrying out often complex and highly skilled projects. It is not a passenger-facing business – though that is not to say it shouldn't be aware of passenger and wider social needs, in terms of accessibility, station facilities and so on. Whilst a consumer-mutual offers an excellent model for a not-for-dividend passenger train company, it is not suitable for Network Rail. A form of governance in which employees are the members would provide a much clearer and focused structure – harking back to the early days of workers' control, but in a much more business-oriented environment. Network Rail's employee profile is overwhelmingly professional, highly-educated and committed. They are exactly the sort of people that Tom Nixton and John Benstead praised in the 1940s – the 'inventive geniuses' whose contribution has never been sufficiently exploited or recognised.

The arguments for and against taking Network Rail into state ownership hinge largely on finance, and giving the company access to cheaper money. However, a disadvantage of renationalisation would be a return to Treasury rules. As one former TOC managing director commented: 'The fact that Network Rail's borrowing is effectively underwritten by government guarantee means they can borrow very cheaply. So it seems to me to be the best of all worlds. When it was a PLC it became too focused on returning dividend to shareholders'.

Bringing Network Rail fully into public ownership would add very substantial sums to the public debt, given that its debt is currently running at £28 billion. However it could cut the cost of servicing the debt, currently around £1.5 billion each year.[7] The authors of *Rebuilding Rail* make the point that this is essentially a political issue: if the whole of Network Rail was structured as a mutual and its debt was transferred into the public sector balance, savings of £156 million a year would ensue, because of the government's superior credit rating. However, in my view it should be possible to reduce the cost of servicing the debt whilst keeping Network Rail off the public sector balance sheet. Of course it is also true, as Taylor and Sloman argue, that 'regardless of how railways are managed in the future, Network Rail's debt is utterly unsustainable for the future of the railway and will have to be shouldered by government eventually'.[8] But to re-nationalise Network Rail would be to use a sledge-hammer to crack a nut, and would run the risk of jeopardising many of the improvements that the company has made in the last few years; and it could also lead to a loss of managerial talent within the company. One Network Rail manager told me that there would be a 'rush to the door by the brightest and the best' if this happened. Network Rail is now winning an international reputation for innovation, efficiency and expertise, and is generally viewed pretty positively amongst railway people, but most of those responsible for these improvements are unlikely to want to stay on for BR Mark 2. This colleague could see advantages in a move towards a more mutual status, which 'could serve to curb silly bonuses', but is dubious about state control, 'given that, frankly, Network Rail is a lot brighter than the DfT'.[9]

This raises the question of what form of mutual governance Network Rail might take. There are arguments for a multi-stakeholder form (i.e. representation of local and regional public bodies, train operators, passengers, etc), which the mutual approach can allow for, but this runs the risk of a weak board, riven with different agendas. An employee-owned Network Rail, on the other hand, would be able to harness the great talent that exists within the company, and ensure a very clear focus on delivering a top-class railway infrastructure. It would also ensure a clear interface between Network Rail, government (via the SRA) and operators, whilst allowing for much greater collaboration in actual delivery.

The operators: InterCity UK

There is a core national network that was formerly the BR InterCity sector and is now divided into several franchises with different rolling stock, different marketing strategies and different pay and conditions for employees. The UK needs a single InterCity operation which connects all the main centres of the country. We had it under BR and it worked: in fact many other European operators copied the idea and you can see it today, operating superbly, in Germany, France, Sweden and many other parts of Europe.

There already exists the organisational infrastructure to bring this about. As we have seen, the government has its own operation called Directly Owned Railways – the ironically-titled 'operator of last resort'. This body currently runs East Coast, a major part of the national network. If it hadn't been politically embarrassing it would also have been given West Coast, effectively putting a majority of the main InterCity network in public ownership. DOR should become the basis of an Intercity UK division, to be run as an arms-length mutually-owned company; this would have a representative governance structure that would include not only government (Department for Transport, devolved governments for Scotland and Wales) but also employees and passengers. This is where the proposals of the Co-operative Party ('People's Rail') come into their own – the creation of a mutual company, operating as a not-for-dividend business, which could combine entrepreneurial flair with quality of service and accountability.

Unfortunately, if the development of a new InterCity organisation is made dependent on taking back franchises as they come up for renewal, the East Coast operation – the success story of DOR – could be one of the last parts of the jigsaw to come into the new body, given that it may soon be back in the private sector. However, the West Coast situation may remain unresolved at a point when a Labour government is able to set up the new body, which means it could be added into the new portfolio; the same could be done with Great Western, which is due for renewal in 2015. Midland Main Line (currently part of East Midlands Trains' franchise) and CrossCountry (currently operated by German state-owned Arriva) could then be included when those franchises expire.

The InterCity UK network should grow into five co-ordinated but devolved business units, each with their own focused management teams reporting to a central strategic team. These would be: West Coast (including Manchester–Scotland); East Coast; Great Western (London–Swansea/Penzance); Cross Country; and Midland Main Line.

A new InterCity UK should not, however, think of the existing InterCity network as immutable. An advantage of having a single overall business is that there would be opportunities to develop new routes beyond the existing network – something that is very difficult in the existing network. And there is plenty of scope to develop the network further, focusing on the long distance journey market. This could lead to some routes – such as Manchester/Liverpool–Edinburgh/Glasgow – forming part of the InterCity UK network, as part of CrossCountry. Large towns or cities currently not served by the InterCity network would be considered for inclusion, with the expectation of a minimum number of services each day to complement the regional routes. It probably makes sense for some 'InterCity' routes to form the core of a regional network, notably London–Norwich and London–Bournemouth/Weymouth. Thus, for example, London–Norwich would become the premier offering of a Great Eastern operation that operated beyond the core London outer suburban network (the latter would form part of a re-constituted Network SouthEast business based on an expanded London Overground).

Such a new system should not be concerned about open access operators. Where they can plug gaps in the InterCity market – for example for larger towns and cities such as Sunderland, Bradford, Halifax, Barrow, Blackburn and elsewhere – they should be encouraged (see below). They would also provide an element of competition to larger operators, thereby encouraging innovation and new thinking.

The regional networks

Great gains are to be made from reforming the regional networks, which currently swallow up a lot of public support, and which are –

with boring regularity – subject to whispering campaigns within government about 'poor value for money'. It doesn't make any sense for the detail of local rail operations to be managed by civil servants in London. Nobody would suggest that bus services should be tendered by the Department for Transport (DfT) – and the same applies with the detail of local and regional services.

The proposed Strategic Rail Agency would take over much of the DfT's role, and could assist in providing basic ground rules, agreed by ministers, for how regional services should be delivered; it should then give regional bodies the money and let them get on with it – and if possible improve on the basic specification. This is much as happens now with Merseyrail and London Overground Ltd.

Structures for delivering transport in the regions are currently changing, and the combined authority approach may be more widely adopted. Here the experience of the metropolitan passenger transport executives and their political overseers in the Integrated Transport Authorities (ITAs) will be invaluable. But transport for the English regions must not ignore the needs of less urbanised areas and – particularly for rail – there should also be strategic authorities that involve the shires. The embryonic consortium of local authorities in the North of England is currently developing an inclusive approach to these considerations, involving partners in the North; and complementary work is also being led by West Midlands PTE, involving neighbouring shire and unitary authorities. Similar bodies will be required elsewhere in the regions. Ultimately, the best approach would be the constitution of region-wide transport authorities that are accountable to democratically elected regional assemblies.[10] However, operating units/concessions would not have to be the same size as the regional authority.[11]

If we were to move away from the current approach of franchising, and towards an approach that is more focused on community needs, a future regional rail network would need to be based on a number of considerations. Firstly, there would need to be a big enough bundle of train services and routes to justify basic overheads – including depot facilities (possibly leased and possibly shared with other operators) – but they should not be so big as to be unwieldy. Second, there would need to be synergy with local and regional government and development agency boundaries (here the emerging city-regions offer the right scale). Third, they should also be able to work across administrative boundaries so that rail services would reflect market needs rather than institutional constraints and barriers. Fourth, there should be a presumption in favour of not-for-dividend train operators that are responsive to community needs and offer value for money, keeping profits within the operation.

There are different ways of delivering such a system, as we saw in chapter nine. One approach would be to create new mutual companies along the lines of Northern Railways and Rail Cymru, which would have strong local roots. However, not every part of the UK would necessarily want to pursue this approach, and there could also be, alongside 'InterCity UK', a regional operation that sits within the Strategic Rail Agency's portfolio of operations ('SRA Regio'!). This could contract with a regional consortium of local authorities, or a devolved government, to provide local and regional services to an agreed specification.

A further option would be for a regional transport authority (such as the emergent consortia of Northern England authorities and similar bodies in the Midlands) to invite bids for the operation of a long-term concession from not-for-dividend companies. This chimes most easily with the current EU proposals, and could help stimulate a new generation of transport-based social enterprises. Bids could be from new mutuals or from existing social enterprises with the right expertise and substance (e.g. larger community transport operators). A further option would be for the commissioning body – whether DfT, devolved government or a regional consortium – to encourage a consortium formed from social enterprises with a mix of business expertise.

For this approach to succeed, the currently massive barriers to entry (an average bid in the UK costs around £10 million) must be removed. How such a company might work is explored further in chapter eleven.

The local railway

In chapter seven we looked at the sustainable branch line concept, which takes a holistic approach towards developing integrated local transport for a discrete network. The best – indeed probably only – way to achieve a truly sustainable branch line is through local management and control, though the extent of that can and will vary. The management team should be small, with a general manager answerable to the board of directors (trustees) and such other staff as appropriate.

The most suitable model will vary, though the most practicable approach in the short term would be a partnership between a local social enterprise and an established train operating company, which could provide safety-critical staff who would work alongside commercial and other staff employed by the local social enterprise. In this scenario, the local company may not be the actual operator: that could be a licensed train operating company that covers a wider area. However, it would have core responsibility for the local railway service and wider business activities outlined below. The licensed train operator would effectively be a partner in a wider enterprise, managed by a new entity – the local sustainable transport company. The LSTC would be responsible for a wide range of activities, but at their core would be a fully co-ordinated local transport network that maximises the benefits of bus and rail.

There is also scope for bringing in new entrants to provide some of the services that would be co-ordinated by the LSTC. But whatever model is adopted should be within the framework of a structure that involves key stakeholders both within the community and the parent train operating company. The mutual company limited by guarantee model, as applied to a local railway or wider transport operation, offers considerable advantages in terms of winning community support, involving a wide range of partners, and access to funding. For a more extended discussion on sustainable branch lines see chapter seven.

The Welsh and Scottish dimensions

An obvious place for community railway to start is Wales, which has a Labour government and a franchise which expires in 2018. The political will is already there: Welsh Labour is currently looking at the feasibility of the Wales and Borders rail franchise being run on a not-for-dividend basis, including using cooperative or social enterprise models.[12] Stuart Cole, based at the University of South Wales, has put forward a number of options for a future rail operation in Wales, and these have relevance for all parts of the UK, including a 'franchised co-operative company', to be owned by the employees or the passengers or some combination of the two.[13]

In Scotland, after a lengthy public consultation during 2012, the SNP-led government has called for legislative changes that would allow the ScotRail franchise to be publicly owned in the future. Alex

Neil, Scotland's infrastructure and capital investment secretary, wrote to transport secretary Justine Greening describing it as 'perverse and verging on the ridiculous' that state-owned rail operators from Europe can bid for UK rail franchises while home-based public bodies cannot.[14]

For the Welsh and Scottish governments to go beyond the current franchise lottery, they need to negotiate some significant changes in their relationships with the Department for Transport that are unlikely to be agreed by the current Westminster government.

The rolling stock challenge

The high cost of leasing rolling stock is one of the biggest stumbling blocks to expanding rail services. One suggestion put forward by Lynn Sloman in *Rebuilding Rail* is for a cap on charges for existing rolling stock (based on an evaluation of a fair price), combined with a shift to direct procurement for new stock.[15] Directly regulating ROSCO profits would perhaps be a more effective approach. At the same time, there should be stronger incentives for operators to own their own trains. In many parts of Europe the public body, e.g. a regional government, is the owner of the fleet and passes the stock on to whoever operates the franchise. A sufficiently large public body, such as the proposed Rail in the North Executive, could, in conjunction with a financial institution (e.g. Co-operative Bank, or pension funds) form its own ROSCO if it was looking to purchase new trains. Similarly, joint ventures – involving, for example, PTEs and devolved governments – could also take on ownership of new trains.

Rail freight

Freight is a hugely important part of what rail can deliver. Currently there is a moratorium (and threat of abolition) on the Freight Facilities Grants, which offer incentives for switching freight to rail. This will stymie future rail freight development just when it needs it: our roads are clogged with freight that should be on the rails – and in some cases, waterways. Investment in infrastructure capacity will benefit freight as well as passenger operations, but there needs to be ongoing investment in depot and rolling stock resources, and without FFG that is far less likely to happen. Freight should be encouraged to win more business, through support in the form of grants and low track-access charges. In the USA and Canada, and in some parts of Australia, there are freight railroads that are co-ops, and it would be good to see that evolve here.

The current much-needed investment in infrastructure, particularly electrification, is helpful to rail freight, but this needs to be network-wide, in order to avoid costly locomotive changes from/to diesel or electric, and it must also provide sufficient track capacity to accommodate a growth in freight. Even allowing for today's faster freight trains, they are still much slower than passenger trains, and capacity is needed to allow faster trains to pass them.

Manufacturing: rebuilding a railway industry in the UK

Britain once led the world in railway manufacturing but it is now trailing behind several other countries, including China, Canada, France, Germany and Spain. The remaining railway manufacturing in the UK is owned by companies based outside the country, notably Bombardier in Derby – which has been hard hit by government decisions to procure new Thameslink trains from Siemens. This would not have been such a major blow were it not for the fact that the UK railway industry is on such a knife edge. The DfT is largely responsible for the market fundamentalism that sees no problem in ordering in stock from overseas – in contrast, the ROSCOs have placed a high proportion of their orders at home. And the DfT also has a predilection for massive orders of five hundred-plus vehicles, which are impossible for any new supplier; and such orders produce a feast and famine situation, which can bankrupt both train builders and the supply chain. In contrast to this, new trains for local lines could be an ideal area for a new entrant, as for example with Stadler in Switzerland: 'What is needed is appropriate encouragement, and allowing a "think local" approach (which despite what the DfT says IS allowed in EU rules)'.[16]

There are several things a proactive government could do to encourage the revival of a UK-based railway industry, supported by a new tier of well-resourced regional development agencies (RDAs). Firstly, rail manufacturing needs long-term planning: a UK-wide rolling stock plan spread over thirty years would give industry the stability and investment horizons that it needs. This should be led by the proposed Strategic Rail Agency, working on behalf of the governments of the UK.

Secondly, encouragement to rail manufacturing would be an ideally suited task for regional and devolved governments seeking to support wider economic growth. The multiplier effects of railway manufacturing in terms of supply industry growth are vast. An interventionist industrial policy, supported by new and accountable RDAs, would aim to encourage development of existing manufacturing and, where appropriate, new plants.

Government procurement policies are widely seen to be unhelpful in supporting domestic industry, the Bombardier saga being only the most well publicised case. An incoming Labour government would need to review its procurement policies and ensure that, whoever takes on future rolling stock procurement (DfT or a new SRA), everything possible within EU rules is done to ensure that British industry is given strong encouragement. Taylor and Sloman point out that EU legislation specifically allows special conditions to be included in contracts which 'may, in particular, concern social and environmental considerations'. The preamble to the EU draft Directive explicitly states that these conditions 'may include the fight against unemployment'.[17]

British rail manufacturing has increasingly lagged behind foreign competitors and it is inevitable that some future rolling stock needs will have to be met by foreign-based firms. However, a condition of such contracts should be that a significant part of the construction of new trains is carried out within the UK, in areas that are suffering from low economic growth. This is already happening with the Hitachi plant in County Durham, which is being constructed on a greenfield site for the new IEP trains. Major orders for new trains are delivered by scores of suppliers rather than one single company. Using the provisions of the Social Value Act, much more could be done to ensure that contracts go to local suppliers.[18]

Strategic business partnerships with foreign manufacturers should be pursued by government agencies at UK, devolved and regional levels, to encourage major foreign companies to invest in the UK, taking advantage of both the UK skill base in railway manufacturing and the likelihood of growing orders for new trains. Links with Chinese manufacturers, several of whom are showing interest in the UK market, should be pursued.

Building up a strong research and development base within the UK is another task of government; UK-based universities should be encouraged to collaborate on innovative projects which can help rebuild the nation's railway manufacturing expertise. Many universities are already collaborating on research projects, and this needs further encouragement and funding.

A rolling programme of light rail schemes (see below) across the UK also has the potential to be good for manufacturing. It's mad that we currently have to buy all our tram equipment from abroad. And here too a condition of procurement policies must be that a large element of the vehicle and infrastructure components should be manufactured and assembled in the UK.

The light rail revolution

Many English cities now have light rail (or 'tram') networks, and Edinburgh will now soon be getting its own trams.[19] But this revolution has been slow in coming; once again we have lagged behind Germany and France. Trams are an obvious solution to problems of bigger cities, but they also have a potential role in highly sensitive areas such as national parks where road traffic is at unacceptably high levels, such as the Lake District and Snowdonia.

As with heavy rail, UK tram schemes appear to be far more expensive than similar projects abroad, and we need to find cost-effective ways of delivering more modern light rail networks that are integrated with heavy rail at one end, and feeder bus and cycle routes at the other. But this is not a 'cheap' option compared to other forms of urban transport, and the last twenty years have seen a battle of ideas – and policy – over the its claims.

However, light rail does have the potential to act as a catalyst for major urban development. We have already seen this along the original Manchester Metrolink corridor between Bury, Manchester city centre and Altrincham. And it can also be a vital tool in traffic management, if it is used as the core element of wider strategies to minimise car access into city centres. Sheffield and Nottingham city centres have been transformed through intelligent traffic management strategies based around tram priority. Part and parcel of this is having good park-and-ride at outlying stations and good connectivity with the heavy rail network and bus services. And this where the problem lies. In most other countries where light rail has experienced a revival, there isn't unbridled on-street competition: in the UK the economics of light rail suffers because a commercial bus operator can undercut tram prices and thus make the business case for light rail unviable. And as a result the prospects for getting good quality urban transport, and bringing wider economic and social benefits to towns and cities, also suffers.

As we saw, early trams undermined existing suburban steam railways, but experience in recent years has been more positive. In most major European cities the tram connects into longer distance and suburban rail networks at major termini, usually with integrated local ticketing systems making interchange even easier. Karlsruhe, Germany, took this approach a big step further by creating a hybrid between light and heavy rail: tram-train. Karlsruhe's main station is about a mile from the city centre, and passengers on local lines from the rural hinterland had to change there in order to proceed into the city centre. Through the pioneering genius of city transport planner Dieter Ludwig, some of these outlying branches were converted to tram operation, but using vehicles that could operate on conventional heavy-rail infrastructure as well as on street tramways, thereby allowing direct routes into the centre. This has become a huge success, and more and more routes have been converted for tram-train operation. An additional benefit has been to free up capacity at the main-line station for longer distance services. Similar schemes are now common across Europe.[20]

The 'tram-train' concept has generated considerable interest in the UK and the last five years have seen the development of studies to test out the idea. That sounds long-winded, and it has been. The Department for Transport, Network Rail and Northern are currently pursuing a pilot based on the Rotherham–Sheffield corridor, allowing tram-trains to run directly onto the Sheffield Supertram network. (Part of the problem with the original – abandoned – pilot project was cost: the project needs to be on a large enough scale to make unit costs viable.) Tram-train certainly has potential in areas like Sheffield (and Karlsruhe) where the main station is distant from the city centre. But it isn't a universal panacea and it can be costly. In Greater Manchester the approach has been to convert existing heavy-rail lines to light rail operation using conventional trams, but using on-street alignments to connect the network, or to go beyond the former railway into the heart of a town or city centre.

It's clear that light rail is good for towns and cities and more are needed. Towns in Europe that have tram networks tend to have a fabulous integrated transport network – instead of a free-for-all with de-regulated buses offering 'choice'. Labour shadow transport secretary Maria Eagle's proposals for 'deregulation exemption zones' would be ideal in cities where light rail is being developed, and would help ensure the best possible integration between bus, light rail and heavy rail. A better term might be 'integrated transport zones' – where there are positive incentives to optimal use of rail, tram and bus, with each co-operating with the others.

It's right that light rail should be promoted at the local level by well-resourced transport authorities in the public sector. But there is also a need for a supportive national policy, with dedicated resources within the Department for Transport that can provide positive assistance rather than discouragement. We need to get away from the current situation whereby each city does its own thing and re-invents wheels: the more standardisation in technology the better it will be. This means closer working between PTEs and transport authorities, the DfT and devolved governments in Wales and Scotland. An incoming Labour government should set up an Urban Transport Challenge Fund that could fund new light rail schemes and other innovative projects to help regenerate our cities, whilst ensuring there are core funding streams available at sub-national level independent of central government.

Finally, most light rail networks in the UK are publicly owned, but their operation is largely contracted to private companies such as Stagecoach – though not in every case. Now that trams have returned to Rochdale, the birthplace of the modern co-operative movement, might we not in the future look to a 'Tram Co-op' owned by its workers and passengers?

Integrated transport and ticketing

One final part of the equation, as we have seen, is transport integration. There are powers in the Transport Act 2000 which could be adapted to allow the integration of the local bus or tram network into a rail concession. This would give the level of integration and efficiency enjoyed in countries like the Netherlands.[21] It also makes possible regionally based ticketing, such as London's popular and successful Oystercard; and such systems, based on smart-card technology, in turn help stimulate the use of public transport. However a de-regulated multi-operator environment runs against any sort of fully integrated ticketing system.

NOTES

1. Richard Brown, *Review of Passenger Rail Franchising*, February 2013.
2. According to one of the authors of *Rebuilding Rail*, in the region of 263 per cent between 2003 and 2011! Taylor and Sloman, op cit.
3. G.F. Fiennes, *I Tried to Run a Railway*, 1973.
4. Stuart Cole, Institute of Welsh Affairs Agenda, 2 August 2012.
5. See Christian Wolmar, 'Sooner or later the big debt issue will have to be tackled', *RAIL*, 1 May 2013; also Taylor and Sloman op cit.
6. Lord Berkeley, 'Time to stop Network Rail's gravy train bonus structure', *Railway Magazine*, June 2013.
7. Wolmar, op cit.
8. Taylor and Sloman, op cit, p37.
9. Private email to author, May 2013.
10. See Paul Salveson, *Socialism with a Northern Accent* (2012) for a discussion on English regional government, which includes a brief consideration of how it might relate to transport.
11. In Germany, for example, the Land governments (or bodies with delegated powers) tend to go for relatively small concessionary networks.
12. See comment by spokesman for former Welsh transport minister Carl Sargeant AM, quoted in Paul Salveson *Rail Cymru: a people's railway for Wales*, Cardiff 2012. Also see this publication for more detailed information on proposal for community railway in Wales.
13. Stuart Cole, Institute of Welsh Affairs Agenda, 2 August 2012.
14. In *Passenger Transport*, June 2012.
15. Taylor and Sloman, op cit.
16. Information from industry expert, private email to author May 2013.
17. Taylor and Sloman, op cit, p37.
18. See *Social Enterprise UK: A Guide to The Public Services (Social Value Act)*, 2012.
19. Colin Ward, op cit, p80.
20. See Salveson, op cit.
21. See Paul Salveson, *Regional Rail in Europe*: and see chapter nine.

11. A PEOPLE'S TRAIN
OPERATING COMPANY

This chapter explores how a social-enterprise train company might provide a very different kind of regional service – combining innovation, high quality service and public accountability. The North of England is used as a model, but the approach is adaptable to any regional or national train operation in the UK.

Northern Rail operates local and regional services throughout the North, as far south as Nottingham and Stoke-on-Trent and as far north as Carlisle and Northumberland; while the TransPennine Express operates faster inter-regional services across the North, particularly on the core Manchester–York corridor, but it also serves Glasgow and Edinburgh and the North-East. The Northern Rail network is desperately in need of investment, and is suffering from the legacy of a franchise that was let by the Department for Transport based on assumptions of nil growth. In fact, since the franchise began in 2004 the operation has achieved passenger growth of around 40 per cent.

When these franchises come up for renewal in February 2016, the likelihood is that they will be merged into a single contract. This seems like a good opportunity to build on the positive achievements of the two operations – and the undoubted enthusiasm of their managers and front-line staff – to create a truly outstanding and mutually owned railway for the North.

The current Northern Rail franchise is unwieldy, based as it is around two very large area directorates (East and West) which are too big to manage effectively.[1] A reorganised company would benefit from strongly devolved management units covering the main centres, but it would be desirable to retain a distinct Northern Railways brand identity, and to continue with certain shared resources, such as depot facilities. This approach – of smaller units collaborating with each other – can bring benefits of scale at the same time as ensuring strong representation from the community and local government.[2] The model outlined below assumes a single operator with highly devolved business units and some peripheral lines run/managed as local sustainable transport companies. The suggested structure would be based on devolved units that align with the emerging city-region 'combined authorities' (see below), coupled with a 'premier' service that would be based on the former TransPennine Express inter-regional network.

A MUTUAL NORTHERN RAILWAYS

As I argued in chapter ten, the Co-operative Party's proposals for Network Rail, published in 2008, are actually much better suited to a passenger train operator than to an infrastructure manager, given that the passenger interface is primarily with the train operator.[3] The Co-operative Party's proposals involve the creation of a company limited by guarantee with two main groups of members: individual passengers who 'buy in' to the company and stakeholders (trades unions, local authorities, businesses and community rail partner-ships). Any passenger can register as a member of the mutual company when they buy a ticket (online or at a booking office) and is then enti-tled to vote in elections for governing bodies. Equally, individual employees would automatically become members of the company.

Such a company could be created by the current Northern consortium, referred to hereafter for convenience as Transport for the North/TfN), who would be 'the banker'. Northern Rail in its current guise requires an annual subsidy of around £500 million, whilst making a profit to its owners of around £40 million. Whilst there should be an objective on the part of TfN to bring this subsidy down over a period of years, the reality is that a continuing high level of support will be needed, however the operator is run. The new mutual would operate as an arms-length company providing a base-line of services required by TfN but having incentives to develop additional services to meet identified demand, and to take some risk on innovative ventures. It would be a not-for-dividend company with profits being recycled into the business instead of exported to shareholders. Risk would be shared between the mutual and TfN, along similar lines to the current Merseyrail franchise with Merseytravel.

Other alternatives include inviting bids from social enterprises to be the operator on a concession basis. Employees and passengers could then create their own mutual company to make a bid (with help from a body such as Co-operatives UK); and there could also be bids from some of the larger well-established community transport operators.

Mission and values

A 'people's railway' needs a clear, simple and visionary mission, and values that can inspire both its workers and customers. The following suggested mission and values are based on those of Euskotren, the highly successful regionally-owned train and bus operator in the Basque Country.

> MISSION: To meet the mobility needs of communities and businesses within the North of England, providing a high quality, accessible and affordable service which respects the environment and promotes sustainable development.

> VISION: To be a leading enterprise in the North, distinguished by its provision of excellent service to customers, value for money to the taxpayer, high levels of employee and community engagement and rewarding careers for its workforce.

The values of the company should include social responsibility; responsiveness to customer needs; a culture of innovation which learns from best practice world-wide; and a commitment to teamwork and partnership, with both internal and external stakeholders. These values need to go beyond traditional private sector hype: to be meaningful they would require regular independent audits.

Improving performance is critical. Getting the fundamentals right is the rock on which everything else should be built: if Northern Railways can offer high quality and reliability they will be in a strong position to develop further. Environmental sustainability should also be fundamental to the social goals of Northern Railways, with best practice in all aspects of its operations – in particular energy and fuel use, which also bring down operating costs.

Northern Railways would be a major employer, with about 6000 employees. Many of its staff would have both safety-critical and sensitive customer-facing roles. High levels of training would be essential, combined with an inclusive approach towards recruitment (including an emphasis on employing 'hard to reach' sections of the community). Encouraging employee involvement in community activities, with agreed time off for volunteering, should be another key aspect of what NR offers to its employees.

Finally, Northern Railways should operate as a responsible business with its customers – above all its passengers – but also its supply chain. Ethical procurement policies should include a presumption of buying local, encouraging positive and fair commercial relationships, and supporting small businesses and in particular social enterprises. The buying power of a large business such as Northern Railways could be used to help small social enterprises and community organisations. Northern Railways should aim to score consistently high in Passenger Focus's passenger satisfaction surveys.[4]

Financial questions

The current subsidy given to the Northern and TransPennine Express franchises, including indirect support via Network Rail's grant, totals £936m per annum.[5] In addition, substantial investment is currently being made in infrastructure through government proposals for electrification and 'the Northern Hub'. The proposed social enterprise train operating company would not impact massively on this current arrangement, though the assumption is that funding the future franchise (or whatever it may become) will be via the Northern authorities, represented by TfN. Northern Railways would continue to receive a considerable financial subsidy from TfN (or DfT), which would take the revenue risk. It should be encouraged to make a surplus from extending and improving its commercial performance, and this surplus would be re-invested into the business through improvements – for example in station facilities, improved information and on-train services – not to shareholders. Neither should there be a culture of excessive executive bonuses (see below). If there is a move away from a franchising model, an additional advantage would be that the costs of managing a franchise – which are considerable – would be reduced.

Whilst there would be some up-front costs in setting up the company, and further costs in monitoring and liaison, these are likely to be lower than the current costs of franchise management.

Creating a real people's railway: Community and 'Northernity'

The privatised railway in the UK has recognised the importance of community involvement in its operations, at least for local and regional services. However, there has been a sense that these are marginal, particularly for some of the longer-distance operators. And the reality of running a complex, long-distance network means that any consultation process, or community involvement, has inevitable limits. So what could Northern Railways do that would really make a difference and give a sense of ownership and involvement? There is a complex relationship between physical size, identity and sense of owning/ belonging to something. British Railways was technically 'owned' by the people of Great Britain but the size was so great (leaving aside any mention of its top-down approach) that it was impossible to develop a sense of ownership. Amongst employees there was a degree of identity with BR, but it was more about a sociological industry identity – which has persisted, despite the efforts of many companies, since privatisation.

A good comparator is Merseyrail, a franchise that is owned by Serco and Abellio and specified by the PTE Merseytravel. Its size is ideal for developing a strong sense of identity and loyalty. Trains and stations are strongly branded and relate closely to a sense of local identity. Northern Railways would be in a similarly strong position to take advantage of its 'Northernity' – in a way that the current jointly-owned Northern and TPE never have been. Building up a strong identity not only as a Northern enterprise, but as one that is the property of the people of the North, offers the sort of advantages that PR people can only dream of.

The branding of Northern Railways should be unequivocally Northern. Its public image should be designed to reflect a modern take on the North, promoting a sense of community as well as heritage. Its profile should extend to every part of the North, not just to stations and trains; and it should have a high profile at major events – festivals and major sporting events but also more local community galas, concerts and celebrations. It should be a sponsor of a range of national and local events and community activities, and have a substantial 'communities' budget.

The direct 'offer' of Northern Railways should symbolise that this is a very different railway company. Stations should be part of the community, building on the success of the 'adopt a station' approach but going much further, with station buildings used for community activities. Where station buildings have been destroyed there should be a programme to rebuild stations, with facilities that are more than fit for purpose, and incorporate retail and community facilities where appropriate. Northern Railways should also have a high-street retail presence at larger towns and cities (including London and Edinburgh as well as within the North), selling not only travel products but also tourist goods from across the North. It should also develop a 'special trains unit' to provide additional services for special occasions or private charter work, on a fully commercial basis (e.g. major sporting events and concerts). Northern Rail currently does this on an ad hoc basis, but there is almost certainly a suppressed demand in this field.

Extending the community rail partnership/station adoption model

There are over twenty well-established community-rail partnerships across the North including the Penistone Line (Huddersfield–Sheffield); Cumbrian Coast (Carlisle–Barrow); East Lancashire (Preston–Colne); Fylde Coast (Preston–Blackpool); Esk Valley (Middlesbrough–Whitby) and Mid-Cheshire (Manchester–Chester). These partnerships should be encouraged to develop their activities further, with additional (and long-term, secure) funding. Their current management varies but most have strong local government involvement, which is of critical importance. The CRPs should look at ways to build on their current activities and identify new opportunities to develop links with local communities. The proposed local sustainable transport company approach (see chapters seven and ten) could be applied to several of these routes, including initially Esk Valley, Cumbrian Coast, and Penistone Lines. In the case of some lines, a route-based co-operative or mutual enterprise (based on the local sustainable transport company) could be formed to promote and develop peripheral services that capitalise on the line's tourist potential, and could possibly bring retail staff back to stations. It is noteworthy that Chester-le-Street is already operated by a private company and Millom is run by a social enterprise; while the Settle-Carlisle Railway Development Company manages station booking offices at Settle and Appleby.

Relationship with central government

The DfT is taking a positive approach towards devolving more respon-sibilities to regions and nations within the UK, so a move towards much greater control of the Northern franchise by the TfN will not, in itself, be a problem. Avoiding the franchising process is a bigger challenge, and this would require political will. Other serious issues are the nature of the decision-making process and the financial risk. It is not likely that the necessary political will be forthcoming with the current Coalition government but an incoming centre-left govern-ment could amend the Railways Act to permit different approaches to the procurement of rail and bus services, provided that a responsible public body can demonstrate that it offers value for money and appro-priate accountability.

A positive relationship with the Department for Transport (or a future Strategic Rail Agency cf chapter ten) is important. The government will retain prime responsibility for the InterCity operations that serve the North (West Coast, Cross Country and East Coast) and TfN should work hard to make sure it can influence those franchises. As suggested in chapter ten, a better approach would be to merge all the InterCity franchises as they come up for renewal, into a single InterCity UK business.

Removing regional railways from the grip of the Treasury is a further necessity. The more that the devolved nations and regions within the UK have control over their own finances for transport and economic development, the better.

Relationship with Transport for the North and local authorities

Northern Railways would have a very strong focus on the distinct markets it would serve – including retaining a 'premier' operation based on the former TPE network. TfN would be the main specifier of the services provided by the company, but the latter could add to the core specification if it could identify commercial opportunities. The emerging 'combined authorities' in the city-regions (e.g. Greater Manchester, West Yorkshire, South Yorkshire), as well as other local authorities (counties and unitaries), could also have a direct input into the operation, both through devolved governance structures and through buying additional services.

Northern Railways should be established through a participatory approach that is led by the Northern transport authorities through TfN, but also involve other stakeholders in creating the company. Specialist legal advice would be required for this. The company should not be a direct part of TfN, but the relationship between the two bodies should be close and friendly, with strong working relationships at senior levels. This is the key to making the project work. Here a good example – again – is Merseyrail, where the senior managers of the train company have close and positive relationships with Merseytravel and also Network Rail. London Overground Ltd has a similar close relationship with Transport for London, with services operated on a similar concessionary arrangement.

TfN would have overall responsibility for the 'concession' (covering a period of at least twenty years), and the company's contract would include key requirements relating to service levels, fares and ticketing, connectivity and accessibility. TfN would also be responsible for funding larger capital projects, possibly with support from city-region combined authorities and local authority partnerships. The concession agreement would include sanctions for poor performance, and there would be an ultimate power to end the concession or take any other action deemed necessary (e.g. to take the operation in-house, as with the DfT's current arrangements with East Coast). There would be a periodic review – about every five years – whereby the whole operation is put under detailed scrutiny, and a report subsequently published by the TfN.

Relationship with the railway industry

The relationship between a not-for-profit train operator and other parts of the railway industry should not present any significant risk. As detailed below, a not-for-profit train operator would have to demonstrate high standards of competence in its dealings with industry partners, including Network Rail and other train operators. It would be a full member of the Association of Train Operating Companies, and also part of the national Rail Settlement Plan, to ensure full inter-availability of tickets. There would also be a very close relationship between Northern Railways and Network Rail at all levels, including train control and planning, route development and station management.

If the train company continued to manage the stations on the Northern rail network, it would also need to have a positive relationship with other train operators, notably East and West Coast and Cross Country. As manager of the stations it would be in a strong position to ensure that the other train operators using its stations provide a good service. There would be also be scope for commercial partnerships with other operators wishing to invest in station improvements – and not just TOCs but also Network Rail and TfN.

The most contentious relationship could be with the rolling stock leasing companies. The cost of leasing trains is one of the main factors driving up costs in rail operation. One option could be for TfN to buy rolling stock outright and lease to the operator, though this would be expensive. Another option may be for TfN to form a consortium with English regions, and/or PTEs and/or devolved governments to create a large not-for-dividend company, which could have substantial benefits of scale and access to capital (see below). This could be structured as a full co-operative.

There would also be opportunities for Northern Railways to assist in the development of supplier companies structured as co-operatives for provision of certain services, such as catering, specialist engineering functions and other services.

Finally, several heritage railways are major players on the Northern tourist scene, and a close and positive relationship with all of them, especially those with a main-line connection, is very important. There may be scope for the short-term leasing of diesel locomotives based at heritage railways for charter services, as well as for using heritage railways for staff training, as occurs on many parts of the UK network already, including the North York Moors Railway.

What would stay the same?

If Northern Railways felt just like any another train operator it would have failed. It needs to excite people and give them a sense, as soon as they get to a station or join a train, that they are in the North. However, in the short term many things would not change dramatically. It is important that change on this scale should not be seen by employees as a risk to their security: there should be assurances that current conditions and pay would be, at a minimum, no worse than the current arrangements – with the potential for being much better. The existing staff would still be working the trains and managing the operation; the same rolling stock would be operating the services and the station fabric would not change overnight. Much of the *technical* aspects of running a train company would remain. Depot facilities at Manchester, Liverpool, Leeds, York and Newcastle would continue to provide the main engineering functions, though, as traffic grows, the arguments for smaller satellite depots at other locations will become greater.

The broader safety environment would not change. Northern Railways would be as much a part of the UK rail network as any other train company and would be subject to the same safety regime and industry standards. On a commercial level, Northern Railways would remain a part of the national Ticketing and Settlement Agreement and the basic fares structure would not change. However, there would be considerable scope for flexibility in local fares, including commuter tickets and multi-modal fares.

Rail is operating in a competitive environment and the main competition is the car. Northern Railways would need to be commercially savvy, and to exploit marketing opportunities, including venturing into areas that may be unfamiliar to many existing TOCs, including retail other than rail tickets, catering etc.

It should be stressed that Northern Railways would not limit its operations to the North alone; the geography of railway operations does not allow it, and the assumption is that Northern Railways would continue to serve major centres outside the North, e.g. Glasgow, Edinburgh, Nottingham and Stoke-on-Trent. At the same time, some parts of the existing Northern network, notably services into Merseyside, may be better transferred to an expanded Merseyrail operation.

What would change?

It is important that Northern Railways positions itself as a very different kind of enterprise, charting 'clear red water' between the private, franchised world of rail operations since 1994 and what it wants to achieve as a social enterprise serving the people of the North. Creating a culture which is based firmly on its values is critical. This should be translated into very tangible activities, including station facilities, trains and customer service.

Northern Railways would take over complete responsibility for stations from Network Rail through much longer leases than currently apply within the railway industry (initially this might apply only to smaller stations on the network). Stations have massive untapped potential.

There are some good examples in the North of station buildings being brought back into use for wider commercial and community activities (see chapter seven). Existing staffed stations would continue to be staffed by railway employees, but the Merseyrail model of having combined booking offices and ticket sales in one 'shop' should be developed, with the Co-op or another reputable retailer as a partner. This approach would work at medium-sized stations, for example Huddersfield, Barnsley, Bolton, Rochdale and Wigan (Wallgate). At smaller stations there is much scope for independent social enterprises to develop retail activities, and, as argued in chapter seven, locating other public services there – e.g. post offices, doctors' surgeries, libraries, tourist information centres – should be considered if the location is appropriate. Stations would continue to be adopted by local community organisations, building on the outstanding work that is already happening in the North of England and elsewhere in the UK.

Northern Railways would inherit a fleet that is mostly diesel, but the imminent arrival of electric trains following completion of electrification schemes will mean that the diesel fleet will be used to enhance non-electrified services elsewhere in the North. All trains in service should have strong Northern Railways branding – with every train named either after an outstanding person or a feature of the Northern landscape. Trains could also be adopted by any relevant local organisation with which the train has an association.

Certain common features should be adopted for all trains, whether new or refurbished. These would include: improved facilities for passengers with disabilities; additional space for luggage and buggies; space for at least four bikes per train; a comfortable environment, with good visibility; the availability of aural and visual information displays; and on-train literature aimed at the tourist market. Customer service is also of vital importance; it can make all the difference between an enjoyable or disastrous journey experience, even when things go wrong. Having on-train staff who are recruited for their customer and 'people' skills, and trained to high standards, is vital to the success of any business, but no more so than in a complex and challenging industry such as railways.

Service development

The existing pattern of services that Northern Railways inherits would provide the bedrock for future development of the network. But nobody would suggest that the existing network is perfect, and Northern Railways should work closely with the TfN, Network Rail and the wider community to develop a network that will become a major improvement of the current one.

Most services already have a reasonable frequency but there are some routes, particularly in more rural areas, where frequencies are poor. A medium-term objective should be to achieve a bedrock minimum frequency of at least an hourly service on all routes. On busy commuter routes, a fifteeen-minute frequency should be aimed for, with strong integration with bus services (see below).

An integrated and developing network

Northern Railways would inherit an already dynamic Northern rail network – with improved frequencies, re-opened lines and an ongoing programme of electrification. As suggested above, TfN would produce its own specification for the line, as is currently done in Scotland. But there would also be opportunities for Northern Railways to influence the thinking of TfN in expanding the network.

Over the next few years there will be powerful logic in extending electrification, not least for freight. The Settle-Carlisle Line is a strategic corridor for both freight and passenger and would be an obvious future contender for electrification.

For re-openings, the following routes should be progressed: Skipton–Colne; Manchester–Sheffield via Woodhead; Ashington Blyth and Tyne; and Penrith–Keswick. [6]

The key issue in the short term is developing an integrated coach and rail network. Closer integration with rail services, including through ticketing, booked connections and shared branding with Northern Railways will offer a truly pan-Northern service. Key routes might be Penrith–Keswick–Workington; Windermere–Keswick; and Buxton–Matlock.

The governance of Northern Railways

Ensuring the right governance structure of Northern Railways will be vital to its success and would be a responsibility of TfN as part of its role in creating the arms-length company. There is a balance to be struck between maximum democratic involvement and a business that has strong management focus; the emphasis should be on creating a dynamic and entrepreneurial business in which decisions can be made quickly.

There are many important stakeholders in a railway operation who need to be represented. These include employees, passengers, government and other rail industry partners including Network Rail. Northern Railways should strive to include all of these interests in its governance, but also to bring in specific expertise where necessary. There should be a two-tier structure that ensures balanced representation across the North, but with a tight management structure at the top. The Northern Railways Board would be the strategic body, with partners representing regional interests, and it would be chaired by someone with strong leadership skills and high-level experience in business, local government or the voluntary sector. Its role would be strategic policy and guidance, leaving the operation of the railway to a highly experienced executive (see below).

At the sub-regional level there should be Area Stakeholder Boards, which could include in their membership local authorities, employees, local managers, passenger groups, community rail partnerships, Network Rail and other relevant rail industry bodies. They would reflect the emerging structure of the Rail in the North Executive, and should as far as possible be based on emerging 'combined authority' boundaries. A suggested division into regions could be based on the following areas: Greater Manchester, Cheshire and Merseyside; Lancashire and Cumbria; North-East and North Yorkshire; West Yorkshire and York; and South Yorkshire, East Riding and Humberside.

A typical membership would include – in addition to employees – representatives of TfN, local authorities, Network Rail's senior manager for the area, other transport operators, a CRP representative and two or three business representatives, possibly with a tourist emphasis. In addition, there would be elected passenger representatives, voted onto the boards by individual members of the mutual company.

The ASB would have considerable influencing power. It would have a strong say in service delivery in its area, but could also look at opportunities for widening Northern Railways' profile in the local community.

The Northern Railways Board would cover the entire network and include representation for employees. There should also be representation from TfN, combined authorities, passengers (individual members elected locally), community rail partnerships, the business community and individual experts nominated by the TfN. The board would be empowered to discuss issues of strategic importance to the company. An executive group of directors (see below) would have day-to-day responsibility for the running of the business.

Management of Northern Railways

The proposed executive management structure of Northern Railways would, to a certain extent, reflect that of other train operating companies. It would be headed up by a Managing Director (appointed by the board), with directors covering key functions (e.g. Commercial, Engineering/Fleet, HR), and with additional director roles for Community and Sustainability and Development. Each of the proposed areas would have their own director with a delivery team answerable to the area director, and there would also be a director for the 'premier' (ex-TransPennine Express) services.

Managers should be primarily recruited from within the railway industry; most would be TUPE'd across from the previous franchise. (It would be important that the new management team be encouraged to develop a firm commitment to the public service and co-operative ethos of the Northern Railways.) However, Northern Railways would need to bring in new areas of expertise to reflect the company's co-operative ethos in areas such as procurement, sustainability and community engagement. Remuneration of managers would be based on current rates within the industry, but the company should set its face against excessive bonuses for senior managers and directors, which achieve little other than create resentment amongst staff and customers.

Northern Railways and its employees

Northern Railways would inherit most of its employees from the previous franchise. Many jobs within the railway industry require many years of training and that generates a high degree of commitment and dedication to the job. Northern Railways would aim to encourage that dedication amongst both the employees it inherits and new entrants.

The proposed new structure would give employees a much stronger stake in their company. Unlike a private for-dividend company there would not be shareholders whose prime interest was the return on their investment; staff would be part of an owning community that also included the TfN and passengers. Having staff on company boards is not new: many large companies have employee directors. But often this does not go beyond tokenism. Northern Railways will address ways in which staff at all levels can feel that they are actively involved in their company.

Each area would have an area employees' forum, open to all employees, and would meet every three months. The forum would elect a representative number of staff to sit on the area stakeholder board alongside senior managers and community/passenger representatives to discuss issues relevant to the area (but these would not include HR issues, which would continue to be the preserve of the existing machinery of negotiation).

Ensuring high levels of customer service should be an integral part of the training received by all staff. Staff would also be encouraged to play an active part in the running of Northern Railways, and in local community life. Staff involved in community activities would be able to apply for small grants to help them. Ways of more actively involving staff in the running of Northern Railways are outlined below.

Northern Railways and its passengers

Finding effective ways of involving passengers is possibly the most difficult challenge for a new company. Passengers would be encouraged to become individual members of the mutual that owned their railway. A starting point might be to offer every season-ticket holder automatic membership (with options to decline if desired). Other options could allow passengers to join for a token amount at staffed stations, or via the railway's website.

Organisations representing passengers also need to be included within the structures of the company. Passenger organisations take a number of different forms, which means some complexity may be required to accommodate them. For example, some of the many rail-user groups on routes in various parts of the North are not as representative as they might be; while community rail partnerships are not 'passenger' bodies as such, although they do involve them; and Passenger Focus is an important statutory body, but it does not have 'Northern' representation per se at present. An appropriate model –

which is bound to be messy and require flexibility – would see an area stakeholder board with representation from all these groups, as well as a number of passenger representatives directly elected by passengers themselves. (Criteria for those offering themselves as candidates for election might include evidence of reasonably regular use of rail, an understanding of the objectives and ethos of Northern Railways and a willingness to engage with fellow passengers.) More locally, there is considerable scope for route-based passenger panels, which could focus on local issues and involve route or station-based managers.

Northern Railways and the wider community

The Northern local authorities would have an input to rail via TfN, but it is also important to ensure that economic development and tourism are represented. So in some cases a specific place should be reserved on the ASBs for such representatives. Community groups are another very important, and by their nature dispersed, constituency. In most parts of the North there are federations of voluntary groups, on a district or county-wide basis – such as the Yorkshire Forum and the Tyne and Wear Public Transport Users Group. These would be the obvious bodies to be represented on the ASBs.

However, it is important to stress that Northern Railways itself should also reach out into the community, and should be involved in community initiatives, sponsor community events and in general have a very high visibility. A Northern Railways Community Unit, accountable to the Director of Sustainability and Community, should be established, part of whose role would be to support the work of the community rail partnerships, but part of which would be to have a direct community presence, for example in areas where a CRP does not exist. It should also have a very high internal profile within the community, encouraging employees to get involved in community activities; these could include managing a company-wide 'day off for your community'. The Community Unit would work closely with other parts of the business to identify suitable premises for community use and suitable community tenants.

In addition the company would seek to build links with other local businesses. There would be a strong commercial element to Northern Railways' external activities. Procurement policies should encourage the company to buy goods and services as locally as possible, with particular encouragement towards using social enterprises operating broadly within the area of Northern Railways' own operations.

Northern Railways need a government of the North

If this vision of a regional authority contracting with an arms-length mutual company is the right way forward to run rail services in the North post-2016, it will require some public investment, probably by TfN. Much will depend on political factors – above all the willingness of a future Westminster government not only to cede powers and funding to the TfN, but also to make significant amendments to the 1993 Railways Act, to allow consideration of the alternative mutual course outlined above. 'Northern Railways' would be a politically radical move, but one that would command strong support within the North and beyond. It could also offer insights and opportunities to other parts of the UK – most obviously Scotland but also to Wales and London.

Unlike Scotland, Wales and London, the North of England does not have an accountable regional government structure. The proposals for a consortium of Northern authorities involve a 'Leaders' Board' of no less than 33 local councils. If any sector demonstrates the desperate need for directly-elected regional government, railways must surely be at the top of the list. The current proposals are the best solution in the absence of a regional government, but few would argue they are ideally suitable for the huge job that Northern authorities will face in managing the rail network.[7]

A regional assembly, ideally elected proportionally, would provide the right level of governance for railways in the North and could make the necessary decisions as to the most appropriate form of delivery. The emerging city-region 'combined authorities' will also have a very important role to play in developing more local networks under the regional assembly's umbrella. Scotland, Wales and London already have the right levels of democratic accountability, and this can be seen in the investment that is going into their rail networks. The North, and the other English regions, need the same powers as Scotland to control and develop their railways.

NOTES

1. A railway serving a population of between five and eight million appears to offer the right scale, allowing for a clear focus on the market whilst getting sufficient economies of scale. The North of England has a population of 15.5 million.
2. A similar approach could work with InterCity – see chapter ten.
3. Co-operative Party, *People's Rail*, 2008.
4. Currently it is at the bottom of the league table. See Passenger Focus, *National Passenger Survey*, 2013.
5. Office of Rail Regulation, op cit.
6. See Chapter 11 for further detail.
7. See Paul Salveson, *Socialism with a Northern Accent* (2012) for a statement of the case for regional evolution.

CONCLUSION

When I started writing this book I had a reasonably clear idea of how I saw rail progressing under a future Labour government. During its writing I've spent a lot of time discussing deliverable ways forward with colleagues in the railway industry whose opinion I respect. Some are acknowledged but others have to remain anonymous. I was pleased with the degree of positive encouragement and support for the core arguments in the book, and equally heartened by some of the more challenging comments: some of these have made me re-think a number of the arguments, not least in relation to the role of the state.

A core question – which emerged with startling clarity – is that concerning the extent to which the state as traditionally understood should take on a much greater role in the rail sector, including the question of whether or not it should have the kind of 'light touch' I suggest in the proposed Strategic Rail Agency. People on the left are most comfortable with state ownership and control, even though we recognise its past failings and the need to move away from the Morrisonian model of state corporation. Even if that was appropriate for immediate post-war Britain with a rail network ravaged by bombing and decades of under-investment, it isn't appropriate today. But neither is the system created by the 1993 Railways Act suitable for a railway which needs stability, development and accountability.

So I have resisted my earlier inclination to argue for a state-owned Network Rail, following discussions with friends in the company and train operators whose views I respect. The current organisation needs space to develop and improve, and the employee-mutual structure I have proposed would both build on its successes and lead to the eradication of some of its less desirable features. Again, train operations need a new business model based on mutualism – something that has hardly been tried in railways (anywhere in the world), but which is commonplace in other sectors. Finding a model which can harness commercial drive with employee and passenger buy-in is a challenge which can be met, with the right political will and the right partners brought together.

Another recurring theme in the book has been size – finding the optimal size of operation and business unit. Everything I have seen in this country and abroad pushes me towards a 'small is beautiful' approach in railways (but not too small to be ugly!). This is almost counter-intuitive for railway people, who are used to large, centralised units. But when you free up local expertise, you start to see innovation, change and involvement. Keep things centralised and life just sloughs along. Yes, of course a railway is a network and you need a balance between local empowerment and central co-ordination; but the stick has a long way to be bent before we get the right balance.

I was largely responsible for the development of community rail partnerships in the 1990s, and on one level it is great to see how successful, and universally welcomed, they have become. But, equally, I think that some of the more radical ideas in *New Futures for Rural Rail*, published almost exactly twenty years ago, need dusting down and re-visiting. The existing trains – local and longer distance – are largely full and the problem here is how to get more trains onto an over-crowded infrastructure. I hope I have made a strong argument for a new, organic, development of the local railway – using the slightly tongue-in-cheek title of sustainable branch line.

I hope that the constant reference to the 'importance of people' has come across without becoming boring. Getting the right people running our railways is absolutely crucial, and keeping them motivated is also essential. I firmly believe that we have the right people there already, at all levels of the railway. The railway needs to improve its gender balance, certainly, but we need also to keep and develop that great tradition of service and professionalism that has been a hallmark of our railways over the last 180 years. I very much hope that the proposals in this book will reinforce that tradition, and re-invigorate those managers and front-line staff who have become cynical after twenty years of substanceless 'empowerment' rhetoric. They know that the most important person in all this is the passenger. We need to find better ways of hearing her voice – and here inviting passengers to become owners of mutual train companies will be transformative.

This is a political book aimed at railway people interested in politics, and politicians who are interested in railways. My own political perspective is centre-left, but I sincerely hope that at least some of the proposals in the book will resonate with politicians from different persuasions and traditions. In a funny and almost mysterious way, railways can act as a unifying force both within communities and amongst politicians.

The need for political change should be apparent in most of the chapters. And this isn't just about electing a Labour government with the will to 'do something' about rail. It is also about the constitutional change that would give Scotland, Wales and the English regions greater freedom to decide what sort of railway they want and how it should be run. For the English regions there is, as yet, no suitable governance structure, and the difficulties we have experienced in developing a body that can represent local authorities across the North of England only serves to highlight the problems in other parts of England.

This book has been a work of evolution and there is plenty more thinking to be done. Getting community groups, unions, social enterprises, political organisations, government bodies and railway people talking to each other about some of the ideas thrown up by this book will be a welcome start.

Summary

SUMMARY

Railways in Britain provide a vital service, for both passengers and freight. Yet the framework provided by the 1993 Railways Act has failed to deliver a railway that passengers, employees and the general public find acceptable. There is a need for a new approach which keeps the best of what has been achieved in the last twenty years but learns from the experience of other parts of Europe in getting the right balance between public and private, national and regional. The alternative is not to go back to a monolithic state-owned British Rail but to go forward with new models of social enterprise, with structures that recognise the changing nature of Britain, in particular devolved governments in Scotland, Wales and London, as well as the radically different structure of railways today.

Big is not necessarily better, and the most successful train companies in recent years have been the smaller ones that have a focus on a distinct geographical market. We need to learn the lessons from this, and get back to manageable sizes of operation that combine scale economies with a strong focus on markets and community needs. New business models should be developed which can show the way forward for other sectors.

It is important to be clear on what we want from the railway. In summary, we want a railway which:

- underpins economic regeneration and supports a growing economy based on the principles of sustainable development, while offering value for money services at an affordable cost to the taxpayer and passenger
- meets the needs of all sections of the community, offering an affordable and accessible form of transport across the UK
- is accountable and responsive to the wider community, including its customers and funders

- forms the core of a co-ordinated transport network and is fully integrated with local, regional and national spatial planning policies
- provides quality employment and maximises opportunities to involve its work-force at all levels
- supports an expanding manufacturing industry backed up by high-quality research and development expertise
- is able to innovate and to both drive and respond to market opportunities and technical change.

THE KEY PROPOSALS IN THIS BOOK

A UK-wide Strategic Rail Agency (SRA) should be created which would be accountable to the British government and to Scottish and Welsh ministers. The SRA would be the 'guiding mind' of rail in the UK, providing a strategic framework for rail to develop, focusing on main routes and operating with a light touch. It should translate government policies into deliverable plans, with as little direct government interference as possible. It would initially manage franchises and ultimately take responsibility for a range of other strategic roles, including major route development.

A democratised Network Rail (structured as a mutually owned business) should continue its job as manager and developer of the railway infrastructure, in close co-operation with the proposed SRA, continuing the development of closer integration with train operators.

The current franchising system is broken, and continuing with the discredited system would be foolish. Existing InterCity franchises, as they come up for renewal, should form part of a new 'InterCity UK', based on the existing Directly Operated Railways (DOR), but with a greater degree of commercial autonomy; InterCity UK would combine a strong focus on the key routes with overall network planning, resource utilisation and marketing. Regional services, including domestic services in Scotland and Wales, should be the responsibility of the devolved governments or consortia of English authorities, with freedom for them to choose what they see as the best form of delivery. This should include encouragement to 'social enterprise' operators, with far fewer barriers to entry into the rail market.

For the longer term, directly elected regional government, working with combined authorities at sub-regional level, would bring the focus, resources and accountability that have proved so successful in countries such as Germany. These bodies may decide to continue with franchising; or establish 'concessions', where the operator provides services at an agreed price; or set up 'arms-length' socially-owned operating companies such as exist in the bus industry.

A new model of 'people's train company', working in partnership with devolved public bodies, should be formed, based on well-established mutual principles, which would allow passengers as well as employees to buy into 'their' train company. Surpluses made by the train company would be re-invested into the railway.

For local railways, innovative approaches based on the sustainable branch line concept should be developed, with community-based social enterprises ('Local Sustainable Transport Companies' - LSTCs) providing complementary services to the core operation and building on the achievements of community rail partnerships. A number of pilot projects based on the Government's *Community Rail Development Strategy* would help test out the most appropriate ways forward; no one size will fit all and innovation should be encouraged. There is considerable scope for combined operations or franchises along a local rail corridor, with rail and bus services fully co-ordinated by one operator or 'enabler', viz the LSTC. Progressively, some of the LSTCs could take on more direct responsibility for providing transport services, both bus and rail. 'Local integrated transport zones', in which bus de-regulation does not apply, would be essential to get the maximum benefit from this approach.

There should be a mixed economy on the railway, with the private sector continuing to provide freight and some open access services, as well as manufacturing and some specialist infrastructure support. Rail freight has huge potential to get more traffic off the roads and contribute to sustainable economic growth; supply-side measures to encourage that shift should include a restoration of freight facilities grants and a more supportive fiscal environment for rail freight. Enhancing infrastructure capacity to meet the needs of an expanding freight sector, as well as passenger traffic, needs co-ordinated and long-term planning.

The current arrangements for rolling stock are not sustainable, with unreasonably high profits being made by rolling stock companies, which are owned by the major banks. New trains could be procured through not-for-profit rolling stock companies or by consortia of public agencies, and a regulated cap should be placed on rolling stock leasing company profits.

Railway manufacturing in the UK is at a low ebb, and the best way to stimulate its revival is through long-term strategies to buy new stock, providing certainty and stability. More should be done to support UK manufacturing through using special conditions in contracts (e.g. measure to combat unemployment) so that areas of economic decline can benefit. New trains, whether built by British or foreign companies, should be constructed mainly in the UK. There is a major role for universities in rail-based research and development, and networking on a regional and national basis with appropriate government and industry funding would help rebuild our lost research capacity.

Britain needs an expanding railway with extra capacity, but it is debatable whether HS2 as currently conceived is either desirable or affordable. A UK-wide strategy to increase capacity, including provision of some new 'high-speed' routes up to speeds of around 250km/h (including a new line to the central belt of Scotland) should be progressed. Relatively short re-openings which help re-connect regional networks are essential.

Rail is a key part of Britain's infrastructure, and its contribution needs to be recognised much more strongly in national, regional and local planning policies that seek to reverse the over-emphasis on roads and put rail at the heart of sustainable development.

A reformed railway would not cost any more than what is currently being spent on railways in the UK. There would be some one-off costs in setting up the proposed Strategic Rail Agency, but these would be more than off-set by avoiding costs of current franchise management and shareholder profits.

Select Bibliography

Aldcroft, D. (ed), *Studies in British Transport History* (Newton Abbott 1974)

Alderman, G., *The Railway Interest* (Leicester 1973)

Alexandersson, Gunnar, *The Accidental Deregulation* (Stockholm 2010)

Association of Community Rail Partnerships, *The Value of Community Rail Partnerships* (Slaithwaite 2008)

Bagwell, P., *The Railwaymen* vol. 1 (London 1963)

Bevir, Mark, *The Making of British Socialism* (Princeton 2012)

Brown, Richard, *Review of Passenger Rail Franchising* February 2013

Buckley, R.J., *History of Tramways* (Newton Abbott 1975)

Campaign for Better Transport, *Going Local* (London 2013)

Cole, G.D.H. and Page Arnot, R., *Trade Unionism on the Railways* (London 1917)

Co-operative Party, *The People's Rail: a mutually run, publicly accountable Network Rail* (London 2008)

Cowie, J., 'The British passenger rail privatisation: conclusions on subsidy and efficiency from the first round of franchises', *Journal of Transport Economics and Policy*, 43 (2009)

Davies, Emil, *The Case for Railway Nationalisation* (London 1912)

Edwards, Clement, *Railway Nationalization* (London 1898)

Faulkner, Richard and Austin, Chris, *Holding the Line – how Britain's railways were saved* (Oxford 2013)

Fienne, G.F., *I Tried to Run a Railway* (Shepperton 1973)

Findlay, G., *The Working and Management of an English Railway* (London 1889)

Griffiths, Robert, *Driven by ideals – a history of ASLEF* (London 2005)

Hamilton, Kerry, and Potter, Stephen, *Losing Track* (London 1985)

Harris, Nigel, and Godward, Ernest, *The Privatisation of British Rail* (1997)

Haywood, Russell, 'Britain's National Railway Network: Fit for Purpose in the Twenty First Century?', *Journal of Transport Geography*, 15 (2007)

–– *Railways, Urban Development and Town Planning in Britain 1948-2008* (Farnham 2009)

Heart of Wales Line Travellers Association Strategic Plan (Llandovery 2010)

Hillman, Mayer, and Whalley, Anne, *The Social Consequences of Line Closures*, 1980

Hole, James, *National Railways – an argument for state purchase* (London 1893)

Holton, Bob, *British Syndicalism 1900-1914* (Michigan 1976)

Howell, David, *British Workers and the Independent Labour Party 1888-1906* (Manchester 1983)

Hylen, Bertil, *Public Transport in Sweden – Deregulation and Intermodal Integration*, VTI (Sweden 2011)

— *Germany and De-regulation of its Railways* (Stockholm 2011)

King, J.S., *Keighley Corporation Transport* (Huddersfield 1964)

Kingsford, P.W., *Victorian Railwaymen* (London 1970)

Knowles, R.D., 'Railway franchising in Great Britain and the effects of the 2008-2009 economic recession', *Environment & Planning A*, 45(1) (2013)

— 'Impacts of privatizing Britain's rail passenger services – franchising, re-franchising and Ten Year Transport Plan targets', *Environment and Planning A*, 36 (2004)

— *Passenger rail privatization in Great Britain and its implications* (1998)

Kynaston, David, *Austerity Britain 1945-1951* (London 2007)

— *A World to Build 1945-48* (London 2007)

McKenna, Frank, *The Railway Workers 1840-1970* (London 1980)

— 'Victorian Railway Workers' in *History Workshop* no. 1 Spring 1976

McNulty, Sir Roy, *Rail Value for Money Study* (DfT and Office of Rail Regulation 2012)

Matheson, Rosa, *Railway Voices: 'Inside' Swindon Works* (Stroud 2008)

Milligan, Edward, *Quakers and Railways* (York 2002)

Morrison, Herbert, *Socialisation and Transport – The organisation of socialised industries with particular reference to the London passenger Transport Bill* (London 1933)

Murray, Andrew, *Off the Rails* (Brooklyn & London 2001)

Nash, C., *European Rail Reform – The Next Steps* (Leeds 2011)

National Audit Office, *HS2: a review of early programme preparation*

National Guilds, *Towards a National Railway Guild* (London 1918)

Nixon, T.E., *First Stages of State Control of the Railways* (Manchester 1948)

Passenger Focus, *National Passenger Survey Autumn 2012* (London)

Passenger Transport Executive Group, *Rail Cities in the 21ˢᵗ century: the case for Devolution* (Leeds 2012)

Preston, J., *A review of passenger rail franchising in Britain*: 1996/1997-2006/2007, *Research in Transportation Economics*, 22 (2008)

Pribićević, Branko, *The Shop Stewards Movement and Workers' Control 1910-1922* (thesis Oxford 1959)

Railway Development Society, *Fighting for Rail* (Bristol 1983)

Reed, M.C., *Railways in the Victorian Economy* (Newton Abbott 1969)

Rolt, L.T.C., *George and Robert Stephenson* (London 1960)

— *Red for Danger* (second ed. London 1966)

Salveson, Paul, *Northern Rail Heritage* (Slaithwaite 2010)

— *British Rail – the Radical Alternative to Privatisation* (Manchester 1989)

— *Regional Rail in Europe, study for HITRANS* (2012)

— *Getting the best from bus and rail in rural communities* (Huddersfield 1999)

— *New Futures for Rural Rail* (Huddersfield 1993)

— *Microfranchising: community control of local railways* (Huddersfield 1994)

— *Socialism with a Northern Accent* (London 2012)

— *Rail Cymru: a people's railway for Wales* (Cardiff 2012)

— *Regional Rail in Europe* (Slaithwaite 2012)

— 'Trams, Trains, Tram-trains', published in *Train Times* (Slaithwaite 2004)

Shaw, J., *Competition, Regulation and the Privatisation of British Rail* (Ashgate 2000)

Simmons, Jack, *The Railways of Britain* (London 1961)

— *The Railway in Town and Country 1830–1914* (Newton Abbott 1986)

Social Enterprise UK, *A Guide to the Public Services (Social Value Act) 2012*

Spaven, David, *Waverley Route: the life, death and re-birth of the Borders Railway* (Glendaruel 2012)

— *The Waverley Line* (2013)

Taylor, Ian, and Sloman, Lynn, *Rebuilding Rail* (Machynlleth 2012)

Thomas, David St John, *The Country Railway* (Newton Abbott 1989)

Thomas, John, *The Callander and Oban Railway* (Newton Abbott 1968)

Transport Scotland, *Fast Track Scotland: making the case for high-speed rail to Scotland* (Glasgow 2013)

Wallace, Malcolm, *Single or Return: the history of the Transport Salaried Staffs Association* (London 1996)

Ward, Colin, *Freedom to Go – after the motor car age* (London 1991)

Wolmar, Christian, *Fire and Steam: a new history of the railways* (London 2008)

Woodcock, George, *Railways and Society: for workers' control of the railways* (London 1943)

Young, Michael, *Small Man–Big World* (London 1948)

Select Index

For individually named stations, see under *Stations*
For local campaign, friends and user groups, see under *Campaigns, CRPs and User Groups*

Lightning Source UK Ltd.
Milton Keynes UK
UKOW04f1804150714

235172UK00004B/179/P